Jesus
The Misunderstood Jew

Jesus
The Misunderstood Jew

What the New Testament *Really* Says about the Man from Nazareth

Robert Kupor, Ph.D.

iUniverse, Inc.
New York Lincoln Shanghai

Jesus the Misunderstood Jew
What the New Testament *Really* Says about the Man from Nazareth

iUniverse books may be ordered through booksellers or by contacting:

iUniverse
2021 Pine Lake Road, Suite 100
Lincoln, NE 68512
www.iuniverse.com
1-800-Authors (1-800-288-4677)

The views expressed in this work are solely those of the author and
do not necessarily reflect the views of the publisher, and the publisher hereby disclaims
any responsibility for them.

New Revised Standard Version Bible, copyright 1989, Division of Christian Education
of the National Council of the Churches of Christ in the United States of America.
Used by permission.
All italics and brackets in the excerpts of the New Revised Standard Version Bible used in
Jesus the Misunderstood Jew are the author's additions.

ISBN: 978-0-595-42404-7 (pbk)
ISBN: 978-0-595-69314-6 (cloth)
ISBN: 978-0-595-86741-7 (ebk)

Printed in the United States of America

To my wife Sandy,
and my daughters Daniella,
Elana, and my personal production editor, Devra

One of the scribes ... asked [Jesus], "Which commandment is the first of all?" Jesus answered, "The first is, 'Hear, O Israel! The Lord our God, the Lord is one; you shall love the Lord your God with all your heart, and with all your soul, with all your mind, and with all your strength.'"

Gospel of Mark, 12:28–30

There was a rich man who ... feasted sumptuously every day. And at his gate lay a poor man named Lazarus, covered with sores ... The poor man died and was carried away by the angels to be with Abraham. The rich man also died ... In Hades ... he looked up and saw Abraham far away with Lazarus by his side. He called out, "Father Abraham, have mercy on me ... for I am in agony in these flames." But Abraham said, "Remember that during your lifetime you received many good things, and Lazarus ... evil things; but now he is comforted here, and you are in agony ..." [The rich man] said, "Then, father I beg you to send him to ... my five brothers—that he may warn them, so that they will not also come into this place of torment." Abraham replied, "They have Moses and the prophets; they should listen to them." He said, "No, father Abraham, but if someone goes to them from the dead, they will repent." He said to him, "If they do not listen to Moses and the prophets, neither will they be convinced even if someone rises from the dead."

Jesus' Parable of Lazarus, from the Gospel of Luke, 16:19–31

CONTENTS

LIST OF ILLUSTRATION AND TABLES

PREFACE

Growing up in a Conservative Jewish neighborhood in New York City, I always felt embarrassed by how little Jews seemed to know about their Bible. I cannot recall a single person who had actually read the entire book. Instead, everyone's knowledge of it seemed to be limited to what they heard in the rabbi's Sabbath sermon and the Bible readings.

Christians seemed so much more knowledgeable about their New Testament. My Jewish neighborhood was surrounded mostly by Irish and Italian Catholics, who appeared to know everything about Jesus and their religion. I was only vaguely aware in those days of the Catholic catechism, and I didn't realize that they were speaking mostly by rote. Still, it made sense that they should know more if only because Western societies are so permeated with Christian references and symbols.

But these thoughts were usually transitory, because I was more interested in science than religion, and generally lived in large, cosmopolitan cities. From New York I moved to Boston to get a Ph.D. in microbiology from Harvard University, and then to San Francisco for further research at the University of California at San Francisco. But life changed abruptly upon arriving in Chattanooga, Tennessee, to become an assistant professor of biology at the University of Tennessee. I was suddenly beset by Gospel-toting students and neighbors trying to save me into Christ. They were so unfailingly polite and enthusiastic that I felt like a celebrity surrounded by his fan club. But my initial amusement changed to uncertainty as I gradually realized that I really did not know why the Jewish people had rejected Jesus. We obviously could not accept a second God, but why had we entirely rejected the man who had preached the Sermon on the Mount, healed the sick, rejoiced in the return of the Prodigal Son, and showed compassion for the poor? I had always instinctively recoiled at his name, yet I was touched as a human by his words and lofty ethics. But who exactly was Jesus? What did he really say? What was his message that we had rejected two millennia ago—or had we, during his lifetime? I felt I had to know.

My stomach knotted when I first opened the New Testament. Jesus Christ. The Holy Spirit. Baptism. I was suddenly in the presence of the man in whose name millions of Jews had been persecuted, exiled, and killed. Every word seemed alien. But as I gained familiarity through constant rereadings, unexpected revelations started to emerge. Jesus began appearing remarkably Jewish in many passages, to the point that I began wondering whether anyone unfamiliar with Judaism could fully understand him. After all, he was really Jeshua of Nazareth, the Holy Spirit was God's Ruach ("Spirit," in Hebrew), and baptism was a form of Jewish ritual cleansing. It became clear that virtually every word Jesus spoke was directed toward fellow Jews, who would have understood his words in their traditional Jewish context. It also became apparent that the New Testament described more than one Jesus. The loving and compassionate figure we usually envision was certainly present in one of the four Gospel accounts of his life, but there was an angry, demanding Jesus in another Gospel, a breathless miracle worker in a third, and a ferociously anti-Semitic Jesus-god—hardly human at all—in the fourth. The portraits seemed irreconcilable. Which was the real Jesus? I began suspecting for the first time that most Christians knew their Scriptures no better than Jews know theirs—that they focused primarily on the weekly sermon and some treasured Bible passages, while overlooking the disquieting or contradictory.

I soon discovered that my newfound knowledge served as an infallible charm against evangelists. After courteously listening for a minute or two, I would borrow their Bible and ask them to explain certain passages that demonstrated that not even Jesus had been Christian. Invariably, they would fall silent and fidget. They would finally admit their perplexity ("We've never really noticed these before"), but they pledged to return as soon as their ministers explained the passages to them. But they never returned. Not once. Because my evidence was irrefutable, for it came from their own Scriptures and could not be denied.

But gratifying as this disappearing-evangelist parlor trick was, it merely whetted my appetite to learn more. Just as Columbus had been stunned to discover that he had landed not in India but in uncharted lands, I was so astonished by Jesus' unexpected outlines that I felt the need for deeper exploration. Even after leaving Tennessee to get an MBA that led to a lengthy career as a Wall Street biomedical analyst, I continued reading additional scholarly books by distinguished Protestant, Catholic, and Jewish authorities. I discovered I had embarked on the most intellectually and emotionally thrilling quest of my life. Jesus was, after all, arguably the most influential figure in Western history. Given his enormous impact, it seemed important to understand him better. Who exactly was he? What was his mission? Was the conventional perception about him oversimplified? That certainly seemed to be the consensus of leading scholars, even if they disagreed over details.

Today, several decades and many dozen books of later, I have come to realize that no one can fairly claim to possess all the answers, because our knowledge of Jesus is incomplete and often contradictory. But I believe that the basic outlines of his life and mission are reasonably clear—and will astonish nearly every Jewish reader and many Christians as well. For Jews, the main roadblock to understanding Jesus is an emotional discomfit with this topic that has dissuaded them from reading either the New Testament or any academic study. The present volume is intended to remedy this situation. It is concise, comprehensive, and assumes no prior knowledge of Jesus or Christianity. Most importantly, it is *authoritative*, because its foundation is not the scholarship of experts whose names would be unfamiliar to most readers, but the *New Testament* itself, along with the *teachings of the world's largest Christian denomination*. Since neither of these sources has any conceivable motivation to exaggerate Jesus' Jewishness, I believe that if Jesus' fidelity to Judaism can be demonstrated from these sources, most Jews will consider such evidence highly persuasive.

For Christians, on the other hand, the main impediment is a lifetime so steeped in Christian thought and theology—much arising many decades after Jesus' death—that understanding the Gospels from the perspective of Jesus' own first-century lifetime can be problematical. Educated priests and ministers are well trained to do so, but, like rabbis, they prefer to concentrate on the spiritually uplifting, to satisfy the emotional needs of their congregants. For Christians, therefore, this book will hopefully acquaint them with aspects of Jesus' life that have been widely discussed for decades and even centuries in seminaries, but infrequently highlighted in community churches. This book is intended to excite interest and provoke fresh thinking in all readers, as befits a subject as central to Western civilization as Jesus of Nazareth.

CHAPTER 1

INTRODUCTION

Would it surprise you to learn that Jesus Christ was faithful to Judaism to the end of his days and that he ministered only to the Jews and never claimed to be God (or even Messiah, publicly)? Would it surprise you even more to learn that these are the *teachings of the Roman Catholic Church*—the Church that was synonymous with Christianity for fifteen hundred years in the Western world and that even today has far more adherents worldwide than all Protestant denominations combined? If so, you are in the company of most Christians and a large majority of Jews.

The Roman Catholic Church teaches these facts for a good reason: they are *revealed in the New Testament itself*, primarily in the Gospels that describe Jesus' life and ministry. But if this is so, why do the Gospels seem to be full of invectives against the Jews? Didn't Jesus constantly refute the Jewish law of the Pharisees? And didn't a Jewish mob in Jerusalem cry out for his crucifixion? On the other hand, how could his fellow Jews have rejected him when the Gospels depict him as being surrounded by adoring crowds wherever he went? And why did he instruct them to obey the Pharisees' teachings, and even exceed them? Yet if he was so Jewish, how did Christianity arise as a separate religion? What *was* his message—the real meaning of his parables and sayings, and of the Sermon on the Mount? The New Testament not only helps answer these questions, but also poses unexpected new ones. Why did Jesus intentionally obscure his message such that the people he tried to teach would not understand him? Why did the people who knew him best think he was "out of his mind"?

Numerous books have plumbed these questions, but many are too long and academic for most readers. This author's hope is to rectify this situation. First, this book is intended to be a primer, so people with no prior knowledge of the New Testament can digest it through a series of well-organized chapters. The writing is straightforward and nonacademic. Second, the book will focus primarily on how Jesus is depicted in the New Testament, rather than on the "historical Jesus," because for both Christians and Jews, Jesus' epochal importance derives from his portrayal in the Gospels. Most people's indelible image of Jesus, which has touched so many lives over the millennia, is based on the Nativity stories, the parables and the Sermon on the Mount, and his death and resurrection. No analysis that strays far from the Gospels is likely to be both emotionally and intellectually fulfilling. Furthermore, studying the Gospels allows Jesus to be understood by means of the very stories and sayings—often so unexpectedly Jewish—that pervade Western culture and daily life. Yet comprehending "Jesus of the Gospels" simultaneously illuminates the "historical Jesus" as well—the actual life of Jesus Christ, based on modern scholarship.

This book's approach is straightforward. It will assume that the New Testament texts are true as written, unless they are contradicted by internal discrepancies, accepted historical fact, or the biblical analysis of arguably the most authoritative Christian Study Bible in the United States. (Study Bibles contains extensive commentary on the biblical text.) Because most American Christians are Protestant, the New Testament translation used in this book is the most popular Protestant translation in the United States, the NRSV (New Revised Standard Version).[1] As for a truly authoritative Study Bible—i.e., one with the official imprimatur of its church—no such Protestant Bible exists, since Protestantism consists of dozens of denominations with divergent ideologies. Therefore, the official Catholic Study Bible (CSB) was chosen. Written by the ruling body of the United States Catholic Church (the U.S. Conference of Catholic Bishops), this is authorized as the *only* Study Bible permitted for use in American Catholic churches. Although the Vatican itself does not formally approve any nation's Study Bible, the Catholic Study Bible bears the "Nihil Obstat" stamp that signifies that all its contents are "not incompatible" (i.e., are consistent) with Vatican doctrine. It may seem unorthodox to apply Roman Catholic commentary to a Protestant Bible, but however sharply Protestants and Catholics disagree on certain issues (the Papacy, the adoration of the Virgin Mary, etc.), their conceptions of Jesus himself are very similar. Moreover, the Roman Catholic Church is the world's largest Christian church and, even in the United States, has as many adherents as the two largest Protestant denominations combined (Baptists and Methodists). The rationale of using American's most popular Bible and sole official Study Bible is simple: inasmuch as neither Protestants nor Roman Catholics have any conceivable motive to exaggerate Jesus' Jewishness, I am assuming that if Jesus' devotion to Judaism can

---

1   Verses from the Jewish Scriptures (Tanakh, or "Old Testament") are from the traditional Jewish translation, the "Masoretic Text." *(The Holy Scriptures: according to the Masoretic Text.* [Philadelphia, Penn.: Jewish Publication Society of America, 1955.])

be proven using primarily these two sources, most readers, whether Christian or Jewish, would consider such evidence highly persuasive.

But before opening the New Testament, it is important to survey what we know about Jesus from the contemporary first-century historical record.

CHAPTER 2

WHAT CONTEMPORARY HISTORY HAD TO SAY ABOUT JESUS

Nothing.

Jesus was never mentioned in any contemporary historical record. He *was* briefly mentioned in 95 CE (sixty-five years after his death) by the major historian of first-century Palestine,[2] Flavius Josephus (c. 37–100 CE).[3] The passage's exact wording is uncertain, because early Christian scribes altered it to make more reverent, leaving modern scholars unsure of its original form. However, the original text is believed to have said that Jesus had been "a wise man. For he was a doer of startling deeds, a teacher of people who receive the truth with pleasure, and he won over many of the Jews and also many Greeks. And the tribe of the Christians, so named after him, has not disappeared to this day."[4] But not a single detail about Jesus' deeds or teachings is provided, let alone any mention of a resurrection. Josephus wrote at greater length about John the Baptist (Jesus' forerunner), who was apparently considered to be more important. The next historical reference to Jesus came in 117 CE from the greatest of Roman historians, Tacitus.

---

2   The term Palestine was first applied to the Jewish nation only after Jesus' death, when the Romans decided to punish the Jews following the Second Jewish Revolt (132–135 CE) by naming the country after the ancient Philistines. Nevertheless, this term will be used because there was no unitary name during Jesus' time that described all the territories of the Jewish nation (primarily Judea and Galilee).

3   Biblical scholars often use CE (Common Era) instead of A.D., and BCE (Before the Common Era) instead of B.C.

4   Josephus, *Antiquities*, 18:63–64.

After describing Christians as "a class hated for their abominations," his entire description of Jesus is that he "suffered the extreme penalty ... at the hands of ... Pontius Pilate."[5]

This historical void is perplexing in light of the momentous events recorded in the Gospels about Jesus' life, including:

- The slaughter of every male Jewish baby under two years of age near Bethlehem at the time of Jesus' birth, because the king of Palestine, Herod the Great, feared that the newborn messiah would ultimately threaten his rule.

- Miracles ranging from raising the dead, mass healings, walking on water, feeding thousands with a few bits of bread, and stilling violent storms, not to mention his own resurrection.

- A three-hour solar eclipse at the time of Jesus' death, accompanied by an earthquake that shook dead Jewish prophets from their tombs, causing them to wander through Jerusalem's streets in broad daylight.

This historical silence is particularly puzzling because Palestine was administered by the Romans and their vassal rulers (such as Herod the Great) throughout Jesus' life. The Romans were of course superb warriors, but above all they excelled in administration. No people, even to our own time, has ever managed to rule and control such a vast, heterogeneous empire for nearly five hundred years. Their secret was discipline and meticulous organization. They placed kings and rulers, centurions, spies, judges, tax collectors, and other functionaries everywhere. They carefully recorded regulatory decisions, legal judgments, revenue receipts, and newsworthy events of every kind. While it is true that many of these records never survived, not a single word about Jesus had been found in any contemporary Roman document, or anywhere else. Nor can anything be found in the oral Jewish tradition of these times, not even the horrific slaughter of the infants. In history's eyes, Jesus lived and died in total obscurity.

This historical gap immeasurably elevates the importance of discovering Jesus within the New Testament itself, as this constitutes the sole account of his life and works.

---

5   Tacitus, *Annals*, 15:44.

CHAPTER 3

THE GOSPELS: AN OVERVIEW

Jesus lived from c. 5 BCE to c. 30 CE[6] and conducted his epochal religious ministry during his final year or two. His life story is recorded in the Gospels written by the four "Evangelists": Mark, Matthew, Luke, and John. These Gospels, along with the momentous Letters of Paul, represent the heart of the New Testament, and more than half its total contents.

The four Evangelists were believed by the early Church to have been among Jesus' Twelve Disciples, or at least the Disciples' intimate friends.[7] However, it is now accepted that none of the Evangelists ever saw Jesus, and that they probably did not know the Disciples either. Tragically, neither Jesus nor his Disciples ever wrote anything. Instead, the Evangelists apparently wrote their Gospels based on stories and sayings that had been circulating about Jesus for several decades.

Of enormous importance, all four Gospels were composed forty to eighty years after Jesus' death, from 70 to 110 CE. This relatively late date distances the Evangelists not only from Jesus, but also from the world he lived in, owing to the intervening cataclysm of the First Jewish Revolt (66–70 CE). In those tragic years, the Romans had destroyed the Jewish heartland of Jerusalem and surrounding Judea. Among the casualties of this calamity was the original synagogue that the Twelve Disciples created in Jerusalem, shortly after their master's death in c. 30 CE. This congregation, called the Mother Synagogue in this book, was led by Peter (St. Peter) himself—Jesus' chief Disciple—along with one lesser Disciple (John) and also Jesus' brother James. As shall become apparent, this synagogue was an authentically *Jewish* congregation that happened to believe that Jesus had been the

---

6   Most dates in this book are accurate within two to three years, since scholars are
     unsure of precise dates. For example, Jesus could have been born as late as 4 BCE and
     died as late as 33 CE.

7   The Twelve Disciples will be designated as "the Disciples" in this book, whereas "dis-
     ciples" will refer to lesser followers of Jesus.

Messiah foretold by the Tanakh (the Jewish Bible, or "Old Testament"). In believing that Jesus had been the Messiah, this congregation was no more heretical than the great sage/rabbi Akiva, who allegedly proclaimed a century later that the real Messiah was Bar Kochba, the leader of the Second Jewish Revolt (132–135 CE).

The Mother Synagogue's destruction during the 60s CE radically transformed the nature of the young Jesus sect. Until the First Jewish Revolt, the sect was centered in Jewish Palestine, even though some of the early Jesus missionaries had established small congregations in the Gentile nations of the Roman Empire. But when the Mother Synagogue was destroyed,[8] the Jesus sect's center of gravity shifted from Palestine to the Gentile lands of Syria, Turkey, Greece, Rome, and elsewhere. It was in these places that the Gospels were written, by Evangelists who spoke only Greek and were largely unfamiliar with Jewish religion or history. The only exception may have been Matthew, who probably lived in Galilee, or at least in nearby Syria. The four Gospels are quite distinct from one another.

Mark

Mark was an unknown Christian, perhaps living in Syria, who in c. 70 CE wrote the first Gospel, possibly based entirely on oral source material. Stylistically it consists of individual episodes in Jesus' life ("pericopes," which include quotations and other details), connected by more general narrative passages. The Gospel portrays Jesus as an impassioned miracle worker and teacher with strong human feelings of surprise, admiration, fear, and anger. Events occur at breakneck speed, linked by words like "immediately" and "at once." The dizzying pace is heightened by the fact that the pericopes and connecting narrative passages seem to proceed in near-random order. The only exception to this is the tightly organized section about Jesus' final days in Jerusalem.

Mark's Gospel is generally regarded as the most historically accurate of the four, both because of its early date and its very human depiction of Jesus. Unfortunately, most Christians consider it the least important Gospel, largely due to this relatively uninspiring portrait of Jesus. Moreover, owing to the early Church's erroneous belief that Mark's Gospel was the second to be written, all versions of the New Testament sandwich it between the Gospels of Matthew and Luke, both of which are longer, stylistically superior, and more spiritually uplifting.

---

8   The Christian tradition that the Mother Synagogue survived by relocating to Pella, Jordan, has no historical support.

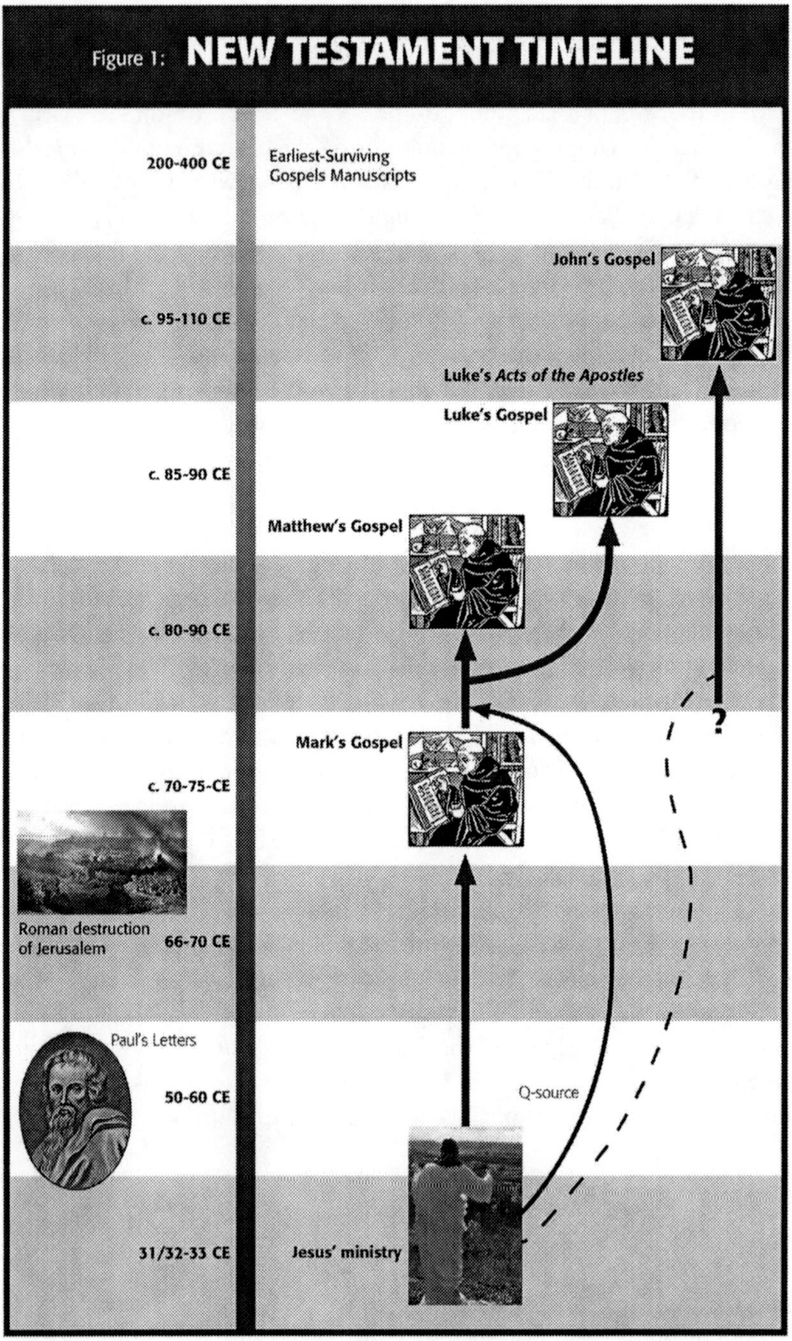
Figure 1: NEW TESTAMENT TIMELINE
200-400 CE
Earliest-Surviving Gospels Manuscripts
John's Gospel
c. 95-110 CE
Luke's Acts of the Apostles
Luke's Gospel
c. 85-90 CE
Matthew's Gospel
c. 80-90 CE
?
Mark's Gospel
c. 70-75-CE
Roman destruction of Jerusalem
66-70 CE
Paul's Letters
50-60 CE
Q-source
31/32-33 CE
Jesus' ministry

Matthew

Matthew may have been the only Judeo-Christian Evangelist,[9] and may even have lived in northern Galilee, which might make this Gospel the only one written in the Jewish homeland. It was written in c. 80–90 CE. Matthew relied very heavily on a copy of Mark's Gospel, although he often rearranged Mark's sequence of events (pericopes) to suit his own taste. More important, he added substantial new material. Some was unique material in his own possession, but most consisted of Jesus' "Q-sayings" (from the German word *Quelle*, for "source"). These sayings may have been orally transmitted, but they probably existed in the form of a document that may have been circulating by 50–60 CE but unfortunately disappeared thereafter. Scholars ascribe great significance to the Q-source, because it constitutes the earliest (and presumably most historically accurate) Gospel material.[10] Unfortunately, many of these Q-sayings provide few clues about to whom they were addressed, or when. Since their original context was unknown, Matthew distributed these sayings throughout his Gospel as he saw fit.

Matthew's Jesus remains human, but he is more dignified than Mark's. He no longer moves at breakneck speed and is more of a teacher (due largely to the many Q-sayings) than a miracle worker. He rarely expresses surprise or fear but overflows with righteous anger, particularly at the Jewish authorities. This anti-Judaic tone is paradoxical,[11] because this Gospel is simultaneously the most devotedly Jewish, as shall be seen. Likewise, it is the most reverent toward the Tanakh, dozens of whose verses are quoted in an attempt to prove that Jesus was the Messiah foretold

---

9 This book will use "Judeo-Christian" to refer to both traditional Jews who happened to believe that Jesus was the Messiah (e.g., the Disciples), and also those whose religious practices were in the process of evolving from Judaism to the new religion of Christianity.

10 The Q-source seems to have originated in Jesus' homeland of Galilee, further supporting its historical validity. The Q "community" appears to have consisted of devout, apocalyptically oriented Judeo-Christians who were viewed with skepticism and hostility by their traditional Jewish neighbors. Because Matthew's version of the Q-sayings is more artistically polished than Luke's, it is considered less authentic. The reasoning is that if both Evangelists used the same Q-source, it is more likely that Matthew tried to burnish Jesus' sayings than that Luke intentionally made them cruder.

11 This book will generally use "anti-Judaic" instead of "anti-Semitic," because the Gospels (except for John) are rarely hostile to the Jewish people (who included Jesus and his Disciples). Nor, as shall become evident, are they generally hostile toward Judaism itself. Instead they are hostile to specific beliefs and practices of some of the Jewish "authorities" (the Sadducees and Pharisees). Since there is no word meaning "hostile to the Jewish authorities," the term "anti-Judaic" will be used instead.

by Jewish Scripture. (These "prophecies" are called proof texts by Christians.) The dramatic tension and burnished literary style of this Gospel has long made it the favorite of Christians, along with the Gospel of John.

Luke

Luke was a Christian who lived somewhere outside of Palestine, possibly in Rome. Many scholars believe he might have accompanied Paul (St. Paul) on some of his journeys. (Although Paul was an extremely important early missionary, he was not a Disciple, and he never saw Jesus [except as a vision, following Jesus' death].) Luke's Gospel was probably the third to be written, in 85–95 CE. He was unaware of Matthew's Gospel, but like Matthew he possessed copies of Mark's Gospel and the Q-source.[12] (The concept that both Luke and Matthew relied primarily on these same two sources, which is accepted by most scholars, is called the Two-Source Hypothesis.)

Nevertheless, these two Gospels are significantly different. One important reason is that Luke often placed the Q-sayings in different parts of the story than Matthew, thereby completely changing their meaning. Moreover, he incorporated substantial material of his own. Finally, he overlaid everything with "irenic" (peaceful, compassionate) overtones. Indeed, Luke created the conventional image of Jesus that exists to this day. Luke's Jesus is notable for his tenderness, loving-kindness, and serenity. His special concern for the poor, women, and the powerless is emphasized, and contentious anti-Judaic elements are minimized.

Several years after writing this Gospel, Luke wrote a second manuscript, entitled the Acts of the Apostles. (The "apostles" were the early missionaries of the Jesus sect, although the term sometimes also includes the Disciples.) This is an extremely important work, being the only New Testament account of the early post-Jesus era of the Jesus sect, from c. 30 to 60 CE.

---

12   Luke's unawareness of Matthew's Gospel was typical of this period. Until the early second century, few Christian congregations were aware that more than one Gospel existed. (L. Michael White, *From Jesus to Christianity* [San Francisco: HarperSanFrancisco, 2004], 450ff). This was partly due to poor communication and the scarcity of expensive manuscripts. Moreover, Christianity was a tiny and scattered sect, with no formal infrastructure until the first half of the second century. Based on the limited available data, one scholar recently estimated that a decade after Jesus' death, in 40 CE, there were a mere one thousand Judeo-Christians and Christians in the world (Stark, *The Rise of Christianity*, 5–7). By 100 CE the number of Christians worldwide was perhaps eight thousand. (Relatively few Judeo-Christians remained by 100 CE, because the two religions were increasingly estranged by then.) In contrast, the Roman Empire contained five or six million Jews, equivalent to 10 percent of its total population.

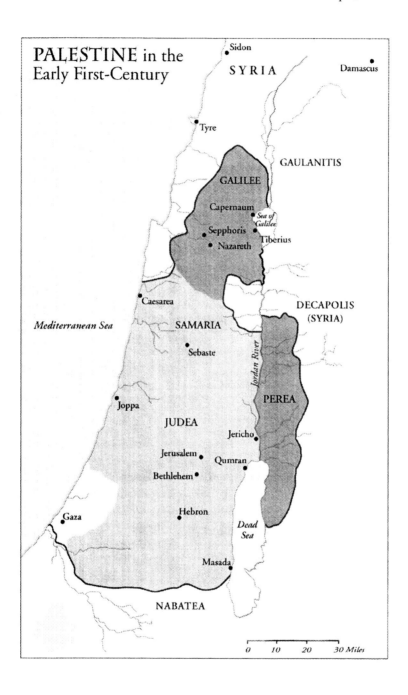

PALESTINE in the
Early First-Century

• Sidon

SYRIA

• Damascus

• Tyre

GAULANITIS

GALILEE

Capernaum •

Sea of
Galilee

Sepphoris •

• Nazareth

Tiberius

• Caesarea

DECAPOLIS
(SYRIA)

Mediterranean Sea

SAMARIA

• Sebaste

Jordan River

PEREA

• Joppa

JUDEA

Jericho •

Jerusalem •

Qumran •

Bethlehem •

• Hebron

*Dead
Sea*

• Gaza

Masada •

NABATEA

0   10   20   30 *Miles*

John

John's Gospel was the last to be written, c. 95–110 CE, by a series of Christian authors, possibly in Antioch or Ephesus (Turkey). John's Gospel is radically different from its predecessors. For all their differences, the three earlier Gospels portray essentially the same man, performing the same deeds and speaking in the same manner. They can therefore be grouped together for interpretation, which is why they became called the "Synoptic" (meaning "to view together," in Greek) Gospels. But 85 percent of John's account is completely new. More important, it contradicts the Synoptic Gospels so fundamentally that scholars still debate whether John was even aware of their existence. For example, the Synoptics' account of Jesus' one- or two-year ministry, centered in Galilee, becomes a three-year Jerusalem-centered ministry. But these differences pale before John's radically new portrait of Jesus. Jesus is now *divine*, shorn almost entirely of humanness. He is God's only Son, who preexisted in heaven before appearing on earth in a human incarnation, as Jesus. His speech is highly symbolic and theological and devoted primarily to expounding his own divinity. The earthy, colorful parables that pervade the Synoptic Gospels are entirely gone. Moreover, he is no longer a Jewish prophet/Messiah trying to guide his people, but rather an anti-Semite who hates most Jews, commoners and religious authorities alike. To Christians, however, this depiction of Jesus as divine makes this Gospel a favorite, along with Matthew's.[13]

John's Gospel creates a serious dilemma for anyone attempting to present a unified image of Jesus. Even the early Church fathers were unsure of what to do with John's Gospel ... once they became aware of it. Not even Church father Justin Martyr, who in c. 150 CE became the first person to realize that three Synoptic Gospels existed, was aware of John.[14] When the Church did discover this Gospel, its initial reaction was mixed. On the one hand, it was delighted to finally have a Gospel depicting a godlike Jesus. On the other hand, the Church was then trying to stamp out the "Gnostic heresy," according to which some Christians believed that Jesus had been *wholly divine* while on earth. The Church had accepted Jesus' divinity by this time (though the full concept of the Trinity would come later), but needed Jesus to be wholly *human* during his earthly visitation. After all, only a

---

13   Readers will immediately appreciate the dramatic dissimilarity between the Synoptics and John's Gospel when reading the excerpts from this Gospel in chapter 17 ("How Jesus Became God").

14   White, *From Jesus to Christianity*, 453. 150 CE was also the earliest date at which any church accepted more than one Gospel as authoritative (Raymond Brown, *An Introduction to the New Testament* [New York: Doubleday, 1997], 13). Until then, each church relied on only a single Gospel.

human Jesus could have "suffered" for humanity's sins and "died" on the cross. The Church finally decided that John's Jesus was just human enough to be acceptable.

This still left John's discrepancies with the Synoptics unresolved. The famous Clement of Alexandria squared the circle in c. 160 CE by calling it the "spiritual" Gospel. That is, it depicted the earthly story of Jesus' divine spirit, rather than his human body. Another major breakthrough in its acceptance occurred when Justin Martyr's student Tatian wrote a unified one-book Gospel (the Diatessaron, c. 170 CE) that incorporated John's material with a "harmonized" account of the more widely accepted Synoptic Gospels. This version of the gospel was initially extremely popular. By artfully editing and interweaving John's material into the familiar Synoptic accounts, the Diatessaron managed to familiarize large numbers of Christians with John's material.[15] By the time this volume fell out of favor, the Church found it much easier to accept John's Gospel as a separate entity. Its acceptance into the canon was set on track in c. 180 CE by the influential bishop of Lyon, Irenaeus. His concern about the schismatic effect of dozens of "authentic" gospels circulating throughout Christendom impelled him to make the first successful effort to establish an official Christian canon of Gospels. Irenaeus argued for John's inclusion as one of four authentic Gospels. His rationale was that "it is not possible that the Gospels can be either more or fewer in number [than four]. For, since there are four zones of the world, and four principal winds ... and the

---

15 The Diatessaron's popularity reveals that even at this late date, the Gospels were not considered Holy Scripture immune to human tampering (David Freeman, editor-in-chief, *The Anchor Bible Dictionary* [New York: Doubleday, 1992], s.v. "Canon, New Testament," I:852ff; Burton H. Throckmorton, Jr., *Gospel Parallels* [Nashville: Thomas Nelson Publishers, 1992], xii–xix). The only Scripture recognized by Christians at this time was the Jewish Tanakh. The Gospels, in contrast, were generally regarded as historical memoirs, until they began to receive Scriptural status in 180–250 CE. That "improving" these non-Scriptural Gospels was considered acceptable until this period is extremely unfortunate, because no *original* Gospel manuscripts have ever been found. The best complete New Testament manuscripts (the Codex Sinaiticus and the Codex Vaticanus) are from the fourth century. Among earlier papyrus fragments, the only substantial one is the "p75" papyrus (c. 200 CE), which contains three-fourths of the Gospels of Luke and John. As a result, no one actually knows the *original contents of any Gospel*. It is essential to remain aware of the time lapse between Jesus' life (died 33 CE), the original Gospels (70–110 CE), and the earliest surviving manuscripts (200–400 CE) that are the source of modern New Testaments. As shall be seen, the Synoptic Gospels found in modern New Testaments contain some surprisingly Christological statements from Jesus (i.e., implying or proclaiming his divinity). Scholars endlessly debate whether such statements originated with Jesus himself, or with the Evangelists, or with later Christian scribes who decided to "improve" the original texts.

pillar ... of the Church is the Gospels ... it is fitting that she should have four pillars."[16] But Irenaeus went even further, by opining that John's "spirituality" made it the most sublime Gospel of all.[17] By c. 250, the four Gospels were firmly established as Scripture throughout the Christian world.

In short, John's Gospel is fundamentally incompatible with the Synoptics (except, of course, to believing Christians). Is it possible that Jesus had really been God and publicly declaimed his divinity at great length, but that Mark and Matthew and Luke, and all their sources of information, *had never noticed*? This seems inconceivable. In the end, one must choose between the three earlier Synoptics and John's Gospel. It is not surprising that the most highly respected general reference work in the English language baldly states that "Scholars have *unanimously* chosen the Synoptic Gospels' version of Jesus' teaching.... They are ... the primary sources for knowledge of the historical Jesus.... John, however, is so different that *it cannot be reconciled with the Synoptics*." (italics added)[18] This book will therefore conform to the accepted convention of relying on the Synoptics.

Still, presenting Jesus' image from the Synoptics is easier said than done. The summaries above have already highlighted some of their differences. Events occurring early during Jesus' ministry in one Gospel occur near the end in another. Sayings associated with a particular pericope in one Gospel may be coupled to an entirely different one elsewhere. Landmark events in one Synoptic may go unmentioned elsewhere. The magnitude of these discrepancies can be dramatically illustrated by comparing their treatment of Jesus' birth, commonly referred to as the Nativity.

Mark

- No Nativity story, as if his birth was not worth mentioning.

Matthew

- An angel tells Joseph, living in Bethlehem, that Mary will conceive a son by divine intervention.
- The Magi pay homage to the newborn Jesus.

---

16   Irenaeus, *Against Heresies*, 3.11.7.

17   White, *From Jesus to Christianity*, 305, 453–55.

18   *Encyclopedia Britannica*, s.v. "Jesus Christ," 22:339.

- King Herod the Great and his religious advisors are so alarmed about the newborn Messiah that soldiers are ordered to kill all male infants around Bethlehem.

- Joseph's family escapes by fleeing to Egypt, at an angel's urging.

- Following King Herod's death, Joseph returns to Palestine, this time to Nazareth.

Luke

- An angel first visits Mary's relative Elizabeth, saying she will give birth to John the Baptist, who will prepare the way for the Messiah.

- The angel later appears to Mary herself, who is living in Nazareth with Joseph, to prophecy Jesus' virgin birth.

- Joseph moves with Mary to his birthplace of Bethlehem, where the baby Jesus is born in the manger of a stable.

- As heavenly angels herald the Messiah's birth, local shepherds rush into the manger to inform Mary and Joseph of the celestial pronouncement.

- Following Jesus' circumcision, his parents bring him to the Jerusalem Temple. Two devout Jews instantly discern his identity and glorify him.

The discrepancies are striking. Mark fails to mention *any* of the signs and wonders documented by Matthew and Luke. Meanwhile, the latter two Gospels are *entirely* different except for two details: the virgin birth,[19] and Jesus' family residence in both Bethlehem and Nazareth (but at different times in their lives).[20]

When the early Church fathers became aware of the existence of three Synoptic Gospels by c. 125–150 CE, they were understandably baffled and distressed by

---

19 The notion of a virgin birth arose from a misunderstanding of *almah*, the Hebrew word for young maiden (girl). An unmarried maiden was expected to be a virgin until she married and conceived with her husband. This is the meaning of the Tanakh's verse "Behold, a young maiden shall conceive" (Isaiah 7:14). Early Christians misunderstood this "proof text" as saying that a virgin would conceive by supernatural means, and applied it to Mary. In fact, this verse explicitly refers to the (quite conventional) birth of the Jewish King Hezekiah, in the seventh century BCE.

20 Bethlehem was important as the birthplace of King David, from whose lineage the Messiah was expected to spring. Nazareth was important, according to the Gospels, so that Jesus could fulfill the Tanakh's prophecy that the Messiah would be a "Nazorean." In fact, no such prophecy exists. The Evangelists might have misinterpreted the word "Nazarite" (one who is consecrated to God) or Nezer (a branch [of the House of David]).

these discrepancies. The desire to harmonize them was of course the main impetus for Tatian's Diatessaron in c. 170 CE. In the end, however, the Church rejected this book owing to concern that too much authentic material may have been deleted. The Church decided instead to retain the four separate Gospels and to try to reconcile their discrepancies by means of carefully crafted interpretations.

But returning to this book's goal, don't the Synoptics' contradictions complicate efforts to present a coherent image of Jesus? The answer is yes. Fortunately, most Synoptic narratives are considerably more consistent than the Nativity stories. Moreover, there is a way to resolve many of these smaller discrepancies, as demonstrated in the next chapter.

CHAPTER 4

THE KEY QUESTION: DID JESUS REJECT JUDAISM AND CREATE A NEW RELIGION?

Let us begin exploring the New Testament's account of Jesus, starting with the most fundamental question: Did Jesus reject Judaism and create a new religion? Most people believe that Jesus repudiated all or part of the Mosaic Law and then disseminated his new teachings to both Gentiles and Jews. (The Mosaic Law, the foundation of Judaism, consists of God's commands as expounded in the first five books of the Bible [Genesis, Exodus, Leviticus, Numbers, and Deuteronomy]). Yet as noted at this book's beginning, not even the Catholic Church believes this. But how can this be, in light of Jesus' well-known Gospel clashes with the Jewish religious authorities?

The answer must begin with our discovery about the Synoptics: they commonly contradict one another, as dramatized by their divergent accounts of the Nativity. Similarly, an anti-Judaic passage in one Gospel may become philo-Judaic in another. Each Gospel is sometimes internally contradictory as well. So how is it possible to determine which accounts are most accurate?

Luckily, there is a solution. Just as maze diagrams are most easily solved by working backward from the final destination, the Synoptics are most easily approached by starting with the only New Testament account of the decades *following* Jesus' death, Acts of the Apostles. Recall that this was written by Luke, the only Evangelist to write accounts of both Jesus' life (the Gospel of Luke) and the years immediately following his death (Acts of the Apostles). Acts of the Disciples particularly focuses on the work of Peter (Jesus' chief Disciple; called Saint Peter by Catholics) and of Paul (called Saint Paul by Catholics), the greatest early missionary. The rationale for starting with Acts is twofold.

Explicitness: "Acts" is more descriptive than the Synoptics.

The Gospels are filled with Jesus' *words*, but we have noted that their interpretation is often complicated by their placement in different pericopes (stories) by the Evangelists. Moreover, the pericopes themselves are arranged in near-random order. The resulting loss of context often obscures the meaning of Jesus' sayings, as will become apparent by chapter 6. Even those sayings found in identical stories are often phrased differently, sometimes significantly so. Interpretation is further complicated by Jesus' fondness for hyperbole—gross exaggeration—in order to create striking verbal effects. Moreover, many of his outbursts against the religious authorities were spoken in anger (particularly in Matthew's Gospel), and may never have been intended as doctrines. A final problem, especially for Christians, is that their religious tradition has taught them to interpret Jesus' words in ways quite different from how his first-century Jewish contemporaries would have.

In short, the Synoptics are filled with often-ambiguous words, but rarely discuss *actions*, which are far more explicit. For example, there is no Synoptic description of a meal that reveals whether or not Jesus and his Disciples kept kosher. But Acts of the Apostles contains many lengthy, unequivocal passages about this and other critical religious practices. Such information is invaluable. For example, had Jesus abrogated the laws of kosher, his Disciples and their acolytes should obviously have followed his example. But if it can be proved that *they strictly kept kosher for many years after Jesus' death*, and even refused to eat the food of (nonkosher) Gentiles, it would **prove** that Jesus must have kept kosher himself. It must be recognized that Acts' unique status as the only description of the post-Jesus years makes it "true," by definition, for anyone who accepts the New Testament. Rejecting the validity of Acts would necessitate rejecting Luke's Gospel as well, eliminating one-fifth of the entire New Testament.

Confirmation: Acts is corroborated by Paul, Christianity's most important figure besides Jesus.

Although Paul never met Jesus, many modern scholars consider him the true founder of Christianity. His Letters constitute the largest and most important section of the New Testament, apart from the Gospels and Acts. Of note, they are the earliest documents in the entire New Testament. Paul lived from c. 10 to 62 CE and wrote his Letters from 50 to 60 CE, ten to twenty years before the first Gospel. These were real letters written to the leaders of congregations throughout the Roman world. They describe historical facts only infrequently (because their primary purpose was to propagate Paul's theology), but they appear to describe those facts straightforwardly. For example, they contain no stories of miracles. Only decades after his death did early Christians decide to collect these letters and ultimately canonize them (accept them as part of the New Testament). They are therefore generally regarded as the most historically accurate writings in the New Testament.[21]

With this rationale in mind, we can begin our examination of these seminal passages from Acts and Paul's Letters. Their *proof* that Jesus was thoroughly Jewish will in turn be the key to unlock the meaning of the Gospels themselves.

***

Acts begins immediately after the resurrection, with Jesus speaking to his Disciples. Before ascending to heaven (the Ascension), he instructed them to remain in Jerusalem, which was to become the site of the Mother Synagogue. Acts continues by detailing the synagogue's early history—rapid membership growth, numerous miracle healings, sporadic Temple persecution, and missionary work in Judea (the overwhelmingly Jewish region surrounding Jerusalem) and Samaria (situated between Judea and Galilee, and home of the Samaritans).

Acts: Peter's Vision, and the Meeting with Cornelius (c. 35–40 CE)

Acts' pivotal turning point begins during one of Peter's missionary trips through Palestine. Peter's importance must be clearly understood. He was the unquestioned leader of Jesus' Disciples, the foremost authority about his master. As he journeyed, a Roman centurion named Cornelius received an angelic visitation. Cornelius was a "God-fearer": a Gentile who revered Judaism and contributed generously to Jewish causes but was unwilling to formally convert by circumcision. The angel informed him that his constant prayers had won God's favor, and

---

21   The Q-source is as old as Paul's Letters. However, since no written Q-document has ever been found, its contents must be inferred by reading Matthew's and Luke's versions of these sayings. Overall, the relative value of these two earliest New Testament sources is as follows: Paul's Letters exist as he actually wrote them, and they appear to be historically accurate. Unfortunately, they rarely mention Jesus' life or teachings, and so are valuable primarily for their insights into the post-Jesus period, particularly outside of Palestine itself. In contrast, the Q-source is focused entirely on Jesus' ministry, and so is more directly relevant to Jesus himself. However, in addition to the fact that the Q-sayings exist only in Matthew and Luke (often in variant versions), it is extremely difficult to determine whether they accurately reflect the actual words of Jesus, who had died twenty years earlier.

that he should send for Peter, who was in the nearby town of Joffa. The next day, as Cornelius' servants approached Joffa at the lunchtime hour, Peter decided to pray, but he became so hungry that he fell into a trance:

> He saw the heaven opened and something like a large sheet coming down, being lowered to the ground by its four corners. In it were all kinds of four-footed creatures and reptiles and birds of the air. Then he heard a voice saying, "Get up, Peter; kill and eat." But Peter said, "By no means, Lord, for I have never eaten anything that is profane or unclean." (Acts 10:11–14)

"I have never eaten anything that is profane or unclean"? Was Peter saying that he had never eaten nonkosher food? That is certainly the Catholic Church's interpretation, for the CSB says, "The vision is intended to prepare Peter to share food with Cornelius' household without qualms of conscience. The necessity of such instructions to Peter reveals that at first not even the apostles fully grasped the implications of Jesus' teaching on the law."[22]

> The voice said to him a second time, "What God has made clean, you must not call profane." This happened three times, and then the thing was suddenly taken up to heaven. Now while Peter was greatly puzzled about what to make of the vision he had seen, suddenly the men sent by Cornelius ... appeared, ... As Peter was still thinking about the vision, the Spirit said to him, "Look, three men are searching for you ... go down." ... So Peter went down to the men and said, "What is the reason for your coming? They answered, "Cornelius ... who is well spoken of by the whole Jewish nation, was directed by a holy angel to send for you to come to his house and to hear what you have to say." [Peter] went with them, and some of the believers from Joppa [Peter's Jewish colleagues] accompanied him. ... Cornelius was expecting them and had called together his relatives and close Friends.... On Peter's arrival ... [Peter] said to them, *"You know that it is unlawful for a Jew to associate with or to visit a Gentile*, but God has shown me that I should not call anyone profane or unclean."
> (Acts 10:15–28; italics and brackets added)

---

22   Donald Senior, general ed., The Catholic Study Bible (New York: Oxford University Press, 1990), 200. Catholic doctrine asserts that many of Jesus' teachings were so subtle that his own Disciples (and often he himself) were unable to fully grasp their meaning. However, it seems unimaginable that the Disciples who lived with Jesus would not have known whether he obeyed such important Mosaic laws as eating kosher food or observing circumcision.

Unlawful for Jews to associate with Gentiles (i.e., non-Jews)? Was it only Peter's recent vision that had convinced him that Jews could mix with Gentiles? Again, the CSB concurs: "The arrival of the Gentile emissaries ... illuminates Peter's vision: he is to be prepared to admit Gentiles, who were considered unclean ... into the Christian community."[23] But how can this be? What about all the Gospel stories of Jesus supposedly rejecting the Jews and embracing Gentiles as the New Israel? Had Jesus actually regarded the Gentiles as unworthy and unclean?[24] The story proceeds as Cornelius recounted his angelic vision, following which Peter said:

"I truly understand that God shows no partiality, but in every nation anyone who fears him and does what is right is acceptable to him."
While Peter was still speaking, the Holy Spirit fell upon all who heard ... the word.
The circumcised believers who had come with Peter
were *astounded* that the gift of the Holy Spirit had been poured out *even on the Gentiles*, for they heard them speaking in tongues and extolling God.
Then Peter said, "Can anyone withhold the water for baptizing these people who have received the Holy Spirit just as we have?" So he ordered them to be baptized in the name of Jesus Christ. (Acts 10:34–48; italics added)

Peter and his companions were so astounded by the Holy Spirit's visitation to the Gentiles that Peter decided that they should be baptized too. (Although a distinctively Christian term, the "Holy Spirit" corresponds to "Ruach" [God's Spirit] in ancient Hebrew.) Can this mean that during Jesus' life, and even for years after his death, only *Jews* were baptized and allowed to participate in the Jesus sect? This is the clear meaning of this passage, as underlined by what happened next:

Now the apostles and the believers who were in Judea[25] heard that the Gentiles had also accepted the word of God. So when Peter went up to Jerusalem the circumcised believers criticized him, saying, "Why did you go to uncircumcised men and eat with them?" Peter began to explain it to them step by step, saying, "I was in the city of Joppa praying, and in a trance I saw a vision. There was something like a large sheet coming down ..." (Acts 11:1–5)

---

23 I.e., the early Jesus sect, which was Jewish.

24 See chapter 9.

25 I.e., members of the Mother Synagogue. Apostles are usually defined as missionaries, but Luke (author of Acts) used the term to include the Disciples as well.

Peter was obviously not the only Jew to be astonished at these events, for the members of the Jerusalem Mother Synagogue now confronted him, Jesus' favored Disciple. Peter had actually entered a Gentile house and eaten their nonkosher food! Such scandalous behavior demanded an explanation, so Peter proceeded to relate the entire episode, nearly verbatim. Repetitions of such length are extremely rare in the Gospels or Acts, and signify the momentousness of the occasion.

Acts: Establishment of the Antioch Synagogue (c. 37 CE); the Council of Jerusalem (c. 48 CE)

The scene in Acts suddenly shifts from Peter to some of the missionary work that had been underway for several years outside of Palestine. Instead of being Palestinian Jews, these missionaries were Diaspora Jews, or converts to Judaism. None appears to have ever met Jesus. They had been proselytizing solely to Jews in the nations surrounding Palestine (Acts 11:19), but as time progressed they began approaching Gentiles also. Acts seems to imply that, at first, the missionaries were converting these Gentiles to Judaism, as a precondition to joining the Jesus movement. Still, the concept of ethnically Gentile congregations was so extraordinary that when the Mother Synagogue heard of this unauthorized activity, it decided to investigate the congregation in Antioch (present-day southern Turkey) by sending a trusted member, Barnabas. He was sufficiently impressed with the Gentiles' zeal that he sent for Paul, so that they could together guide the synagogue/church. Paul, who will be discussed at length (chapter 16), was a Cilician Jew who had joined the Jesus sect. (Cilicia was a Roman province in southern Turkey, slightly north of Antioch.) Together Paul and Barnabas guided the congregation for one year, and it was here, in Antioch, that Jesus followers were first called "Christians" (Acts 11:26).

Acts is ambiguous as to whether these Gentile "Christians" (followers of Jesus the Messiah [Christ]) had converted to Judaism or not. Either way, it is clear that Paul began admitting unconverted Gentiles within the next year or two. So for the *first time*, probably in c. 40 (ten years after Jesus' death), a group of non-Jews devoted to his teachings arose. Whether the Mother Synagogue was initially aware of these distant events is unclear. However, during Paul's continued stay in Antioch, some members of the Mother Synagogue arrived and insisted that only Jews could follow Jesus, saying:

> "Unless you are circumcised according to the custom of Moses,
> you cannot be saved." And after Paul and Barnabas had no small
> dissension and debate with them ...
> Paul [and] Barnabas ... were appointed to go up to Jerusalem ...

and discuss this question with the apostles and the elders
[i.e., the Mother Synagogue].
(Acts 15:1–2, brackets added)

This was the impetus for the epochal Council of Jerusalem, c. 48 CE. The meeting quickly grew contentious, because "Some of the believers who belonged to the sect of the Pharisees stood up and said, 'It is necessary for them to be circumcised and ordered to keep the Law of Moses.' The apostles and the elders met together to consider this matter. After there had been much debate, Peter stood up …" (Acts 15:5–7).

Much debate? This is odd. The Mother Synagogue was run primarily by Peter and James, Jesus' own brother (see next chapter). (A third leader, the Disciple John, is rarely mentioned in Acts.) Why the need for debate? We have seen that Peter had already informed the synagogue, years previously, of his staggering encounter with Cornelius. Didn't everyone already understand that Gentiles could be Jesus followers? Apparently not, for the CSB notes that "The Jewish Christians of Jerusalem [i.e., the Mother Synagogue] … [had] concluded that the setting aside of the legal barrier between Jew and Gentile [i.e., Cornelius and his associates] was an *exceptional ordinance* of God."[26] So Peter himself had believed that Cornelius was a unique exception. This explains why Peter was being asked for the *first time*, nearly *twenty years* after Jesus' death, whether unconverted Gentiles could become Jesus followers. Peter finally arose, and declared his opinion:

"My brothers, you know that in the early days God made a choice …
among you, that I should be the one through whom the Gentiles would hear the
word of the good news and become believers. And God … testified to them by
giving them the Holy Spirit, just as he did to us … he made no distinction
between them and us.
Now therefore why are you now … placing on the neck
of the disciples a yoke that neither our ancestors nor we have been able to bear?[27]
On the contrary, we believe that we will be saved through the grace of the
Lord Jesus, just as they will." The whole assembly kept silence, and listened
to Barnabas and Paul as they told of all the signs and wonders God had done
through them among the Gentiles. (Acts 15:7–12)

---

26   The Catholic Study Bible, 201, italics and brackets added.

27   This is a curious statement in view of Peter's adherence to Judaism even after this time, as shall be seen.

But the matter was not yet resolved, because Jesus' brother James wanted to ensure that the Gentiles followed at least the laws of God's covenant with Noah: to abstain from fornication, things polluted by idols, and meat undrained of its blood. James seemed comfortable with this compromise because he knew these Gentiles had ample opportunity to become real Jews: "For in every city, for generations past, Moses has had those who proclaim him, for he has been read aloud every Sabbath in the synagogues" (Acts 15:13–21).

Thus, James—whose position carried the day—decreed a dual approach. Jews would continue to maintain the Mosaic Law, as taught in every synagogue. Gentiles who refused full conversion, though, would be allowed to embrace Jesus as long as they maintained the basic commandments of Noah. But whatever the details, it is clear that it was the Council of Jerusalem that decided, for the first time, that non-Jews could follow Jesus. Note that Paul, the main champion of this "mission to the Gentiles," never tried to justify his stance by referring to any of Jesus' own sayings or deeds. The clear implication is that Jesus had never advocated such action (see chapter 9). The CSB agrees. It states that during the early post-resurrection years, **"there was little or no thought of any dividing line between Christianity and Judaism."**[28] By definition, if there was no dividing line between Christianity and Judaism, it follows that the early Judeo-Christians were all *observant Jews.* The Disciples and other Jesus followers were simply traditional Jews who happened to believe that Jesus had been the Messiah foretold by the Tanakh. They were Jews by both birth and religious observance. What was novel was the concept that even non-Jews could become Jesus followers. As stated by the CSB, **"Only ... at the Council ... does the evangelization of the Gentiles become the official position of the church leadership in Jerusalem."**[29] In short, Acts of the Apostles *proves* that *Jesus remained faithful to Judaism, ministered only to Jews, and regarded Gentiles with indifference or worse.*

Paul: Letter to the Galatians

The above conclusion, from Luke's Acts, is so momentous that it is fortunately corroborated by an equally unimpeachable New Testament source: Paul. Paul provided his own account of the Council of Jerusalem in his Letter to the Galatians (50–56 CE). We have noted that scholars accord great weight to Paul's Letters, because they represent the oldest part of the New Testament (along with the Q-source) and they seem exceptionally objective. Paul's account is terse, but will become much clearer when we revisit it in chapter 16. The key point is that Paul acknowledged that it was the Council of Jerusalem that decided that he could

---

28   The Catholic Study Bible, 188.

29   The Catholic Study Bible, 201.

continue his special mission to the Gentiles, whereas those who had actually known Jesus (Peter, James, etc.) would continue living as Jews, as they always had. Describing his trip from Antioch to the Council of Jerusalem, Paul said:

> I went up again to Jerusalem with Barnabas.... I laid before them ... the gospel that I proclaim among the Gentiles.... When they saw that I had been entrusted with the gospel for the uncircumcised, just as Peter had been entrusted with the gospel to the circumcised ...
> and when James and Cephas[30] ... recognized the grace that had been given to me, they gave
> to Barnabas and me the right hand of fellowship, agreeing that we should go the Gentiles and they to the circumcised. (Gal 2:1–9)

Paul thus corroborates that it was the Council of Jerusalem that officially decided, for the first time, that non-Jews could follow Jesus; i.e., that *Jesus' early followers had all been practicing Jews.* He repeats James' decision that Paul could continue his work with the Gentiles, whereas James and Peter would continue their work with the Jews and Judeo-Christians. However, a fascinating epilogue in the Letter to the Galatians reveals that Peter was not completely comfortable with Paul's activities. Peter personally visited the Antioch church a year or so later and initially intermingled with the Gentile Jesus followers. But after several members of the Jerusalem Synagogue also arrived at Antioch, Peter's behavior changed, to the great chagrin of Paul:

> I opposed him [Peter] to his face, because he stood self-condemned, for ...
> he drew back and kept himself separate [from the Gentiles]
> for fear of the circumcision faction. And the rest of the Jews also
> joined him in this hypocrisy, so that even Barnabas was led astray.... When I saw that they were not acting consistently with the truth of the gospel, I said to Cephas before them all, "If you though a Jew, live like a Gentile ... how can you compel the Gentiles to live like Jews?"[31]
> (Gal 2:11–14, brackets added)

---

30 Peter's real name was Simeon, but Jesus nicknamed him the Rock (Cephas in Aramaic, Petros [Peter] in Greek) because of his position as chief Disciple.

31 Peter did not "live like a Gentile," but Paul was accusing him of hypocrisy and bad faith, for Peter had initially tried his best to treat the Gentiles as equals. Paul, being a Hellenistic Diaspora Jew, was well versed in Greek rhetoric, including the use of sophistry to win arguments.

So Peter apparently became ashamed or unsure of his willingness to socialize with Gentiles. This is further evidence that he remained fully Jewish at home in Jerusalem. Thus the ironic finale: Paul, *who had never met Jesus*, publicly upbraiding *Jesus' chief Disciple* for "ignoring" Jesus' teachings. Would Paul would have been so self-assured if he had known Jesus personally?

***

So both Luke and Paul—the sole sources for the early post-Jesus period—concur that Jesus followed the Mosaic Law and ministered exclusively to Jews during his life, and even during his post-resurrection return. Peter, James, and other Mother Synagogue congregants were simply traditional Jews who happened to believe that Jesus had been the Messiah. The turning point was the Council of Jerusalem's decision, fifteen years after Jesus' death, to approve Paul's mission to the gentiles. The Council of Jerusalem "*may be judged the most important meeting ever held in the history of Christianity,*" echoes a renowned Christian scholar, because it "decided that *the followers of Jesus would soon move beyond Judaism and become a separate religion.*"[32]

With this confirmation of Jesus' Jewish identity, we can begin to unlock the meaning of the Gospels themselves. The first question we will ask is why, if Jesus was so Jewish, do the Gospels seem to depict him as continually arguing with the Jewish religious authorities? But first, some words about how to understand the Gospels would be useful

Postscript: Did Peter Die a Jew or a Christian?

It is clear that Peter was Jewish at the time of the Council of Jerusalem. His age at this time is unknown, but he would have been nearly fifty if he had been five years younger than Jesus. Because he died less than twenty years later, by 67 CE, it is worth asking whether he remained Jewish to the very end, or whether, as Christian tradition holds, he died as the first bishop (pope) of the Roman Church, and was ultimately buried in the Vatican, beneath today's St. Peter's Basilica.

We know tantalizingly little about this subject. Acts of the Apostles says nothing further about Peter following the Council. Nor does Paul record any interaction with Peter following their clash at Antioch (c. 49 CE). However, Paul's last mention of Peter, in his First Letter to the Corinthians (c. 56 CE), suggests that the two men continued to clash on religious doctrines, to the extent that the Corinthian congregation confronted possible schism. "For it has been reported to

---

32   Brown, *Introduction to the New Testament*, 306.

me … that there are rivalries among you. I mean that each of you is saying, 'I belong to Paul,' or … 'I belong to Cephas [Peter]'" (1 Cor 1:10–13). He also expressed his irritation that Peter was broadly regarded as Jesus' authentic representative, because the Corinthians provided Peter with free room and board whenever he visited, while denying this honor to Paul (1 Cor 9:1–6).

This Letter strongly implies that a mere decade before his death, Peter was continuing to teach a different—presumably more Jewish—gospel, than Paul. Sadly, Peter disappears entirely from the New Testament at this point. (The two "Letters from Peter" in the New Testament were written by others.) However, a tenuous historical trail remains. It is generally accepted that Peter probably visited or even lived in Rome as early as 59 CE, and died there by 67 CE. The strongest evidence comes from Clement of Rome, an early Roman pope who, writing about his own city thirty years later (c. 95 CE), said that: "Peter … by reason of wicked jealousy … frequently endured suffering and thus, bearing his witness, [died.] … [He] … who lived such [a] holy [life] … joined a great multitude of the elect who by reason of rivalry were victims of many outrages and tortures and who became outstanding examples among us" (Clement of Rome, *Letter to the Corinthians*, 5:4, 6:1).

Clement's statement about the cause of Peter's death is perplexing. Most experts believe that Peter died along with thousands of other Judeo-Christians and Christians in 64–67 CE, following the notorious Roman fire of 64 CE. The Emperor Nero was so rattled by popular suspicions that he had ordered the fire so as to obtain additional land for his palace that he decided to accuse the "Christians" of deliberate arson. He instituted a vicious, indiscriminate persecution of Christian men, women, and children. (Many Jews were likewise ensnared, since the Romans, properly enough, considered "Christianity" to be no more than an obscure Jewish sect.) Did Clement's allusion to rivalry and envy suggest that enemies of Peter brought him to the attention of the Roman authorities? Or was Peter's death unrelated to the general tragedy?

Peter's life, however, is of greater interest to us than his death. Did he end his life a Jew (i.e., Judeo-Christian) or as a Paul-like Christian? No one knows, but it is important to note that despite his enormous visibility as Jesus' chief Disciple, there exists no evidence that he founded the Roman Church (as held by Christian tradition), served as its first bishop/pope, or even actively participated in it.[33] Extensive study of the writing of the early Church Fathers and the early Roman popes (e.g., Clement, the third pontiff) fail to disclose any allusions to Peter's

---

33 Daniel Wm. O'Conner, *Peter in Rome* (New York and London: Columbia University Press, 1969) 3–11, 70–75, 207–09; Bart Ehrman, *Peter, Paul, and Mary Magdalene* (New York: Oxford University Press, 2006), 80–84.

activities. "That Peter founded the Church at Rome is extremely doubtful and that he served as its first bishop ... for even one year, much less the twenty-five-year period that is claimed for him, is an unfounded tradition that can be traced back to a point no earlier than the third century.... Nothing can be determined ... about when he came to Rome, how long he stayed, or what function of leadership, if any, he exercised within the Roman Church."[34]

What then might Peter have been doing in Rome? Perhaps he was spending his declining years in the city's innumerable synagogues, doing what he had done so long: spreading the word about Jesus to his fellow Jews. We are so accustomed to envisioning Jews as a tiny minority that it is easy to forget how numerous they once were. In 50–100 CE, Rome was the world largest Jewish city, with as many as 650,000 Jewish inhabitants.[35] (Jerusalem contained only 25,000 people.) Overall, there were roughly 6 million Jews in the Roman Empire, representing 10 percent of its entire population. (Perhaps one-third of them lived in Palestine, with the remainder dispersed in such cosmopolitan cities as Alexandria [Egypt], Ephesus [Turkey], Corinth [Greece], and Antioch and Damascus [Syria].) By contrast, the world's entire population of Judeo-Christians and Christians may have been a mere 1,000 in 40 CE. In Rome itself, they may have numbered only a few hundred during Peter's time. The worldwide number may have reached 8,000 in 100 CE. (Most would have been real Christians by this period, owing to increased friction between Judaism and Christianity.) They increased to 220,000 by 200 CE, but still represented less than one-half of 1 percent of the Empire's population. As late as 250 CE, the Church father Origen could still write that there were "just a few" Christians. But their numbers suddenly soared at that time and, by 300 CE, reached perhaps 6 million, or 10 percent of the total population. After the Roman emperor Constantine legalized Christianity in 313 CE and made it the Empire's official religion in 325 CE, the number jumped to approximately 35 million by 350 CE, or 55 percent of the population.

In short, Peter may well have died a Mosaic Law—observant Jew, just like Jesus. His passing represented a watershed for the initial phase of the Jesus movement, because his death followed on the heels of James, who had become leader of

---

34   O'Conner, *Peter in Rome*, 207. In assessing Peter's role in Rome, scholars disregard Jesus' famous saying, in Matthew's Gospel (Mt 16:19), that Peter would become the "rock" upon which Jesus would build his "church" (i.e., the Roman Church). Among other problems, Matthew is the only Synoptic Evangelist to make this statement, or to imply that Jesus intended to build a "church," or even to use the word "church" in his Gospel. (In all Synoptics, "synagogue" is the standard word for a religious meeting place or congregation.)

35   Stark, *The Rise of Christianity*, 5–7, 131.

the Mother Synagogue during its latter years. James was executed in Jerusalem by the Sanhedrin in 62 CE, during the tumultuous run-up to the First Jewish Revolt. (Paul too was killed in this decade, probably following imprisonment in Rome, in the early 60's CE.) With the passing of the original Jewish leadership from the Jesus movement, which unquestionably accelerated during the First Revolt, the stage was set for the increasing Christianization of the Jesus sect.

CHAPTER 5

UNDERSTANDING
THE GOSPELS

The key to understanding the Gospel Jesus is to forget everything you've ever heard about him.

This is not easy. The story of Jesus is like a two thousand year-old ship's keel—thickly encrusted by barnacles that must be scraped away to reveal its real contours. We must likewise scrape from our memory everything that happened decades, centuries, and millennia after he died—all the paintings, books, movies, sermons, and the entire history of Christianity as it later unfolded. Instead, we must attempt to see him *as he was seen by the first-century Palestinian Jews he lived among*. After all, these were the people who actually witnessed his teachings and deeds firsthand.

So how did his people view Jesus? He was one of many preachers, prophets, and miracle workers crisscrossing Palestine, although he was unusual in being all three simultaneously.[36] He spoke common Aramaic, the lingua franca of the Jews and surrounding Semitic peoples. (Hebrew, a related language, had not been spoken for five hundred years except in religious liturgies.) Because he may not have known the Greek language in which the Gospels would later be written, he might have found many of its terms as alien as they are to modern Jews:

Jesus:	Jeshua (Yoshua, short for Yehoshua; Hebrew)
Christ:	Messiah (Hebrew)
Gospel:	Good news (Old English)
Baptism:	Mikva (water immersion for removing ritual sins; Hebrew)
Holy Spirit:	Ruach (God's spirit; Hebrew)
Repentance:	Tshuvah (repentance; Hebrew)

---

36   John P. Meier, *A Marginal Jew* (New York: Doubleday, 1994), 2:407.

Jesus' ministry was primarily in Galilee, a fertile agricultural and fishing region in northern Palestine. Since he generally avoided Gentiles (chapter 9), the vast majority of the people he spoke to were Jewish. Like himself, a woodworker from the small town of Nazareth, they were overwhelmingly rural, from villages and small towns. He apparently never entered any of the cities of Galilee, not even Sepphoris (Galilee's largest city, a mere four miles from Nazareth) or Tiberias (eight miles from Capernaum, the lakeside village that became the center of his ministry). Even though these cities were mostly Jewish, they may have contained an uncomfortable number of Gentiles and semi-Hellenized Jews.

Jesus' Jewish audiences were relatively poor, meagerly educated, and highly traditional—typical of any rural population in ancient times. They toiled endlessly to support their families and remain free from debt. They adhered to their ancient Jewish religion as their forebears had done for a thousand years. They considered it the world's most ethical religion, the only monotheism. Their Judaism revolved around the Sabbath—the blessed day of rest, after six days of toil—the holy festival days, the Temple, and the laws about food, marriage, and other fundamentals of daily life. They were perhaps dimly aware that their religion had begun splintering during the Maccabean Revolt against their former Syrian rulers (c. 167–164 BCE), creating new sects such as the Pharisees and the Essenes. These sects and others, along with the Sadducees (the descendants of the preexisting priestly class), were constantly debating amongst themselves about the proper interpretation of the Tanakh. Indeed, there were even disputes about which writings merited inclusion in the Tanakh, which was not fully canonized until c. 100 CE. In any case, these sects' arguments were often heated, often interesting, but of little practical interest to these common people, who were generally content to continue in the ways of their ancestors. This was especially so in Galilee, which was a religious backwater compared to the Jewish heartland of Jerusalem and Judea, home of most religious authorities.[37] Most of these sectarian arguments would ultimately disappear following the First Jewish Revolt against the Romans (66–70 CE), which decimated the Sadducees and Essenes, leaving the Pharisees as sole survivors. These Pharisees gradually evolved into the sage/rabbis[38] who compiled the monumental Mishnah

---

37 Geza Vermes, *Jesus the Jew* (Philadelphia: Fortress Press, 1973), 42–57; Meier, *A Marginal Jew*, 3:617.

38 "Modern" rabbis did not appear until c. 700–800 CE, when Jewish leaders began to take charge of synagogues and live among their lay congregants (Shaye J. D. Cohen, *From the Maccabees to the Mishnah* [Philadelphia: Westminster Press, 1987], 221–4). Until this time, they were pious scholars who associated primarily with one another.

(c. 200 CE) and Talmuds (c. 500–600 CE), which gave rise to modern Judaism. But all this was yet to come.

These were the people Jesus spoke to, and he undoubtedly realized that his mission would fail if he couldn't communicate with them. So he had to choose his words carefully, especially because there was no guarantee that these people would see him more than once during his peripatetic ministry. He knew that when he spoke of religion and his own ministry, they would interpret everything in the context of their Jewish tradition. To them, God was the Jewish God, religion was Judaism, and so on. They had never heard (and probably would never hear, in their lifetimes) of Christianity or the Trinity. Subtle allusions or cryptic asides would mean nothing to these people, especially in the absence of newspapers or television to preserve Jesus' words. Occasional criticisms of the established Jewish authorities would probably soon be forgotten, because the sects had been directing similar criticism at each other for a couple of centuries.

So Jesus knew he had to choose his words carefully, especially if his message was really different, even radical—such as calling on these people to abandon the religion they had lived for a millennium and which defined them as a people. A radical message would have to be unmistakable—trumpeted, with fanfares.

***

That Jesus' words must be interpreted through the ears of his contemporaries may seem self-evident. Far less self-evident is the importance of envisioning what he *looked* like. Much anti-Semitism has historically been rooted in Christian perceptions that Jesus' appearance was so sublimely noble that only the truly wicked—such as some of the Jewish authorities—could fail to accept his leadership. This is an unfortunate misconception, because Jesus looked quite ordinary. No halo crowned his head, and no reverential background music accompanied him. His voice too was unremarkable, and did not cause the breeze to drop or birds to fall silent.

How can we be so sure? By reading the Gospels' description of how Jesus was regarded by those who knew him best: his family, kinfolk, and neighbors. His family surely knew him intimately. After all, the Nativity stories relate that his parents were visited by angels announcing his virgin birth and special mission, that they fled to Egypt to escape King Herod's wrath, that magi and celestial angels announced his birth, and so on. These miraculous events were manifest not only to Jesus' parents but also to many others. And because Jesus' hometown of

These post–First Jewish Revolt scholars will be called "sage/rabbis" in this book. Many historians refer to them as the sages.

Nazareth may have contained as few as four hundred people,[39] his neighbors must also have known him exceedingly well. Although the Gospels are silent about Jesus' life until the age of thirty-three (apart from the Nativity stories), it is generally assumed that "Jesus of Nazareth" had lived there virtually all his life. Then, at age thirty-three, he traveled south to the Jordan River, to be baptized by John the Baptist, the Jewish holy man. It is with this baptism that all three Synoptic Gospels begin the story of Jesus' epochal ministry. Shortly thereafter, he returned to Nazareth for the first time. How was he received?

Upon his return, he first began preaching around his own house. According to Mark's Gospel: "The crowd came together … [and] when his family heard it [his teaching], they went out to restrain him, for people were saying, 'He is gone *out of his mind*'" (Mk 3:20–21; italics and brackets added). This translation is from the NRSV Bible,[40] but the CSB translation differs. The CSB believes that it was his *relatives* who were bewildered.[41] Its translation of this verse is therefore, "When his relatives heard of this they set out to seize him, for they said, 'He is out of his mind.'"

But certainly his own *mother* knew his God-chosen identity. But she did not. Apparently hearing about Jesus' strange behavior from the relatives, his mother and brothers rushed over (his father Joseph had passed away) while Jesus was still speaking to the crowd in the house. When the crowd informed Jesus that his family was outside, wishing to talk to him, he replied: "'Who are my mother and my brothers?' And looking at those who sat around him, he said, 'Here are my mother and my brothers! Whoever does the will of God is my brother and sister and mother'" (Mk 3:33–35).

This depiction is dramatically at odds with the innumerable images of Mary and Jesus with halos, contemplating each other in adoration. Jesus didn't even have the courtesy to talk to his family. "Jesus puts distance between himself and his uncomprehending family," notes the CSB.[42] Things continued downhill when he returned after some preaching and healings in the surrounding countryside:

---

39 Jonathan Reed, *Archeology and the Galilean Jesus* (Harrisburg, Pa.: Trinity Press International, 2000), 131–32. Archaeological excavations show that Nazareth occupied 48,000 square yards (equivalent to a square with sides 220 yards long), with houses whose dimensions and adjoining yards/gardens suggest a population of four hundred. Non-archaeologists have suggested numbers of one or two thousand.

40 As stated in chapter 1, this New Revised Standard Version translation is the most widely used Protestant Bible in the United States and is the source for virtually all New Testament passages in this book.

41 The Catholic Study Bible, 72.

42 Ibid., RG 411.

> On the Sabbath he began to teach in the synagogue, and
> many who heard him were astounded. They said,
> "Where did this man get all this? What is this wisdom
> that has been given to him? What deeds of power are being done by his hands!
> Is this not the carpenter, the son of
> Mary and brother of James and Joses and Judas and Simon, and are not his
> sisters here with us?"[43] And they took offense at him. (Mk 6:2–3)

This event is called the Rejection at Nazareth. Jesus was "amazed at their unbelief" (Mk 6:6). The people who had watched him grow up and still knew him and his family rejected his claim to authority and considered him more arrogant than holy. With the memory of his earlier rejection by his family and kinfolk fresh in his mind, Jesus ruefully declared, "Prophets are not without honor except in their *hometown*, and among their *own kin*, and in their *own house*" (Mk 6:4; italics added). Jesus responded to this stinging rebuke by moving twenty miles away to establish a new center for his ministry in the small fishing town of Capernaum,[44] on Lake Galilee. He seems never to have returned to Nazareth, or to have seen his family or anyone else from there again. (After his death, his brother James became a leader of the Mother Synagogue, and his mother briefly attended.) This is remarkable. If he was so extraordinary—the Messiah himself—why didn't his brothers leap at the chance to join him, instead of frittering away their lives at home? Why didn't his mother bother to see him again, or even to visit his post-crucifixion tomb? The conclusion seems inescapable: Mary and his siblings viewed him as just another family member, just as his neighbors viewed him as just another villager. In sum, everyone who knew him best considered him unexceptional.

In fact, *no one* seems to have heard of Jesus until his ministry started at age thirty-three, except for John the Baptist, who had recently baptized him. Jesus did not have a single disciple/Disciple as he began his ministry, which lasted one or

---

43   Based on their names, Jesus' family seems to have been quite Jewish. His father (who had died by this time) was Joseph, his mother was Miriam (Mary), and his brothers were Jacob (James), Joseph (Joses), Simeon (Simon), and Judah (Judas) [Meier, *A Marginal Jew*, 2:616]. Many Christian scholars have suggested that Jesus' "brothers and sisters" were really stepbrothers and stepsisters (i.e., that Mary had remarried after her husband Joseph's death), but this is speculation.

44   Capernaum was somewhat larger than Nazareth, with a probable population of one thousand (Reed, *Archeology and the Galilean Jesus*, 139–69). Its modest size is confirmed by the fact that it was unmentioned in any ancient writing until Josephus (late first century), who called it a "village."

two years. Even during his ministry, virtually no one seems to have heard anything about him except for his great healing skills. Not once did anybody ask Jesus, "Are you the one whose birth was attended by miracles?" or "Did not John the Baptist hail you as Messiah?" Whatever signs and wonders had marked his life had been completely forgotten. Jesus seems to have been surprisingly anonymous.

Recall the irreconcilable discrepancies between Matthew's and Luke's Nativity narratives, and the absence of any such account in Mark's, as if the birth had been quite ordinary. Everything discussed in this section suggests that the Nativity stories were just that—stories. The CSB concurs, by noting, for example, that Luke's Nativity story "is largely … the composition of Luke who writes in imitation of Old Testament birth stories.… The focus of the narrative, therefore, is primarily Christological."[45] ("Christological" refers to any story or doctrine that emphasizes Jesus' Messiahship or divinity.) In fact, miraculous birth stories were so common in contemporary biographies ("lives") throughout the Roman Empire that the absence of miracles was a sign of the subject's unimportance.

With this understanding that Jesus looked too ordinary for others to automatically defer to him, it is time to consider his interactions with the Jewish authorities.

Postscript: Jesus' Reception in Nazareth

Alert readers may have noticed that Mark's Gospel is the source for all the Nazareth passages above. Since some of them are not reported in Matthew's or Luke's Gospels, are we justified in focusing primarily on Mark's account?

The answer seems to be yes. Scholars broadly agree about how to assess the relative authenticity of Gospel passages. The first benchmark is simple: earlier writings are assumed to be more historical than later ones. On this basis, Mark's is considered the most historical Gospel. It not only preceded the others by ten to twenty-five years, but also provides the most human portrait, suggesting that Mark was more intent on presenting the truth than on embellishing it. (The only sources older than Mark's Gospel [Paul's Letters, and the Q-source] mention nothing about Nazareth, and so provide no insights.)

Scholars also rely on another half dozen criteria to assess credibility. Some are rather controversial, but one of the best accepted is the Criterion of Embarrassment. This states that the Evangelists had no conceivable motive to

---

45   The Catholic Study Bible, 97. Further evidence that the Nativity stories were fanciful is that both Matthew and Luke scrupulously avoided mentioning any of the Nativity details in the rest of their Gospels, presumably out of respect for Mark's original account. This explains why no one in the Synoptics seems to have heard of these events.

embarrass or denigrate the man they literally worshipped. This is why, for example, Jesus' crucifixion is universally agreed to be historical. Early Christians trying to spread their new religion throughout the Roman Empire had no reason to falsely claim that the Romans had killed their master like a common criminal. (Of course, early Christians eventually turned his gruesome death to their advantage by formulating the "suffering servant" theology.) And apart from the crucifixion, the most embarrassing event in Jesus' life was his humiliating rejection by his family and neighbors.

This Criterion's validity is apparent in any side-by-side comparison of the three Synoptics, for any pericope. Matthew and Luke, who used Mark's Gospel as a template, routinely omitted or softened offensive details or added ennobling new ones. On the other hand, they *never* changed a flattering statement to one less favorable. In the case of the Nazareth material, Matthew was reasonably faithful to Mark. He omitted the "out of his mind" quotation from the home preaching scene, but included Jesus' refusal to speak to his family. The entire synagogue scene was also retained, although Jesus' "prophet" saying ("Prophets are not without honor, except in their hometown, and among their own kin, and in their own house") was trimmed by omitting "among their own kin" (Mt 13:57). Luke went further. He truncated this saying to a bare-boned, "No prophet is accepted in the prophet's hometown" (Lk 4:24). He omitted both the "out of his mind" quotation and also Jesus' refusal to see his family. He also softened the synagogue scene. Yet despite these changes, both Evangelists broadly accepted Mark's depiction. Even as they downplayed Jesus' discord with his kin, they never claimed that anyone in his family (including Mary) *ever* said anything good about him, or paid him any attention. This is extraordinary, inasmuch as these Evangelists' Nativity stories abound with miraculous revelations to Mary about her son's glorious selection by God. These Evangelists also agree that Jesus' Rejection at Nazareth motivated him to relocate from Nazareth to Capernaum. Thus, all Synoptics agree that apart from his supreme self-confidence, Jesus was regarded as ordinary (apart from his healing ability) by those who knew him best. This is consistent with the fact that all Synoptics lack even a single detail about his life until his ministry began at age thirty-three.

CHAPTER 6

JESUS' CONFLICTS WITH THE JEWISH AUTHORITIES

Jesus is constantly castigating the Jewish religious authorities in the three Synoptic accounts of his life ... or so it seems.[46] His cries of hypocrisy, evil-mongering, and "woe unto you" fill page after page. How can this possibly be reconciled with the clear evidence of Jesus' Jewishness from the Acts of the Apostles?

The answer is provided by an examination of these stories. Some will be discussed here, and others later. Fortunately, no narrative context will be lost as we shift from one story to another, because the Synoptics' story line is minimal. Following an initial Nativity story (absent in Mark), Jesus disappears until he is thirty-three years old. He then travels to John the Baptist, the revered Jewish holy man who seemingly proclaims him the Messiah (but see chapter 12). Jesus subsequently commences his one- to-two year ministry, during which he heals and teaches as he travels primarily through Galilee. But the Gospels' accounts of his ministry are organized as self-contained episodes (pericopes) that are typically unrelated to whatever precedes and follows them. Once a pericope is concluded, it is never referred to again. Even references to the changing seasons are absent. In fact, the only reason Jesus' ministry is believed to have been one or two years is that scholars assume that he would have made regular Temple festival pilgrimages, yet only one such pilgrimage (on Passover) is mentioned. The sparseness of

---

46   Even Luke's Gospel contains conflict stories, despite Luke's acknowledgment in Acts of Jesus' Jewishness. The Gospels were written as faith-documents, not pure histories. For example, Luke's Gospel states that Jesus spent one day on earth after his resurrection, whereas Acts increases it to forty days. Luke probably saw no inconsistency, for his intent was to emphasize the event's grandeur by providing a biblical time frame ("forty days and forty nights"). In exactly the same way, he inserted into his Gospel account several sayings of Jesus that, in light of Acts, sounds extremely improbable.

detail is also due to the Gospels' brevity, for even the longest Synoptic Gospel is only two-thirds the length of Genesis, the first book of the Tanakh. A true "story plot" emerges only during Jesus' final days in Jerusalem, when events follow one another in a logical, climactic order.

The Greatest Commandment

Any discussion of the conflict stories must begin with the "Greatest Commandment," which presents Jesus' core religious precepts. According to the Gospel of Matthew, when Jesus began preaching in the Jerusalem Temple during what would prove to be his last week of life, he quickly locked horns with religious authorities who demanded to know the justification for his teachings (Mt 22:23). Jesus began defending himself, while the authorities tried to trap him into saying something foolish or seditious. But Jesus silenced them with his astute answers. Then a Pharisee tried his luck, by asking which of God's commandments was the greatest. Jesus replied: "'You shall love the Lord your God with all your heart, with all your soul, and with all your mind.' This is the greatest and first commandment. And a second is like it: 'You shall love your neighbor as yourself.' On these two commandments hang all the law and the prophets" (Mt 22:36–40).

The story ends there, with no response from the Pharisee. The abrupt ending seems to imply that the Pharisee gave up when he realized his trap had failed. After all, Jesus had expounded the classic Jewish view of Judaism by linking a verse of its most famous prayer—the Shema (Deuteronomy 6:4)—with its most famous ethical summary (Leviticus 19:18). He had followed this by stating that these momentous verses were the basis of the "law" (Torah/Mosaic Law) and the "prophets" (the prophetic books of Isaiah, Ezekiel, etc.) which were the cornerstones of Judaism.

But the background tension of Matthew's account is absent in Mark's version, for when a "scribe" asked the same question:

> Jesus answered, "The first is, 'Hear, O Israel! The Lord our God, the
> Lord is one; you shall love the Lord your God with all your heart, and with
> all your soul, with all your mind, and with all your strength.' The second
> is this, 'You shall love your neighbor as yourself.' There is no other
> commandment greater than these." Then the scribe said to him, "You are right,
> Teacher; you have truly said that, 'he is One, and besides him there is no other';
> and 'to love him with all the heart, with all the understanding,
> and with all the strength,'—
> this is much more important than all burnt
> offerings and sacrifices." And when Jesus saw that he answered

wisely, he said to him, "You are not far from the
Kingdom of God." After that no one dared to ask him any questions.
(Mk 12:29–34)

The significance of this passage cannot be overstated. When asked to relate the greatest of all religious commandments, Jesus recited the opening lines of the most famous Jewish prayer of all times: *"Shema yisra'el adonay eloheynu adonay ehad … Ve'ahavta et adonay eloheha behol levaveha uvhol nafsheha uvhol me'odeha."* This very prayer, along with the Ten Commandments, was the centerpiece of the daily priestly service in the very Temple he was standing in.[47] It was (and remains) so quintessentially Jewish that it virtually defines Judaism. A century later, Jewish tradition holds that the great sage/rabbi Akiva recited the Shema as he died from Roman torture for participating in the Second Jewish Revolt. The Shema remains, to this day, the prayer than Jews traditionally recite before their death. This is why the authorities dared not ask Jesus any more questions—how could they possibly entrap someone so thoroughly Jewish? Who could imagine an adherent of any other religion—from Zeus worship to Hinduism to Christianity—proclaiming the Shema as the greatest religious precept of all?

Note too the significance of the Shema's opening verse: "Hear, O Israel! The Lord our God, the Lord is one." These words, from Jesus' lips, make clear that he did not believe that he was God. When the scribe responded, "You are right, Teacher," Jesus did not interrupt him by saying, "But you must understand, *I* am that God." Instead, Jesus praised his wise answer. Jesus undoubtedly knew that the scribe was referring to the heavenly, ineffable God of Israel. Jesus' approval demonstrates that he, too, believed that everyone's greatest obligation was to embrace the one God of the Jews. Jesus never called himself a god in the Synoptics. Indeed, when a rich man addressed him as "Good Teacher," Jesus replied, "Why do you call me good? No one is good but God alone" (Mk 10:18). He corrected a woman who cried out, "Blessed is the womb that bore you," by responding, "Blessed rather are those who hear the word of God and obey it!" (Lk 11:27). Instead, he viewed himself as God's messenger; as he said: "Whoever welcomes me, welcomes not me but the One who sent me" (Mk 9:37).

Only one small question remains. When Jesus told the scribe that he was "not far" from the kingdom of God, was he implying that something more was required—such as faith in Jesus? Or was he merely hedging because he could not be sure the scribe would always remain righteous? The answer seems to be provided in the Gospel of Luke, where this incident occurs during the journey to Jerusalem, rather than in it. A "lawyer" ("scholar of the law," according to the

---

47 Cohen, *From the Maccabees to the Mishnah,* 69.

CSB translation) tested Jesus by asking what was necessary to win God's favor. When Jesus turned the question back on the lawyer, by asking his own opinion, the lawyer recited the Shema. Thereupon, Jesus responded, "You have given the right answer; do this and you will live" (Lk 10:28). In short, Heaven could be won by simply following traditional Judaism; nothing more was needed. And although the tone of the three Gospel accounts varies, all highlight Jesus' profound allegiance to the religion of his birth.[48]

Pouring New Wine into New Skins
This brief passage has often been interpreted by Christians as signifying that Jesus' teachings ("new wine") could only be contained within "new skins" (Christians, the new Israel), rather than in the Jews. According to Mark and Matthew, Jesus said:

> No one pours new wine into old wineskins; otherwise, the wine will burst
> the skins, and the wine is lost, and so are the skins; but one puts
> new wine into fresh wineskins. (Mk 2:22)

But neither Mark nor Matthew explicitly states whether the "new" is better or worse than the "old." Only Luke does, for he concludes the verses above by saying: "And no one after drinking old wine desires new wine, but says, 'The old is good'" (Lk 5:39).[49]

The *old* is better, as any wine drinker knows. More substantively, most first-century peoples believed that their civilizations had declined from earlier Golden Ages, and that the ancient was superior to the new. Jews yearned for the days of Moses and the great prophets, and of the First Temple and its forever-lost Ark of

---

48 Although these three versions have been presented in a particular order (most anti-Judaic to most philo-Judaic), it is impossible to determine which version is most authentic, especially given their fundamental similarity. Instead, the purpose of this comparison, and others to come, is to display the differences—sometimes subtle, sometimes dramatic—often found among the Gospels. Christians have, not surprisingly, tended to focus on the versions that emphasize Jesus' differences with individual Jews and their religious practices. If, on the other hand, one focuses on the very large number of versions that emphasize his allegiance to traditional Judaism, a far different Jesus emerges. (When Gospel versions are—unlike here—incompatible, scholars rely on criteria such as date of composition, and the Criterion of Embarrassment.)

49 Luke's concluding verse was intentionally omitted from many early copies of his Gospel, presumably by Christian scribes unable to believe that Jesus could have said such a thing (Bart Ehrman, *Misquoting Jesus* [San Francisco: HarperSanFrancisco, 2002], 96).

the Covenant. The Greeks bemoaned the lost glory of Athens, and even the ascendant Romans felt the loss of the heroic days of the Roman Republic. Judaism was respected throughout the Roman Empire precisely because of its antiquity, which was equated with truth and wisdom. This is one reason why the early Church adopted the Tanakh as its sole Scripture until the New Testament began to take shape in the late second century: it was far easier to disseminate Christianity as the culmination of an old, established religion than as a new one.

The "Woes": Jewish Hypocrisy and Evil-doing

The Gospels are so crammed with Jesus' castigations of the religious authorities' hypocrisy and "evil-doing" that quoting even a fraction would quickly become redundant. The most scorching example is Jesus' lengthy condemnation of the Pharisees and scribes in Jerusalem, in Matthew's Gospel. Because it comes shortly before Jesus' arrest and crucifixion, it packs enormous emotional impact. This close juxtaposition of events seems to taint the Pharisees with guilt, despite the Synoptics' agreement that they played no role in Jesus' death. Cried Jesus:

> The scribes and the Pharisees ... tie up heavy burdens ... and lay them on the shoulders of others; but they themselves are unwilling to lift a finger to move them. They do all their work to be seen by others ... but woe to you, scribes and Pharisees, hypocrites!
> For you lock people out of the kingdom of heaven. For you do not go in yourselves, and when others are going in, you stop them.... Woe to you ... for you tithe mint and dill[50] ... and have neglected the weightier things of the law: justice and mercy and faith.... Woe to you ... you are like whitewashed tombs, which on the outside look beautiful, but inside they are full of the bones of the dead and of all kinds of filth ... how can you escape being sentenced to hell? (Mt 23: 2–36)

The vitriol of this lengthy tirade (thirty-six verses) is shocking, and has been a source of much anti-Semitism over the millennia. How could such a searing indictment be uttered by a Jewish Jesus? Actually, the answer is twofold. First, this condemnation was in fact squarely in the tradition of such classical Jewish prophets as Ezekiel and Hosea, for it was a resolutely Jewish attack on the Pharisees for (allegedly) *betraying* their sacred religion. This becomes obvious if the first verse of Jesus' harangue (omitted above) is presented, and if some of the verses above are presented in their entirety:

---

50   I.e., pay a voluntary Temple-support tax on these purchases.

> Jesus said "The scribes and the Pharisees
> *sit on Moses' seat; therefore, do*
> *whatever they teach you and follow it,* but do not do what
> they do, for they do not practice what they teach.... Woe to you, scribes and
> Pharisees, you hypocrites. For you tithe of mint and dill ... and have neglected the
> weightier things of the law: justice and mercy and faith. It is these
> you ought to have practiced, *without neglecting the others."*
> (Mt:23:1–36; italics added)

So the religious authorities *did* proclaim the truth, but failed, in Jesus' view, to observe their own teachings. The CSB agrees that "The crowds and the disciples [Jesus' audience] are exhorted not to follow the example of Jewish leaders, whose deeds do not conform to their teaching.... Matthew ... portrays the time of Jesus' ministry as marked by fidelity to the law (italics added)."[51] Still, Jesus' apparent hatred of the Pharisees in his final days is certainly disturbing ... that is, if this incident actually happened. This leads to the second important insight: it probably didn't. Matthew is actually a minority voice, for both Mark and Luke agree that Jesus' *actual* words on this fateful occasion were:

> Beware of the scribes, who like to walk around in long robes,
> and to be greeted with respect in the marketplaces, and to have the
> best seats in the synagogues, and places of honor at banquets.
> They devour widows'
> houses and for the sake of appearances say long prayers. They will
> receive the greater condemnation. (Mk:12:37–40)

Thus, Matthew's extended, withering diatribe against the Pharisees and scribes was most likely a brief, relatively mild attack on the scribes alone.[52] (The identity of these scribes is uncertain; see chapter 12.) But why would Matthew have created such a fictitious scene? Once again, the CSB provides the answer: "This speech reflects an opposition that goes beyond that of Jesus' ministry and must be seen as expressing the bitter conflict between Pharisaic Judaism and *the*

---

51   The Catholic Study Bible, 50.

52   Luke's Gospel does contain some of these anti-Pharisee verses (which are Q-sayings), but incorporates most of them into the Hand Washing conflict story (discussed next). In this setting, the verses have little emotional impact, because Luke's Hand Washing story occurs while Jesus is dining in a Pharisee's home in peaceful Galilee (see chapter 12).

church of Matthew at the time when *the gospel was composed.*"[53] "The sharp edge to Matthew's critique may stem from the tragic division and hostility that grew between Judaism and Jewish Christianity in the early decades of the church [i.e., after Jesus' death]. For Matthew, the fact that most of Israel did not accept Jesus … was a baffling and unexpected turn … and his telling of the story of Jesus reflects this." [54]

Matthew's Gospel is so important, being many Christians' favorite Synoptic, that these comments merit amplification. This Gospel is a paradox. On the one hand, it is the most Jewish Gospel. It is the most insistent about the *ongoing* sanctity of the Mosaic Law. It also tries the hardest to prove that Jesus' coming was foretold by the Tanakh itself, via proof-texts. Yet it is also the most stridently condemnatory of the religious authorities, especially the Pharisees. It even goes out of its way to introduce Pharisees into pericopes so that they can be denounced. Note that in this case, "the scribes" in Mark's original version of the pericope was replaced with "the scribes and the Pharisees." Why this love/hate paradox? Recall that Mark and Luke were late-first-century Christians who lived outside of Palestine. Their contacts with Jews may have been quite limited. But Matthew may have lived in Galilee, which experienced such a huge influx of Jews following Jerusalem's destruction in the First Jewish Revolt that it literally supplanted Jerusalem as the center of Jewish learning. Living in a predominantly Jewish area meant that Matthew's synagogue/church probably included many Jews who still followed the Law (i.e., Judeo-Christians), or at least retained strong emotional ties to it. He therefore wanted his Gospel to emphasize Jesus' fidelity to the Law. However, he may well have been frequently castigated by local sage/rabbis for apostasy from traditional Judaism. (Recall that the Pharisees seem to have evolved into the so-called sage/rabbis following the First Jewish Revolt.) Unsurprisingly, he probably developed a strong personal animus against them. Since they were the descendants of the pre-Revolt Pharisees, Matthew seems to have projected his own hostilities back into the time of Jesus, by exaggerating or creating anti-Pharisaic diatribes that are usually absent from the other Synoptics.[55] Note that the most anti-Judaic version of the Greatest Commandment was also penned by Matthew.

---

53   The Catholic Study Bible, 49, italics added.

54   Ibid., RG 389.

55   A striking example of Matthew's interpolation of contemporary materials into his Gospel is found in this Gospel's eighteenth chapter. This entire chapter is commonly called "The Church Order Discourse," because Jesus is represented as reciting the rules of conduct that were apparently enforced in Matthew's late-first-century congregation (Catholic Study Bible, 38).

Hand Washing before Meals

Although Mark's is the least popular of the four Gospels, its hand washing story is famous because it has traditionally convinced Christians that Jesus nullified the Mosaic Laws mandating that only kosher foods could be eaten. In this story, several Pharisees and scribes noticed that some of Jesus' Disciples had not ritually washed their hands before eating. They asked Jesus:

> "Why do your disciples not live according to the tradition of the elders,
> but eat with defiled hands?" He said to them, "Isaiah prophesied rightly
> about you hypocrites ... as it is written, 'This people honors me with their lips,
> but their hearts are far from me....' "You abandon the commandments of God and
> hold to human tradition.... You have a fine way of rejecting the
> commandment of God in order to keep your tradition! ...
> There is nothing outside a person that by going in can defile, but the things
> that come out can defile.... (Thus he declared all foods clean.)
> And he said, "It is what comes out of a person that defiles ... theft, murder,
> adultery, avarice, wickedness."
> (Mk 7:5–22; parentheses in original)

However, despite the unambiguous statement that "Thus he declared all foods clean," Jesus said no such thing. This is why the NRSV translation above puts parentheses around this important verse. The NRSV's editors believe it was added to Mark's original Gospel by a later scribe.[56] The CSB believes that Mark may have written this, but that he was mistaken, since it is wholly incompatible with Paul's Letters and Luke's Acts of the Apostles.[57] Tellingly, Luke's version of this pericope makes it clear that Jesus was objecting only to the tradition of hand washing (Lk 11:37–39). Matthew was even more explicit, for Jesus concluded his teaching in this Gospel with, "These [theft, murder, etc.] are what defile a person, but to *eat with unwashed hands does not defile*" (Mt 15:20; italics and brackets added).

So the real crux of Mark's story is that Jesus was accusing the Pharisees of *abandoning* the Mosaic Law ("commandments of God"), in favor of "human tradition." What was this "tradition"? It was an early form of what modern Judaism calls the "oral law." Orthodox Jews have long believed that on Mount Sinai, God presented Moses not only with the Mosaic Law, but also with an unwritten (oral) law required to interpret it. This oral law was supposedly transmitted intact over the centuries, all the way to the Pharisees, who called it the "tradition." The

---

56   The New Oxford Annotated Bible (NRSV translation), xii.

57   The Catholic Study Bible, 79.

Pharisees will be discussed later (chapter 12), but it suffices for now to know that they were a small group of very pious Jewish laymen who had no official religious or legal standing. Following the First Jewish Revolt (66–70 CE), the tradition was supposedly transmitted intact, as the "oral law," to the subsequent sage/rabbis. This law was finally codified in c. 200 CE into the Mishnah, a cornerstone of modern Judaism.

Scholars, however, dispute this scenario.[58] While it is extremely likely that the Mosaic Law was initially accompanied by oral teachings that clarified some of its cryptic commands, the relationship between these ancient teachings and the Pharisees' much later "tradition" is unknown. So is the relationship between this tradition and the later oral law. The oral law undoubtedly adopted parts of the tradition but probably modified other parts, and/or incorporated many new elements as well.

The critical point is that in Jesus' time, the Pharisees were a small sect of very pious Jews who seem to have been the *only* people who seriously observed this *"tradition."* And even Pharisees were split into factions (e.g., the schools of Hillel and Shammai) that incessantly debated the tradition's specifics (e.g., whether hand washing was required daily, or only on Sabbath and Festival days).[59] The Sadducees, the priestly class that maintained Judaism's holiest institution, the Temple, rejected it entirely. (For simplicity's sake, this book will henceforth use the term "oral law" for both "tradition" and the oral law). Ordinary Jews, who represented most of the population, generally ignored it, especially in rural areas such as Galilee. Yet no one has ever claimed that the Sadducees or commoners were not Jewish. It was the Mosaic Law, and *only* the Mosaic Law, that was Judaism's defining foundation. *And Jesus himself insisted on the primacy of the Mosaic Law*, as highlighted by his attack on the authorities for supposedly disregarding it. Thus, the real lesson of this pericope is that despite Jesus' dismissal of the oral law, he staunchly upheld the Mosaic Law and was never accused of violating it in *any* Synoptic story.[60]

---

58 Cohen, *From the Maccabees to the Mishnah*, 221ff, 143ff; Martin Jaffee, *Ancient Judaism* (Upper Saddle River, N.J.: Prentice-Hall, 1997), 74 ff.

59 E. P. Sanders, *The Historical Figure of Jesus* (London: Allan Lane, Penguin Press, 1993), 45.

60 Exactly how the Mosaic Law was interpreted in Jesus' time is unclear, because the Tanakh's description of the Law of Moses sometimes cryptic. For example, the Mosaic Law states that the Sabbath is to be a "sanctified day of rest," but provides little detail on what exactly this means. Nevertheless, Jesus was never criticized in the Gospels for violating the bedrock practices of Judaism, should as keeping kosher, Temple wor-

The Sabbath Work Stories: Plucking Grain

The Synoptics contain five stories about working on the Sabbath, which is forbidden by the Mosaic Law. These stories have convinced many Christians that Jesus nullified the Jewish Sabbath, in whole or in part.

In the most trivial story (Mk 3:23–28), some Pharisees rebuked the hungry Disciples for "working" on the Sabbath by hand-crushing some grain in order to eat the flour. Jesus defended his Disciples by comparing their infraction to one King David committed during his youth. The Pharisees made no response, perhaps because of the obvious pettiness of their criticism. But what elevates this episode beyond pettiness was Jesus' final riposte to the Pharisees:

> The sabbath was made for humankind, not humankind for the sabbath;
> so the Son of Man is lord even of the Sabbath. (Mk 2:27–28)

The first sentence is innocuous enough: that God created Sabbath to provide people with much-needed rest and spiritual rejuvenation, not to entangle them in rules. (The Mishnah [200 CE] later echoed this sentiment, by saying, "The Sabbath is delivered to you, and not you to the Sabbath."[61]) The second sentence sounds weightier. Since Jesus often referred to himself as the Son of Man, this passage seems to say that Jesus considered himself unbound by Sabbath laws. However, this is unlikely, as will become evident when the meaning of Son of Man is explained (chapter 10). The CSB is also skeptical, and believes that Jesus never spoke this sentence; Mark invented it. "The early public use of the designation 'Son of Man' ... is most unlikely ... Mark's comment on the theological meaning of the incident is to benefit his Christian readers."[62] It is also crucial to recognize that the prohibition of grain-crushing was merely a Pharisaic tradition: the only Sabbath work explicitly forbidden by Mosaic Law involves lighting fires and cooking, strenuous or business-oriented work, and extended travel. (Because some of the Law's Sabbath commandments are too cryptic to be completely explicit, others might add another rule or two, but it seems clear that ordinary activities were permitted.) Rural Jews, like rural people throughout history, probably chewed on an occasional grain or seed without even thinking about it.[63]

---

ship, circumcision, observing the Festivals, maintaining the Sabbath (further detail in text), and so on.

61 Mehilta on Exodus 31:14.

62 The Catholic Study Bible, 70, 71.

63 *Encyclopedia Judaica* (New York: Macmillan, 1971–72), s.v. "Oral Law," 12:143–45. It is revealing that unlike the Babylonian Talmud (c. 600 CE), which was compiled in a major city, the Palestinian Talmud (c. 500 CE, in Galilee) contains few restric-

The Sabbath Work Stories: Miracle Healings
The Gospels' other Sabbath work stories involve miracle healing. Judaism has always permitted the treatment of severely ill people on Sabbath, but not of people who could easily wait until Sabbath ended. However, this prohibition was presumably designed to prevent actual work—for example, preparing or carrying medicines, and charging and accepting payment. But healing the sick solely by freely offered *words* involved no work, and thus was permitted in this period.[64] (After all, Jews have always prayed on Sabbath for the recovery of the sick.) Whether healing by touch (laying on of hands) was also acceptable during this period is more ambiguous. Jesus merely touched people, and requested no fee. Many scholars therefore believe it was permissible. Perhaps the only truly controversial aspect of Jesus' Sabbath healings was that they were usually performed in synagogues, which might have offended the pious by disrupting the service.

The individual pericopes can now be examined. The first three can barely be called conflict stories, because the congregants were dazzled by Jesus' cures, and the few protesters quickly acquiesced to his rationale. Everyone in the synagogue was so delighted by the healing of the Man Possessed by Evil Spirits that Jesus' fame began to spread throughout the surrounding regions of Galilee (Mk 1:21–28). The healing of the Crippled Woman incensed the synagogue leader (a layman) but thrilled the congregants. After Jesus' healing, this leader rebuked the woman for not waiting until Sabbath ended. But Jesus replied: "You hypocrites! Does not each of you on the Sabbath untie his ox or his donkey … and lead it away to give it water?" And when he said this "all his opponents were put to shame; and the whole crowd was rejoicing at all the wonderful things that he was doing" (Lk 13:15–17).

The healing of the Man with Dropsy was virtually identical, except that the "adversaries" were Pharisees and the lawyers. But they were silent throughout and never challenged Jesus' rationale (Lk 14:3–6). However, the final story, of the Man with the Withered Hand, is a puzzler. It is by far the most venomous Sabbath work story, even though Jesus healed solely by words. The Pharisees asked Jesus:

"Is it lawful to cure on the sabbath?" so that they might accuse him. He said to them, "Suppose one of you has only one

---

tions regarding agricultural work during the Sabbath, because religious interference was deeply resented by the farming majority of Galilee (Geza Vermes, *The Authentic Gospel of Jesus* [London: Penguin Press, 2003], 48).

64 *Encyclopedia Judaica*, s.v. "Jesus," 14:10–14; Geza Vermes, *The Changing Faces of Jesus* (New York: Penguin Press, 2000), 210.

> sheep and it falls into a pit on the sabbath; will you not lay
> hands on it and lift it out?
> How much more valuable is a human being than a sheep!"
> Then he said to the [sick] man,
> "Stretch out your hand." He stretched it out, and it was restored....
> But the Pharisees went out and conspired against him, how to destroy him."[65]
> (Mt 12:10–14, brackets added)

This episode is truly enigmatic, because Jesus' verbal cure broke no laws. Perhaps these particular Pharisees were unusually fastidious about "tradition" or synagogue decorum. Or perhaps this pericope was exaggerated by the Evangelists. The only thing that is absolutely certain is that however angry these Pharisees may have been, they must have calmed down quickly, for *not a single Pharisee ever threatened (or even touched) Jesus or his Disciples*, in *any* Synoptic story.

***

A quick recap might be useful at this point:

- Jesus never annulled any element of the Mosaic Law (the Sabbath and Holy Days, keeping kosher, circumcision, etc.) in the Synoptics. In fact, he often sought to make the Law *stricter* (see next chapter). This is consistent with this chapter's observation that many of the "conflicts" were initiated by his demands that the authorities hew more closely to Judaism. He did ignore much of the oral law, but this was the norm for that period.

- Many "conflict stories" become attenuated or even disappear completely when the different gospel versions are compared. This reflects the fact that Matthew, in particular, tended to exaggerate or possibly create many of them.

- Jesus was never threatened or physically touched by any Jewish authority (or any Jew, with one possible exception[66]) until he disrupted Temple

---

65 Luke softens this by saying they "were filled with fury" and began discussing what they might "do" to Jesus (Lk 6:11).

66 In the previously discussed "Rejection at Nazareth," both Mark and Matthew report that after the synagogue congregants rebuked Jesus for his claim to special authority, Jesus left peacefully. In Luke's version, however, the congregants *accepted* his authority. Thereupon, Jesus unaccountably insulted them by saying that they probably wanted

operations in Jerusalem in his last week of life (chapter 13). Until then, no one even raised his voice at Jesus. Quite the opposite; we have seen that Jesus himself triggered many of the conflicts, owing to his belief that the authorities were insufficiently Jewish, or that the Pharisaic traditions were irrelevant. In other cases (discussed later), conflicts arose from his conviction that God had chosen him for a special mission, so that everyone should automatically defer to him. But whenever authorities justifiably questioned his claims (as his family and neighbors did in Nazareth), he tended to reflexively accuse them of hypocrisy and wickedness.

• The Gospels' tight focus on Jesus makes it easy to forget that his disagreements with the authorities were generally quite run-of-the-mill—no different from those among the Jewish sects themselves. Judaism was exceptionally splintered in this period, and religious disputes were the norm. Moreover, it is often difficult to know whom Jesus actually clashed with, owing to the Evangelists' tendency to conflate such words as Pharisees, scribes, lawyers, and even "the people."

• The value of understanding Jesus by starting with Acts of the Apostles and Paul's Letters should now be apparent, for their explicitness stands in sharp contrast with the conflicting or ambiguous sayings ascribed to Jesus by the various Evangelists.

This chapter has highlighted the discrepancies amongst the Synoptics, to demonstrate that passages that initially seem anti-Jewish or anti-Judaic turn out to be much less so away upon further inspection. But, as noted earlier, these same contradictions make it difficult to prove, directly from the Gospels, that Jesus was as rigorously Jewish as illuminated by Acts of the Apostles and Paul's Letters. The case would be far stronger if the Gospels contained a lengthy, internally coherent teaching from Jesus that erased all reasonable doubt. Fortunately, it does, in the form of Jesus' most famous teaching in the entire New Testament. And by clearly expounding Jesus' religious and ethical precepts, this teaching also allows us, for the first time, to begin uncovering his ministry's meaning and purpose.

---

him to perform some miracles, but that they were unworthy. This insult so enraged the congregants that they unsuccessfully tried to throw him off a cliff. Since this account contradicts that of the two earlier Synoptics, its veracity seems questionable.

CHAPTER 7

JESUS' MESSAGE, PART I: ETHICAL MESSAGE—THE SERMON ON THE MOUNT

The Sermon on the Mount, from the Gospel of Matthew, is accepted as the heart of Jesus' religious and ethical teachings. Matthew certainly thought so, because it is not only the longest sermon in his (or any other) Gospel, but it is Jesus' first sermon, delivered before a multitude of listeners. It has often been cited as proof of Christianity's ethical superiority over Judaism.

But recall that if we are to understand the Sermon, we must listen with the ears of early-first-century Palestinian Jews. The large majority of the massed crowds were Jewish peasants and townsfolk who had lived as Jews for many generations. They had never heard of "Christianity" or even "Jesus Christ"; it was Jeshua of Nazareth standing before them. In short, they would inevitably interpret the Sermon in a Jewish context unless Jesus told them otherwise … which he did not, as seen below. He was a Jew preaching to fellow Jews.

So let us now listen to the Sermon, not only to hear what Jesus said, but also to understand why the CSB states that "How to live with the Sermon on the Mount has been a constant point of discussion in the church."[67] It began with a series of "Beatitudes" (blessings) reminiscent of the Prophetic writings and the Psalms ("Blessed are the poor in spirit, for theirs is the kingdom of heaven. Blessed are they who mourn, for they will be comforted …") The Sermon then shifted to its core religious and ethical message:

> *"Do not think that I have come to abolish the law or the prophets;*
> *I have come not to abolish but to fulfill. For truly I tell you, until*

---

67   The Catholic Study Bible, RG 394.

heaven and earth pass away, not one letter, not one stroke of a letter will pass from the law until all is accomplished.
Therefore, whoever breaks one of the least of these commandments, and teaches others to do the same *will be called least in the kingdom of heaven*; but whoever does them and teaches them will be called great in the kingdom of heaven."[68] (Mt 5:17–19; italics added)

This passage's meaning would have been perfectly clear to his contemporaries: obey the Mosaic Law *fully*. The CSB admits, in its commentary on this passage, that Jesus' mission "remains within the framework of the law."[69] Like Acts, this passage—indeed, the entire Sermon—casts serious doubt on any Gospel story that implies Jesus' annulment of the Law. The Law had to be followed … to the uttermost:

"For I tell you, unless your righteousness *exceeds* that of the scribes and the Pharisees, *you will never enter the kingdom of heaven.* You have heard that it was said to those of ancient times, 'You shall not murder'; and 'whoever murders shall be liable to judgment.' But I say to you that if you are angry with a brother or sister, you will be liable to judgment … and if you say, 'You fool,' you will be liable to the hell of fire … You have heard that it was said, 'You shall not commit adultery.' But I say to you, that everyone who looks at a woman with lust has already committed adultery with her in his heart. If your right eye causes you to sin, tear it out and throw it away; it is better for you to lose one of your members than for your whole body to be thrown into hell. And if your right hand causes you to sin, cut it off and throw it away.… You have heard that it was said, 'An eye for an eye and a tooth for a tooth.' But I say to you, Do not resist an evildoer. But if anyone strikes you on the right cheek, turn the other also; and if anyone wants to sue and take your coat, give your cloak as well.… You have heard that it was said, 'You shall love your neighbor and hate your enemy.'[70] But I say to you, love your enemies, and pray for those who persecute you.… For if you love those who love you, what reward do you have? … Be perfect, therefore, as your heavenly Father is perfect." (Mt 5:20–48; italics added)

---

68 Called the Kingdom of God by the other Evangelists.

69 The Catholic Study Bible, 13.

70 No such commandment exists in the Tanakh.

This is emotionally moving, but was Jesus tightening the Law to the point of unattainability? Was he really saying that anger must be treated as if it were murder? That merely looking at a woman was adultery? That the evil should be free to torment the righteous? And that people should be perfect ... as perfect as God? If *this* was the benchmark, who could possibly hope to attain Heaven?

> Whenever you pray, do not be like the hypocrites; for they love to stand
> and pray in the synagogues and at the street corners, so that they may be
> seen by others. But whenever you pray go into your room
> and shut the door, and your
> Father who sees in secret will reward you. (Mt 6:6)

Once again, Jesus was excoriating the showy style of (some) Jewish religious authorities, but hallowing their practices. There is no indication here that he was asking the people to change any of their Jewish prayers.

> Do not worry about your life, what you will eat or what you will drink, or ...
> what you will wear. Is not life more than
> food, and the body more than clothing? Look at the birds of the air; they neither
> sow nor reap ... yet your heavenly Father feeds them. Are not you of more
> value than they? ... Consider the lilies of the field, how they grow; they
> neither toil nor spin. Yet I tell you, even Solomon
> in all his glory was not clothed like one of these. But if God
> so clothes the grass of the field ... will He not much more
> provide for you, O you of little faith! ... your heavenly Father knows that
> you need all these things. But strive first for the kingdom of God and his
> righteousness, and all these things will be given to you as well. (Mt 6:25–33)

This is heart-stopping in its sublimity. But it is thrilling precisely because we know it is not true: God does not always provide our every need, however much we may wish it were so. The words of Genesis, "you shall live by the sweat of your brows," have unfortunately been humankind's lot since the banishment from the Garden of Eden. No one could possibly adhere to these precepts.

> Ask, and it will be given you; search, and you will find; knock, and the
> door will be opened for you. For everyone who asks receives, and everyone
> who searches finds, and for everyone who knocks, the door will be open.... In
> everything do to others as you would have them do to you; for this is the law and
> the prophets. (Mt 7: 7–12)

Here we have more gorgeous imagery, culminating in the recitation of the Golden Rule of Leviticus (Lev19:18). But now the Sermon ends on a chilling note:

> Enter through the narrow gate; for the gate is wide and the road
> is easy that leads to destruction, and there are many who take it.
> *For the gate is narrow and the road is hard that leads to life....*
> *And there are few who find it....* Not everyone who says to me,
> 'Lord, Lord,' will enter the kingdom of heaven, but only the one who
> does the will of my Father in heaven. On that day many will say to me, "Lord, Lord,
> did we not ... do many deeds of power in your
> name?" Then I will declare to them, "I never knew you. Go away
> from me, you evildoers." (Mt 7:13–23; italics added)

Only a *few* of those seeking heaven will attain it.[71] Jesus' most famous sermon suddenly becomes uncomfortably understandable. It was a fire-and-brimstone sermon, not a compassionate homiletic about becoming better people. And his most famous saying—"Love thy enemy"—was not a plea, but rather a *command* that eternally condemned anyone incapable of obeying it. Of course, Jesus did not intend every one of his words to be strictly followed. He was an orator who frequently used hyperbole and poetic imagery for effect. His command to "tear out your right eye" was not meant to be taken literally. Still, the overall message of the Sermon seems clear enough—only the near-perfect would be accepted.

✳✳✳

Christian religious leaders have struggled with the Sermon on the Mount for centuries, for two reasons. First, it is so Jewish—even radically so—that many of them have labored for years to allegorically interpret it in an acceptably Christian way. They have done so primarily by reinterpreting Jesus' introductory words. ("Do not think I have come to abolish the law or the prophets; I have come not to abolish but to fulfill. For ... until heaven and earth pass away, not one letter ... will pass from the law until all is accomplished.... Therefore ... whoever does them ... will be called great in the kingdom of heaven.") The meaning of these words is so self-explanatory that it may seem difficult to imagine how they could be interpreted as annulling the Law. However, the next chapter will show that

---

71 Of course, this pessimism was hardly unique in Jewish history, for many of the great Jewish prophets (e.g., Ezekiel and Jeremiah) expected only a holy "remnant" of Jews to find favor in God's eyes. In Jesus' own day, the Essenes and some other Jewish sects were similarly convinced that only their own members were destined for heaven.

within fifty years of Jesus' death, many of his followers began to believe that Jesus' mere *presence* on earth had *already* made the old ways of heaven and earth "pass away." Thus, they felt that God's Plan had already been "accomplished" (fulfilled) by the time the Sermon was delivered, making the Law obsolete. Although such beliefs were new in 80–100 CE, they soon became so embedded in Christian theology that many modern believers cannot interpret the "fulfillment" saying in any other way. Notwithstanding, *the Jews who actually heard the Sermon* in c. 29 CE would have construed everything in a traditional Jewish context. Jesus said nothing to imply that heaven and earth had passed away, or that the Mosaic Law was moribund. Quite the opposite. Commenting on the Sermon, the CSB states that "Jesus' ministry … remains within the framework of the law."[72] Likewise, he never claimed to be God, the founder of a new religion, or, publicly, the Messiah. He did secretly reveal his Messiahship to his Disciples, as shall be seen. But even had he proclaimed it publicly, it would not have changed anyone's thinking about the Law's primacy. From the very beginning, Jews have expected their Messiah to help establish an earthly Kingdom in which *the Law would be perfectly obeyed*, bringing eternal peace and harmony. A Messiah who would *annul* God's Law was inconceivable. In short, Jesus' audience could have interpreted the Sermon in only one way: we must embrace our Judaism, but more stringently and urgently than ever.

The second reason for Christianity's struggle with the Sermon is that its insupportable demands contradict the image of a compassionate Jesus. How could this possibly represent his core ethical message? As the CSB comments, "How to live with the Sermon on the Mount has been a constant point of discussion in the church. *Are these demanding words to be taken as impossible ideals*, meant only for a *perfect world or for perfect people?*" [73] Or, continues the CSB, "Do they make sense *only in the setting of Jesus' own time, when people thought the end of the world was near* and so might be capable of responding heroically in such an emergency situation?" For indeed, many people *did* anticipate the world's imminent end. In fact, we shall now see that *this* was the second major component of Jesus' message. Indeed, it was his "gospel."

Postscript: Sermon on the Mount, or Sermon on the Plain?

The Sermon on the Mount has been examined in detail because of its enormous religious importance. However, the Sermon may never have happened as described, because it is a large collection of Q-sayings (one-third of the total) that Matthew decided to consolidate into one unit. It seems unlikely that these sayings

---

72   The Catholic Study Bible, 13.

73   Ibid., RG 394; italics added.

came from a single sermon, because many of them (omitted above) contradict one another. As noted in the CSB, Matthew "organized many … sayings into discourses or speeches…. These are not 'transcripts' of actual talks … because there is little logical progression…. Rather the Evangelist has clustered the sayings of Jesus around basic motifs."[74]

Luke, who also possessed the Q-source, instead assembled a smaller number of Q-sayings into his "Sermon on the Plain," and dispersed the rest throughout his Gospel. The Sermon on the Plain's brevity makes it less impressive than the Sermon on the Mount. It is also less impressive because Luke's Q-sayings are less artistically polished than Matthew's, which is why scholars consider them more authentic. (This is in accord with the Criterion of Embarrassment, since Luke would have had no reason to rob Jesus' words of their original majesty, whereas Matthew had obvious motivation to enhance them.) Of greater importance, Luke did not employ Matthew's dramatic "thesis/antithesis" technique of stating a Mosaic Commandment ("You have heard that it was said …") and then tightening it ("But I say to you"), as seen in this comparison:

Matthew 5:38–46	Luke 6:27–30
"You have heard that it was said, 'An eye for an eye and a tooth for a tooth.' But I say to you, Do not resist an evildoer. But if anyone strikes you on the right cheek, turn the other also; and if anyone wants to sue you and take your coat, give your cloak as well. You have heard that it was said, 'You shall love your neighbor and hate your enemy.' But I say to you, love your enemies and pray for those who persecute you, so that you may be children of your Father in heaven; for he makes his sun rise on the evil and on the good."	"If anyone strikes you on the cheek, offer the other also; and from anyone who takes away your coat do not withhold even your shirt. But I say to you that listen, Love your enemies, do good to those who hate you, bless those who curse you, pray for those who abuse you."

74 Ibid., RG 389.

Thus, Luke's Jesus did not try to increase the Mosaic Law's rigor or to present his statements as commandments. (The only Mosaic Law that all Synoptics agree was changed by Jesus was the law on divorce, which he *stiffened* either by prohibiting it altogether or restricting it to cases of adultery [depending on the differing Gospel versions].) Even his warnings to the crowds were milder. For example, Matthew's "Be perfect, just as your heavenly Father is perfect" became "Be merciful, just as your Father is merciful" (Lk: 6:36). Meanwhile, Matthew's ominous warning about the "narrow gate" was shifted by Luke into a less conspicuous pericope. In sum, Luke's Sermon is the loving homiletic that Christians imagine the Sermon on the Mount to be, but it has fallen into obscurity due to its inferior literary quality. As a final comment on the Sermon on the Mount, it seems remarkable that Christians have always been so keenly attuned to its anti-Judaic attacks on the Pharisees, yet so unable to recognize its firm allegiance to Judaism.

CHAPTER 8

JESUS' MESSAGE, PART II: THE GOSPEL

Understanding Jesus' urgent cry for strict adherence to Judaism requires nothing more than recalling that "gospel" means "good news." Jesus believed he had good news—electrifying, really—and he did what anyone else would have done: shout it out. In fact, this is literally how the two earliest Synoptics begin their account of his ministry. They are his very first words to the people:

> Jesus came to Galilee, proclaiming the good news [gospel] of God, and saying, "The time is fulfilled, and *the kingdom of God has come near; repent*, and believe in the good news." (Mk 1:14–15, italics and brackets added)
> He withdrew to Galilee … [and] from that time Jesus began to proclaim, "Repent, for the kingdom of heaven has come near." (Mt 4:12–17, italics and brackets added)

This was the gospel: the world was ending, for the Day of the Lord[75] (Judgment Day) was rapidly approaching, when God would be gathering the righteous into His Kingdom. Repent! This apocalyptic message is hammered home even before Jesus appears on the scene, for the Synoptics actually begin their narratives (apart from the Nativity stories) with the jeremiads of John the Baptist, the Jewish holy man who would soon baptize Jesus. To the multitudes seeking his baptism of repentance on the Jordan River, John thundered:

> "You brood of vipers! Who warned you to flee the wrath to come? …
> Even now the ax is lying at the root of the trees; every tree therefore

---

75 Called simply "That Day" in the Gospels, due to Jews' reluctance to use God's name in vain.

that does not bear good fruit is cut down and thrown into the fire.
One ... is coming ... to gather the wheat [i.e., the righteous] into
his granary [the Kingdom], but the chaff [evildoers]
he will burn with unquenchable fire." So ... he proclaimed the good
news [gospel] to the people. (Lk 3:7–17, brackets added)

This, then, was the gospel. For as Jesus told his Disciples and the multitudes in all three Gospels, in two variant forms:

Truly I tell you, this generation will not pass away until
all these things [the Day of the Lord, and coming of
the Kingdom] have taken place.
(Mk 13:30–32; Mt 24:34–36; Lk 21:32–33)
Truly I tell you, there are some standing here who will not
taste death before they see the Son of Man coming in his kingdom.[76]
(Mk 9:1; Mt 16:28; Lk 9:27)

The day and hour were unknown, but the Day of the Lord would come in *this lifetime*. It might even come within days. As Jesus approached Jerusalem, the Disciples "supposed that the Kingdom of God was to appear immediately" (Lk 19:11). Indeed, Jesus apparently believed that his own ability to exorcise demons proved that the Kingdom was so near that evil's grip on humanity was already weakening. He exalted by saying he had already witnessed Satan "fall from heaven" (Lk 10:18), for "If it is by the finger of God that I drive out demons, then the Kingdom of God has come upon you" (Lk 11:20). Now the stern message of the Sermon on the Mount becomes crystal clear. Jews had to become perfect because they would soon face the final judgment. Anyone wishing deliverance had to cast aside all impurities, avarice, and enmities. Only those who could conquer their human imperfections were worthy of the Kingdom.

This apocalyptic message clarifies Jesus' entire ministry. It helps explain his relentless diatribes against the Jewish religious authorities. The authorities were correct in their religious preaching but had failed to live it to the utmost, to perfection. They were thus hypocrites and even stumbling blocks for the people, who had been lulled into thinking that these were normal times when normal conduct sufficed. But these were very special days, the prelude to the apocalypse. Repent!

This also explains many of Jesus' actions that otherwise sound cruel and even immoral. When an aspiring disciple said to him:

---

76 The term "Son of Man" will be discussed in chapter 10, but, broadly speaking, it refers here to the coming of the Kingdom.

"I will follow you, Lord; but let me first say farewell
to those at my home." Jesus said to him, "No one who puts a hand to the plow
and looks back is fit for the kingdom of God." (Lk 9:61–62)
Another of his disciples said to him, "Lord, first let me go and bury my father."
But Jesus said to him, "Follow me, and let the dead bury their own dead."
(Mt 8:21–22)

Let the dead bury the dead! For a son to walk off without burying his own father was to break one of the Ten Commandments. Why could not Jesus wait several hours to allow this man to fulfill his sacred burial obligations? Or one more hour to allow the other to bid his family farewell? It was because the Day of the Lord was so *close.* Jesus had to keep on moving in order to spread his gospel; he could not tarry for anything, even sacred family obligations. Indeed, families meant nothing anymore.

Do you think I have come to bring peace to the earth? No, I tell you,
but rather division! From now on five in one household will be divided,
three against two … they will be divided father against
son and son against father, mother against daughter and daughter
against mother. (Lk 12: 51–53)
Whoever loves father or mother more than me is not worthy of me; and whoever
loves son or daughter more than me is not worthy of me. (Mt 10:37)

Because redemption was only for the perfect, only the perfect could follow Jesus. A prosperous young man who admired Jesus ran up to ask what was required to enter the Kingdom. When Jesus responded by reciting the Ten Commandments, the young man announced that he had always followed them:

Jesus, looking at him,
loved him and said, "You lack one thing; go, sell what you own,
and give the money to the poor … then come, follow me."
When he heard this he was shocked and went away grieving, for he had many
possessions. Then Jesus … said to his disciples, "How hard it will be for those who
have wealth to enter the kingdom of God! … It is easier for a camel to go through
the eye of a needle than for someone who is rich to enter the kingdom of God."
They were greatly astounded and said to one another,
"Then who can be saved?" (Mk 10:21–26)

Not even this man, who merited Jesus' love for his obedience to the Law, was worthy. He had to dispense everything to the poor and follow Jesus as a mendicant. What value had wealth with the Day of the Lord impeding? It was so close that constant vigilance was required:

> But about that day or hour, no one knows, neither the angels in heaven
> nor the Son, but only the Father. Beware, keep alert; for you do not know when
> the time will come.... Therefore, keep awake—for you do not know when the lord
> of the house [God] will come in the evening, or at midnight, or at cockcrow,
> or at dawn, or else he may find you
> asleep.... And what I say to you I say to all: Keep awake.
> (Mk 13:32–37, brackets added)

This is one of the many Watchfulness parables that fill the pre-Jerusalem section of the Synoptics: the Parable of the Wedding Feast, the Ten Bridesmaids, the Watchful House Owner, and so on. In every one, the explicit or implicit time frame is the same: weeks, months, possibly years. Jesus' statement that "some are standing here who will not taste death until they see the kingdom of God" indicated that it might be delayed up to several decades ... but certainly not a century or millennium. No, the urgency was palpable. When Disciples asked when it would happen, Jesus said:

> When you hear of wars and rumors of wars, do not be alarmed;
> this must take place, but the end is still to come. For nation will
> rise against nation, and kingdom against kingdom; there will be
> earthquakes ... and famines. This is but the beginning of the birth pains....
> But when you see the desolating sacrilege set up where it ought not to be [pagan
> idols in the Jewish Temple[77]] ... those in Judea must flee to the mountains ...
> and the one in the field must not turn back to get a coat. Woe to those who are
> pregnant and to those who are nursing infants in those days!
> (Mk 13:7–17, brackets added)

Note Jesus' belief, shared by virtually every Jew of his generation, that the desecration of the Jewish Temple was the most calamitous event that could befall humanity. Meanwhile, Jesus' own prayer, the "Lord's Prayer," was equally apocalyptic:

---

77   The Catholic Study Bible, 53 (see also verse Daniel 5:27, from the Tanakh)

Our Father in heaven, hallowed be your name. *Your kingdom come.*
Your will be done on earth as it is in heaven. Give us this day our
daily bread. *And forgive us our debts* [better translated as "our sins"],[78] as we
also have forgiven our debtors. *And do not bring us to*
the time of trial, but rescue us from the evil one ...
(Mt 6:9–13; italics and brackets added[79]

***

Of the Synoptics, only Luke's fails to begin Jesus' ministry with "The Kingdom of God is at hand. Repent ..." This quotation has instead been relegated to a less conspicuous place. One can only speculate why, but recall that Luke's was the last Synoptic, composed in 85–95 CE. By that time, anyone who had actually seen Jesus would have been at least sixty-five years old, in an era when most people died at half that age. Was Luke trying to deemphasize the embarrassing failure of Jesus' core prophecy to materialize? This would certainly explain Luke's emphasis on a radical theological concept not found in Mark's original Gospel. Asked by some people when the Kingdom would come, Jesus replied, "The kingdom of God is not coming with things that can be observed; nor will they say, 'Look, here it is!,' or 'There it is!' For, in fact, the kingdom of God is among you" (Lk 17:20–21).

The Kingdom was already here! This certainly blunted the sting of the unfulfilled prophecy. As the CSB comments, "The emphasis has thus been shifted from an imminent observable coming of the kingdom to something that is already present."[80] "By reinterpreting the meaning of [Mark's Gospel], [Luke] has come to terms with what seemed to the early Christian community to be a delay in the Parousia [the Second Coming, when Jesus was expected to introduce the Kingdom]."[81] This is not to say that Luke was trying to expunge the prophecy. He was simply prolonging the "incoming"—the Kingdom of God *had* already begun,

---

78 Meier, *A Marginal Jew*, 2:293.

79 The same spirit is captured in the beginning of the famous Jewish prayer, the Kiddush, which is also probably from the first century:
Exalted and sanctified be His great Name
in the world which He created according to His will and *may*
He rule His kingdom in your lifetime and in your days, and in the
lifetime of the entire House of Israel,
Speedily and in the near future—and say Amen.

80 The Catholic Study Bible, 131.

81 Ibid., 137.

but was not completely *fulfilled.*[82] But the delay would be short, for Luke too concludes with "this generation will not pass away until all things have taken place" (Lk 21: 32). So the Kingdom had been delayed ... but only briefly.

Interestingly, Luke's attempt to downplay the Kingdom's imminence is part of a far broader pattern. We shall discover that the New Testament's earliest writings, Paul's Letters (50–60 CE), are extremely apocalyptic (chapter 15), as is the earliest Gospel, Mark's (c. 70 CE). What happens in the successive Gospels of Matthew and especially Luke (c. 80–95 CE) is revealing. They too are apocalyptic, but noticeably less so. The reason is fascinating: virtually their entire apocalyptic content derives from their earliest source materials: i.e., borrowings from Mark's Gospel and the Q-source. Their *new* material, which they themselves wrote, is essentially devoid of it. (The last Gospel, John's [95–110 CE] not only avoids it entirely but even states that "the coming of the Kingdom" *already occurred* the moment Jesus' ministry began. This Gospel is one of Christianity's earliest sources for the belief that Jesus himself was the Kingdom, as mentioned in the discussion of the Sermon on the Mount.[83]) In short, as the people of Jesus' generation began passing away in the decades after his death, the Evangelists progressively downplayed his core prediction about the Kingdom's coming. Significantly, this trend,

---

82 This is often called Luke's "already/not yet" theology. Luke is also the source of Jesus' statements that his healing powers provided proof of the incoming Kingdom.

83 John's Gospel was to be "last but not least," because its reinterpretation of the Day of the Lord/Coming of the Kingdom to mean Jesus' own presence in the world has become standard Christian theology since the early second century. This reinterpretation was probably inevitable, for Jesus' failure to return by 100 CE meant either that (a) he was not the Messiah, or (b) his prophecies were never intended to be interpreted in their literal, apocalyptic sense. It was far easier to accept the latter than the former. For this reason, many Christians find it difficult to recognize the apocalyptic nature of the Synoptics or Paul's Letters (chapter 15). Even the greatest Christian scholars overlooked this until a century ago. Then, in 1906, the renowned humanitarian/Bible scholar Albert Schweitzer rocked the academic world by demonstrating in his *The Quest for the Historical Jesus* that the failure to recognize Jesus' apocalyptic essence had brought New Testament studies into a blind alley. *The Quest* remains immensely influential, although the pendulum has begun to swing back during the last few decades. Whether this recent tendency among Christian scholars to deemphasize the apocalyptic is the result of superior understanding, or simply of nervousness about accepting the possibility that Jesus' key prophecy was wrong, is in the eye of the beholder. It might be noted that many of the great Jewish prophets were also mistaken in their prophecies, but these errors have never represented a theological challenge for Judaism, because the prophets were always understood to be humans. For its God to be wrong, however, is a challenge for Christianity.

in turn, largely explains Jesus' evolving image in the Synoptics. In Mark's Gospel, Jesus is a miracle worker who seems to be breathlessly racing against the clock to complete his mission before the apocalypse begins. Matthew's Gospel remains edgy due to the combination of apocalyptic and anti-Judaic material, but Jesus no longer seems so pressed for time, allowing him more opportunity to focus on teaching. (The inclusion of the Q-sayings also contributes to the emphasis on teaching). In Luke's Gospel, the apocalyptic message is so toned down that Jesus is steadfastly serene, always with sufficient time for more good deeds and loving words.

***

Apocalyptic expectations were hardly unique in this period. What was the origin of this worldview, and how did it shape the world into which Jesus was born?

Early Development

The Jewish people have long believed in a Messiah, but over half a millennium would pass before they began to also believe in an apocalypse—a titanic conflagration that would usher in a the Day of the Lord (Judgment Day) and the Kingdom. The earlier idea, of a Messiah, arose in response to the disintegration of the Israelite nation following the Golden Age of King David and Solomon (c. 1000–930 BCE). These kings had unified the twelve tribes into the United Kingdom of Israel, expanded its territory through military conquest, and built the First (Solomon's) Temple in Jerusalem. But the country split into two weaker nations after Solomon's death. The northern kingdom, which inherited the name of Israel and contained ten of the tribes, was destroyed in 721 BCE by the Assyrians. Its peoples were slaughtered and scattered, blotting out the Ten Lost Tribes from history. The southern kingdom, Judea (composed of the tribes of Judah and Benjamin), centering on Jerusalem, was overrun in 586 BCE by the Babylonians. The First Temple was destroyed, including its only truly holy object: God's sacred residence, the Ark of the Covenant. Great numbers of Judeans were killed, enslaved, or sent into exile to Babylon.

This tragic decline unleashed a yearning for a Messiah—a ruler, presumably descended from King David, who would reunite the people (including the Lost Tribes) and militarily overthrow their foreign despots. The final battle would be as bloody as any major battle but would lack apocalyptic elements such as earthquakes and pestilence. Nor would God hold a Final Judgment, for the Messiah would rule his new kingdom so righteously that every Jew would see the light and become good. Even the Gentile nations would see Israel's glory and begin worshipping its holy God. A Temple surpassing even Solomon's would be rebuilt, and the sacred Ark of the Covenant somehow restored.

Figure 2: JEWISH HISTORY OF PALESTINE

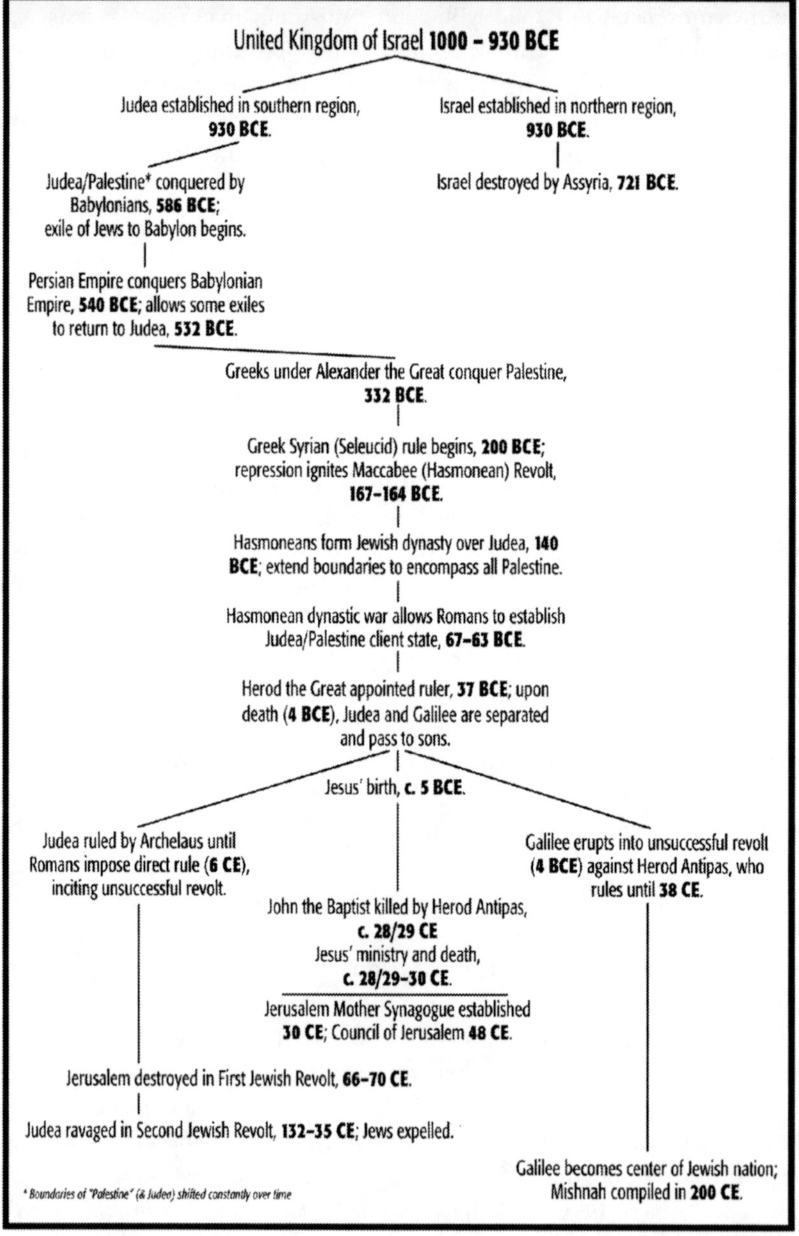

United Kingdom of Israel **1000 – 930 BCE**

Judea established in southern region, **930 BCE.**

Israel established in northern region, **930 BCE.**

Judea/Palestine* conquered by Babylonians, **586 BCE**; exile of Jews to Babylon begins.

Israel destroyed by Assyria, **721 BCE.**

Persian Empire conquers Babylonian Empire, **540 BCE**; allows some exiles to return to Judea, **532 BCE.**

Greeks under Alexander the Great conquer Palestine, **332 BCE.**

Greek Syrian (Seleucid) rule begins, **200 BCE**; repression ignites Maccabee (Hasmonean) Revolt, **167–164 BCE.**

Hasmoneans form Jewish dynasty over Judea, **140 BCE**; extend boundaries to encompass all Palestine.

Hasmonean dynastic war allows Romans to establish Judea/Palestine client state, **67–63 BCE.**

Herod the Great appointed ruler, **37 BCE**; upon death (**4 BCE**), Judea and Galilee are separated and pass to sons.

Jesus' birth, **c. 5 BCE.**

Judea ruled by Archelaus until Romans impose direct rule (**6 CE**), inciting unsuccessful revolt.

Galilee erupts into unsuccessful revolt (**4 BCE**) against Herod Antipas, who rules until **38 CE.**

John the Baptist killed by Herod Antipas, **c. 28/29 CE**
Jesus' ministry and death, **c. 28/29–30 CE.**

Jerusalem Mother Synagogue established **30 CE**; Council of Jerusalem **48 CE.**

Jerusalem destroyed in First Jewish Revolt, **66–70 CE.**

Judea ravaged in Second Jewish Revolt, **132–35 CE**; Jews expelled.

Boundaries of "Palestine" (& Judea) shifted constantly over time

Galilee becomes center of Jewish nation; Mishnah compiled in **200 CE.**

But the Messiah never came, despite the prophets' predictions. Why had God allowed his Chosen People to suffer so under the heels of the foreign pagans? The traditional Jewish answer to any question about evil was that God was punishing them for their transgressions. Later, the idea that humans were too insignificant to understand God's inscrutable plan began to gain currency. But a third explanation began to take root after c. 540 BCE, when the mighty Persian Empire conquered Babylonia and most of the Middle East. Because Persia ruled Judea for the next two centuries, and proved relatively benign—King Cyrus even allowed some of Babylonia's Jewish exiles to return to Jerusalem in 521 BCE, to try to rebuild the city and construct a Second Temple—Jews were inevitably exposed to Persia's religion, Zoroastrianism. This "dualistic" religion taught that the world was the stage of a titanic struggle between a powerful god of Goodness and an almost equally powerful god of Evil, who would eventually be defeated in a cataclysmic struggle that would shake the earth. Jews had long believed in demons, but only as occasional troublemakers, and there was no room in monotheistic Judaism for the existence of an actual god of evil. But the idea that perhaps God co-cohabited the heavens with angels—both good and evil (devils)—slowly entered their imaginations, ready to germinate with the next calamity.

In 332 BCE, Alexander the Great conquered Persia, sweeping Judea into his fast-growing Greek Hellenistic empire. The initial impact was minimal, because Judea was governed at first by the tolerant Greek rulers of Egypt. Then came tragedy. In 200 BCE, dominion passed to the Greek Seleucid rulers of Syria. They were adamant about imposing a homogenous Hellenistic culture throughout their lands, and saw Judaism as an intractable roadblock. Thus, after replacing the Jewish high priest in 175 BCE, they demanded, on pain of death, that the Jews reject their religion in favor of Greek polytheism. The book 1 Maccabees[84] captures the horror of their plight in its story of seven brothers and their mother being tortured by the Seleucid king to induce them to eat pork, in violation of Mosaic Law. When one of the brothers defiantly cried out his willingness to die for his God:

> The king, in a fury, gave orders to have pans and caldrons heated.
> While they were being quickly heated, he commanded his
> executioners to cut out the tongue of the one who had spoken ... to scalp

---

84 Ironically, although 1 Maccabees and 2 Maccabees are our primary source about the Maccabean revolt (and the origin of Chanukah), they were canonized into the New Testament but not into the Tanakh. The reason is probably that the original Hebrew (or Aramaic) manuscripts were lost, leaving behind only Greek translations that the early rabbi/sages considered unacceptable for canonization.

> him and cut off his hands and feet, while the rest of his brothers
> and mother looked on. When he was completely maimed but still
> breathing, the king ordered them to carry him to the fire and fry him.
> As a cloud of smoke spread from the pan, the brothers and their mother
> encouraged one another to die bravely, saying ... "The Lord God
> is looking on, and he truly has compassion on us." (2 Mac 7:3–6)

And each of the seven brothers died similarly, followed by their mother.

Jewish resistance to Seleucid persecution finally exploded into the Maccabean Revolt of 167–164 BCE. The revolt succeeded, although the Seleucids retained some power for another two decades. But in 140 BCE, the victorious Maccabean leaders created a Hasmonean dynasty that would rule a fully independent Jewish nation for nearly a century. But the persecutions and the revolt had traumatized the Jewish psyche, and they gave birth to three new religious concepts. The first, described in the passage above, was actually "something new under the sun"—martyrology—the conviction that death was preferable to abandoning one's religion. No people in history had ever died in the resolute defense of their religion. Their suffering inevitably introduced a second new concept: the resurrection of the dead. Surely there had to be a final reward for all those who had agonizingly died in God's name. By extension, it seemed only just that the same everlasting reward be shared by all the generations of righteous dead, who had endured their own suffering. Hitherto, Jews had believed that when the Messiah finally restored their nation, only those alive at that time would inhabit it. The dead would remain in their shadowy netherworld of Sheol. But now, in the conclusion of the Tanakh's Book of Daniel, dating from the Seleucid period, the idea of resurrection of the dead was expounded explicitly for the first time:

> There shall be a time of trouble, such as never was....
> And at that time thy people shall be delivered, every one that shall be found
> written in the book [God's book of virtuous Jews]. And may of them that sleep in
> the dust of the earth shall awake, some to everlasting life, and some to reproaches
> and everlasting abhorrence. And they that are wise shall shine
> as the brightness of the firmament; and they that turn the many to
> righteousness [shall become] as the stars for ever and ever.
> (Dan 12:1–3, brackets added)

In this seminal passage is also mentioned the third great, recent innovation: that the resurrection would be preceded by a terrifying apocalypse—"a time of trouble such as never was." The apocalypse represented the belated impact of Zoroastrianism on Jewish thinking. Daniel had no need to describe the apocalypse in detail, for it had already been presented in full a few decades earlier, in 1 Enoch. Unlike Daniel, which is the only apocalyptic writing to be canonized into the Tanakh, 1 Enoch never received scriptural status in any religion. Yet it is probably the most famous unknown book in history, for its story is universally known. It taught that evil arose when a group of celestial angels, led by Semyaz (Satan), rebelled against God. They were cast out of heaven but continued their malign deeds on earth. Their evil would grow until God could no longer tolerate humanity's suffering. Then, assisted by his archangels, he would destroy Satan and his evil cohorts. The struggle would be cosmic. The Heavens would shake; stars would fall from heaven. This celestial Armageddon would be mirrored on earth by an apocalypse: earthquakes, pestilence, and indescribable horrors. Finally, with God's final victory, earthly victory would come also to the Jews, whose foreign overlords would be defeated. Interestingly, God's centrality in the conquest of evil raised the question of whether a Messiah was really needed for earthly victory, although most Jews continued to assume so.

Finally, implied in this passage, although not a new concept, is the Day of the Lord (Judgment Day). In the original Messianic concept, everyone was welcome into the Kingdom, for even the sinful would be gradually transformed to righteousness. But the centuries of catastrophes—the Assyrian and Babylonian conquests, the Seleucid horrors, and intermittent internecine conflict—had hardened hearts. With so much evil in the world, it seemed unimaginable that everyone could freely enter the Kingdom. There had to be a Judgment Day when the wicked—both living and resurrected—would be winnowed into everlasting agony. Only the upright deserved entrance to the glorious Kingdom. Every human would be judged for eternity; there would be no second chance. Suddenly, the stakes of the Day of the Lord were immeasurably high. In short, the Seleucid period was immensely influential, by introducing martyrology, the resurrection of the dead, and the apocalypse, and reemphasizing the Day of the Lord.

Continuation, and Emergence of the World of Jesus
We must briefly return to Jewish history, both to continue tracing the apocalyptic outlook of the Jewish people and to understand the milieu of the early-first-century world that Jesus lived in. As noted, the Jewish Hasmonean dynasty was established in 140 BCE and ruled in relative peace for nearly one century. It generally enjoyed broad public support, particularly when its conquest of Samaria, Galilee, and the Mediterranean coast dramatically expanded the nation's boundaries. Many of the conquered Gentiles in these new territories were forcibly converted

to Judaism.[85] For the first time since King David and Solomon, all of "Palestine" consisted of an autonomous Jewish homeland, named Judea.

As this century progressed, however, fissures developed between the Hasmoneans and a small minority of pious Jews, including the Pharisees and the Essenes, who apparently arose in this era. These groups were outraged that the Hasmoneans began appointing family members to the Temple's high priesthood, a position hitherto reserved for the Zadokite priestly class (direct descendants of Moses' brother, Aaron). The position of high priest was supremely important. In reaction to these sacrilegious appointments, the apocalyptic *Testament of the Twelve Patriarchs* was written to prophecy the Hasmoneans' doom. Friction also mounted over the Hasmoneans' gradual assimilation of Hellenistic culture. By 67 BCE, a dynastic civil war erupted between two Hasmonean brothers competing for the crown. An exhausting stalemate forced them to seek mediation from the ever-expanding Roman Empire, whose armies were already at the door. The Romans decided to support the compliant Hyrcanus II, who was installed in 63 BCE. But in addition to destroying part of Jerusalem in their efforts to capture Hyrcanus' brother, the Romans exacted a steep price. Judea was annexed into the Empire and stripped of its non-Jewish regions, such as Samaria and the Mediterranean coast. This infamy provoked the appearance of the Psalms of Solomon, which promised the coming of a Messiah who would crush the pagan Romans and their Hasmonean underlings.

When Hasmonean infighting resumed, Rome finally swept away the splintered dynasty by crowning the ambitious half-Jewish leader, Herod the Great. He ruled

---

85 This fact, along with several ancient texts (including the Gospel of Mark's reference to "Galilee of the Gentiles") has led some scholars to question whether Galilee was truly Jewish in the early first century. However, other documents that do support Galilee's Jewishness have recently gained substantial credibility through extensive archaeological studies of the region that began in the 1970s (Reed, *Archeology and the Galilean Jesus*, 23–61). These studies have revealed that Galilee was entirely depopulated by the Assyrian invasion of 721 BCE and was only spottily resettled during the Persian and early Hellenistic periods (586 to 167 BCE). Significant repopulation began only following its conquest by the Jewish Hasmoneans. The migration began at the Judean border and progressed northward. By the first century CE, its predominantly Jewish character could be discerned, in both cities and rural areas, in several ways: (a) complete absence of pig bones anywhere in Galilee; (b) distinctively Jewish tombs (ossuaries), always situated outside the boundaries of villages or cities (to avoid the corpses' ritual impurity); c) widespread distribution of mikvas (for ritual washing); and (d) near-universal use of Judean pottery, which was not used in surrounding Gentile regions. The only exceptions (e.g., some stylized idols) were found in a few upper-class dwellings of Gentiles and highly Hellenized Jews.

from 37 to 4 BCE, and expanded the borders of Judea to include, once again, all of Palestine. Jesus was born in the last years of his reign, c. 5 BCE. Herod was ruthless but efficient. He instituted both economic prosperity and a spectacular building campaign that extended from Judea/Palestine to the large Diaspora communities of surrounding Roman provinces. A centerpiece of this program was an enlargement of the Temple so monumental that eighty years were required for its completion (20 BCE–60 CE). By the time of Jesus' ministry, the Second Temple was the largest and most renowned religious edifice in the Roman Empire, a true wonder of the world. Herod's ancestry prevented him from becoming installing himself or his family members as high priests, but he carefully selected loyal Zadokites.

With Herod's death in 4 BCE, the predominantly Jewish regions of his kingdom were bequeathed to two of his sons.

Judea (and Samaria)

Judea, the Jewish heartland, was allotted to Herod's son Archelaus. But Archelaus' unpopularity forced the Romans to replace him with a series of military governors (procurators), from 6 to 41 CE. The procurator during Jesus' ministry, Pontius Pilate, occupied this post from 26 to 36 CE.

This transition to direct Roman rule in 6 CE was disastrous. The Judeans were accustomed to foreign domination, but only through vassal Jewish leaders, such as Hyrcanus II, Herod the Great, and Archelaus. Never had a foreign empire ruled directly and stationed its own troops on Jewish soil. The tension exploded when Rome initiated a tax census in 6 CE to collect money for its coffers. With the rallying cry "No King but God," a revolutionary named Judas of Galilee triggered the bloodiest anti-Roman revolt of Jesus' lifetime. (Jesus was about ten years old.) Roman troops crushed the rebellion and, according to the historian Josephus, left two thousand Jews hanging on crucifixes.

Judea settled down to a state of simmering tension, but without active rebellions, for the rest of Jesus' life. Because the Jewish people were humiliated by direct military rule by pagan Rome, the unpopular procurators needed Jewish assistance in maintaining order and collecting taxes. They therefore co-opted the highly Hellenized Jewish upper class. This consisted largely of the Herodian family (Herod the Great's sons and relatives), other Jewish aristocrats, and the Sadducees who controlled the Jerusalem Temple. The Romans took special pains to ensure the loyalty of the high priest of the Temple, Judaism's most prestigious and wealthiest institution. Inevitably, the Sadducees became widely unpopular among their fellow Jews, both for their collaborationist activities and their wealth, since most ordinary Jews of this period were impoverished. The most apocalyptic of all writings, the War Scroll, may have originated in this period. Starting with the opening sentence, "This is the war of the Sons of Light against the Sons of

Darkness," this scroll was a virtual military manual against the Romans and their collaborators. It was not widely known because it was written by the separatist Essene community at Qumram, but the Essenes may have influenced John the Baptist.

Despite (or because of) these tensions, the early procurators tried to provide enough autonomy to satisfy the masses. But there were inevitable missteps. In the early years of Pontius Pilate's rule (26–36 CE), while Jesus was probably still alive, Roman troops bearing standards emblazoned with idolatrous imperial imagery were stationed in Jerusalem. Massive protests forced Pilate to back down. But he became sterner in the years after Jesus. When angry Jerusalem crowds protested his diversion of Temple funds for aqueduct construction, they were slaughtered by concealed Roman soldiers. Pilate was finally recalled to Rome in 36 CE for ordering the massacre of Samaritans praying at their own holy "Temple," on Mount Gerizin.

Galilee

This fertile backwater agricultural territory (along with Perea, east of the Jordan River) was bequeathed to another of Herod the Great's sons, Herod Antipas. The transition, in 4 BCE, was violent. The death of the brutal Herod the Great unleashed insurrectionary passions, particularly in the city of Sepphoris, a mere four miles from Nazareth. Rebels led by Judah, son of Ezekias (possibly the same "Judas of Galilee" who later instigated the 6 CE Judean revolt), sacked Sepphoris' military armory. The Roman Legion retaliated by burning the city to the ground and selling its inhabitants into slavery. Jesus was only two years old, but he must have grown up knowing many people whose family members had been killed or enslaved in the tragedy.

Once peace allowed Herod Antipas to begin governing, he appears to have ruled efficiently, for the Romans retained him in office for decades, until 38 CE. Galilee was generally peaceful, partly because Herod was Jewish, and partly because people were aware of the iron fist inside the glove. Like all rulers in the Roman Empire, Herod maintained the peace by eliminating problems before they festered. His firsthand exposure to Jewish firebrands like Judas, son of Ezekias, motivated him, c. 28–29 CE, to arrest John the Baptist, who was living along the Jordan River, in Perea (governed by Antipas). The Synoptics state that Herod was alarmed that a holy man of such charismatic power was denouncing his religiously illicit marriage to his brother's wife. The Baptist was beheaded at Herod's order. We will later read Josephus' fuller account of the murder.

In any case, this was the world that Jesus was raised in. Memories of the mass crucifixions from the Judean uprising and the sack of Sepphoris must still have been searing. His own mentor, John the Baptist, had been arrested and killed.

John seemed to be a transformative figure for Jesus. Jesus came to John for baptism, and the two men shared a virtually identical message of apocalyptic repentance. The Synoptics concur that Jesus' ministry began perhaps two months after the Baptist's arrest, as if Jesus felt he had to fulfill the Baptist's mission. In short, Jesus' apocalyptic worldview is easy to understand, for he was a personal witness to the spiritual and political unrest that had preoccupied the Jewish people since the days of the Maccabees.

CHAPTER 9

JESUS' MESSAGE, PART III: MISSION TO THE GENTILES AND SALVATION THROUGH FAITH?

Jesus' mission and message should now be clear: he had come to warn his people to repent in order to triumphantly enter the Kingdom of God. But was this his entire message? Didn't he also preach to the Gentiles and offer a new path—faith in himself, the Christ—to achieve salvation? The answer is no, as will soon become evident.

Relations with Gentiles
Consistent with the evidence from Acts that Jesus cared little for Gentiles, the Synoptic accounts of his life mention Gentiles only infrequently, and usually with hostility. It must be recognized the term Gentiles refers to any non-Jew of any religious persuasion; the term Christian is wholly absent from the Synoptics. The most dramatic example of Jesus' relations with Gentiles was his shocking behavior toward a Syrophenician (Canaanite) Woman while in a non-Jewish region north of Galilee. The woman begged him to cure her demon-possessed daughter, but:

He did not answer her at all, and his disciples came and urged him, saying "Send her away." He answered, "I was sent only to the lost sheep of the house of Israel."
But she came and knelt before him, saying, "Lord, help me." He answered,
"It is not fair to take the children's food and throw it to the dogs."
She said, "Yes, Lord, yet even the dogs eat the crumbs that fall from
their master's table." Then Jesus answered ... "Woman,

> great is your faith! Let it be done for you as you wish." And her daughter
> was healed. (Mt 15:23–28)

Jesus not only initially repulsed this grieving mother, but even after her humble obeisance to her Jewish "masters," he maligned her as a "dog" unworthy of the spiritual food of Judaism. Only her persistence persuaded him to relent. Jesus expressed identical sentiments toward Gentiles in the Sermon on the Mount, when he warned the crowd, "Do not give what is holy to dogs; and do not throw your pearls before swine, or they will trample them underfoot and turn and maul you" (Mt 7:6). (*Dogs* and *swine* were common Jewish terms of contempt for Gentiles, according to the CSB.[86]) Jesus' only other references to Gentiles in the Sermon on the Mount were criticisms of their greed (Mt 5:47) and babbling prayers (Mt 6:7).

His exclusive mission to the Jews was reemphasized in one Gospel when he commissioned his Disciples to disperse and preach his gospel through Palestine, saying, "Go nowhere among the Gentiles, and enter no town of the Samaritans, but go rather to the lost sheep of the house of Israel"[87] (Mt 10:5–6). Unfortunately, he later ignored his own advice by traveling from Galilee to Jerusalem through Samaria. In his only recorded visit to a Samaritan village, the people "did not receive him, because his face was set toward Jerusalem [i.e., he was obviously Jewish]. When his disciples James and John saw it, they said, 'Lord, do you want us to command fire to come down from heaven and consume them?'" (Luke 9:53–54). But Jesus refused, so they continued on to seek another resting place.[88]

---

86   The Catholic Study Bible, 17.

87   Mark and Luke do not mention this restriction, but all three Synoptics emphasize Jesus' focus on the Jews.

88   It was precisely the intense animosity between the Jews and Samaritans—the kind that festers deepest between estranged relatives—that explains Jesus' renowned parable of the Good Samaritan. The Samaritans are believed to have descended from the small numbers of Israelites living north of Judea who survived the Assyrian conquest of 721 BCE. Over time, they intermarried extensively with the new pagan settlers, while remaining Jewish. However, their form of Judaism evolved independently from Judean Judaism (i.e., normative Judaism) for the next six hundred years. They were therefore viewed as heretics and renegades by the Jews of Judea and Galilee.

This background allows the Parable of the Good Samaritan Parable to be understood. This parable is actually the conclusion of Luke's version of the Greatest Commandment story (chapter 6). After the Jewish lawyer had agreed with Jesus that "you shall love thy neighbor as thyself," the lawyer asked, "And who is my neighbor?" Jesus replied with this story: A Jew traveler was beset by robbers who beat him severely and dumped him on the roadside. A Jewish priest who later came across the

These pericopes demonstrate that Jesus occasionally did pass through Gentile or Samaritan lands, but it seems significant that he never attempted to preach to the people. He did heal some people, as in the case of the Syrophoenician woman, but sometimes with strange results. Once, in another Gentile territory, he encountered a man possessed by many demons. Jesus exorcised the demons, which entered into pigs that flung themselves into the sea. But when the neighboring Gentiles rushed to the site of the miracle, they all asked him to leave their district, for they were seized with "great fear" (Lk 8:37). This is the only Synoptic healing story in which the onlookers, rather than responding with awe and delight, asked Jesus to depart.

There are a few other stories of Jesus healing Gentiles, but these are exceptions. Yet Jesus' overall distaste for Gentiles seems to be contradicted by one pericope that demands attention. As Jesus entered Capernaum, the center of his Galilean ministry, a Gentile centurion approached him, saying that his servant lay paralyzed at home, suffering greatly. When Jesus agreed to cure the servant, the centurion responded:

> "Lord, I am not worthy to have you come under my roof; but only speak the word
> and my servant will be healed." When Jesus heard him,
> he was amazed and said, ...
> "Truly, I tell you, in no one in Israel have I found such faith.
> I tell you, many will come from east and west, and will eat
> with Abraham and Isaac and Jacob in the kingdom of
> Heaven, while the heirs of the kingdom will be thrown into
> the outer darkness, where there will be weeping and gnashing of teeth."
> (Mt 8:7–12)

This apparent prediction that Gentiles would supplant the Jewish people in God's favor is jolting; it seems to contradict the concept of a Jewish Jesus. It

---

prostrate victim ignored him, as did a second Jew. But a Samaritan traveler who saw him was filled with pity and carried him to an inn in order to feed and heal him (Lk 11:29–37). Jesus then asked the lawyer, which of the three travelers was the victim's true neighbor? The lawyer instantly answered that it was the Samaritan, for he fully agreed with Jesus that merely being Jewish was worth little without compassion and good deeds. In short, Jesus' parable had nothing to with Samaritans; it was simply a strikingly original way of dramatizing the critical importance of ethical behavior in Judaism. (The dramatic value of Jesus' choice of a Samaritan becomes apparent by modernizing the parable. If an Israeli rabbi recounted a story of an injured Jewish soldier who was ignored by Palestinians but rescued by a fellow Jewish soldier, the story would be meaningless. But making a Palestinian the hero provides impact.)

does not, however. We will soon see, for example, that the centurion's "faith" is not what it sounds like. More important, note that this passage was written by Matthew, who often filled Jesus' mouth with anti-Judaic invective. When we turn to Luke's version (the only other Synoptic account), it is dramatically different. The centurion is no longer an ordinary Gentile, but a "God-fearer" who first asked his Jewish friends for assistance in approaching Jesus. More strikingly, the angry warning to the Jewish people is gone. Why? Luke decided that the "weeping and gnashing" sayings (from the Q-source) should instead go into a pericope in which Jesus was traveling through Galilee. When a villager asked him whether only a few would be accepted into the Kingdom, Jesus answered:

> Strive to enter through the narrow door; for many ... will try to
> enter but will not be able.... There will
> be weeping and gnashing of teeth when you see Abraham and Isaac and Jacob
> and all the prophets in the kingdom of God, and you yourselves
> thrown out. Then people will come from east and west,
> from north and south, and will eat in the kingdom of God. (Lk 13:24–29)

Thus, according to Luke, Jesus' warning was addressed not to a Gentile, but rather to some Jewish villagers, to encourage their quick repentance if they hoped to join the other Jews throughout Palestine who were striving to enter the Kingdom. Although the relative validity of these two versions is impossible to judge in isolation, Luke's pericope is so much more consistent with Acts, the Letter to the Galatians, the Greatest Commandment, the Sermon on the Mount, and so forth, that his placement of these verses seems far more sensible than Matthew's.

Salvation through Faith?

Christians believe Jesus provided a non-Jewish (i.e., Christian) way to gain God's favor: by "faith in Jesus," which would "save" them by providing "forgiveness of sins." But the CSB's statement that "there was little or no thought of any dividing line between Christianity and Judaism" proves, by itself, that this is impossible.[89] Only God can judge a person's fate in Judaism. The idea of worshiping Jesus—a man who ate and slept like themselves—would have been inconceivable to Jesus' contemporaries. He himself never claimed to be God or divine in any way, just as he never claimed to be creating a new religion.

It therefore comes as no surprise that a careful reading of the Synoptics shows that none of the references to "faith," "saving," or "forgiveness of sins" refer to a theological belief that Jesus was a God who could "save" people. We emphasize

---

89 The Catholic Study Bible, 188.

careful reading, and the importance of understanding the Gospels from the perspective of first-century Jewish minds. Today, people have heard of "faith in Jesus" so often that faith is automatically interpreted in a theological sense. But faith would *not* have been interpreted so during Jesus' life, when almost everyone regarded him as an ordinary man, as illustrated by his reception in Nazareth. Therefore, unless *explicitly* stated in the Gospels, the most logical way to interpret "faith in Jesus" is in its ordinary sense: that people trusted him, or believed in his message or healing powers. This said, these terms can now be examined in order.

Faith

Jesus never asked people to have faith in him as a savior. The only time he ever instructed people to have faith in a savior was when he was referring to *God*. For example, when the Disciples expressed amazement at one of his miracles, he said, "Have faith in God. Truly I tell you, if you say to this mountain, 'Be taken up and thrown into the sea' ... it will be done for you" (Mk 11:22–23).

More frequently, Jesus used "faith" in a more generic sense by urging people to "have more faith," or by accusing them of not having enough. But occasionally he would say, after healing a patient, "Your faith has saved you." (The word "saved" is discussed below.) But such faith always meant *belief in his healing powers.*[90] And Palestinian Jews could easily believe in Jesus' miraculous powers without believing he was more than human. After all, Moses had been mortal, yet had performed far more spectacular miracles than Jesus (such as the Ten Plagues of Egypt). The Gospels never even claim that Jesus was the greatest miracle worker of his own time, as shall be seen.

That "faith" simply meant belief in Jesus' curative skills is easily illustrated by the centurion pericope. Since Jesus was so amazed at the centurion's faith, it should be simple to glean the word's meaning from this story. Here is the same pericope in greater detail:

The centurion answered, "Lord, I am not worthy to have you come under my roof; but only speak the word, and my servant will be healed. For I also am a man under authority, with soldiers under me. And I say to one, 'Go', and he goes, and to another, 'Come', and he comes, and to my slave, 'Do this', and the slave does it." When Jesus heard him, he was amazed and said ... "Truly I tell you, in no one in Israel have I found such faith." (Mt 8:8–10)

---

90   Meier, *A Marginal Jew*, 2:639.

Thus, the centurion was so accustomed to being immediately obeyed by his underlings that he assumed from Jesus' authoritative manner that Jesus' words would similarly be executed. There is absolutely no suggestion here that the centurion believed that Jesus was God, or that he should be worshiped. Nor is there any suggestion that the centurion was morally transformed in any way by his encounter with Jesus, or that he was meritorious to begin with (in Matthew's version, above). His minions' quick response to his orders was probably due to their anticipation of harsh punishment for any delay. As for his reverent-sounding statement that "I am not worthy to have you enter under my roof," the CSB believes it was merely a polite acknowledgment that Jesus, like all Jews, would consider a Gentile's home too unclean to enter.[91] (We encountered this sentiment previously, with Peter and Cornelius.) Thus, this pericope demonstrates that "faith" had nothing to do worship, theological belief, or repentance.[92]

Save/Salvation
These terms were usually used in the sense of saving people from physical death, or exclusion from the Kingdom. Nevertheless, it is easy to understand how they could be interpreted theologically in other contexts. It was mentioned above that Jesus sometimes said, "Your faith has saved you" to those he healed. In this setting, however, Jesus was *automatically* "saving" them, for a primary meaning of the Greek word "save" (sozo) is "to heal." (This meaning is captured in the English word "salve," a healing ointment.) When Jesus said, "Your faith has saved you," he was merely affirming the universal truth that healing is most effective in those who believe their healer's powers.

There is one superficially theological-sounding use of the word "save" in the Synoptics. Jesus told a crowd: "If any want to become my followers, let them deny themselves and take up their cross, and follow me. For those who want to save their life will lose it, and those who lose their life for my sake, and for the sake of the gospel, will save it" (Mk 8:34–35). However, considering the powerful evidence of Jesus' Jewishness, this passage is most easily understood by recalling his certitude that he had been chosen by God to save as many Jews as possible on the Day of the Lord. By extension, he naturally believed that whoever assisted him, no

---

91 The Catholic Study Bible, 111.

92 Incidentally, fundamentalists who believe in the literal accuracy of Scriptures see no discrepancies among the differing versions of various pericopes. They simply believe that each pericope records a different episode. The centurion story is a challenging test of this notion, for it seems difficult to imagine that Jesus effected long-distance cures of the slaves of two different centurions, each of whom manifested the greatest faith Jesus had ever seen.

matter the hardships, was guaranteed entrance to the Kingdom. Conversely, those who ignored him might be rejected. This interpretation is supported by the juxta-position of "lose their life for my sake/for the sake of the gospel," which indicates that he equated "his sake" with his mission of spreading the gospel. In any event, this passage is certainly not an explicit statement that he was the source of human salvation. Explicit declarations of this kind *can* be found in the Gospels—but only in John's Gospel, where Jesus is depicted as God. In this unique Gospel, Jesus pro-claims: "I tell you, *I* am the gate.... All who came before me are thieves and ban-dits; but ... whoever enters by *me* will be saved" (Jn 10:7–9; italics added). And again, "God did not send the Son [Jesus] ... to condemn the world, but in order that the world might be saved through him. Those who believe in him are not condemned; but those who do not ... are condemned" (Jn 3:17–18). Nothing remotely comparable is contained in the three Synoptics.

Forgiveness of Sins

On several occasions, Jesus said to people he had cured, "Your sins are forgiven."[93] It is easy to misinterpret this expression to mean that Jesus possessed a godlike power to offer forgiveness. Instead, this statement merely reflects the fact that in those days all illnesses were believed to be God's punishment for sin. Thus, Jews recognized that faith healers or exorcists could succeed only if God had cho-sen to forgive the patient's sins. As the CSB notes, "The connection between the forgiveness of sins and ... cure ... reflects the belief of first-century Palestine ... that sickness and infirmity are the result of sin, one's own or that of one's ances-tors."[94] That Jesus was speaking of *God's* forgiveness is supported by his invariant use of the passive voice ("Your sins are forgiven [i.e., by God]"), never the active "I forgive your sins." Whenever Jesus *explicitly* named the ultimate authority of forgiveness of sins, it was God. Jesus' famous Lord's Prayer begins: "Our Father in heaven, hallowed be your name. Your kingdom come ... *Forgive us our debts* [bet-ter translated as "sins," which is the word found in Luke's version of this prayer (Lk 11:4)]." Likewise, he instructed his Disciples to constantly forgive others in their prayers, so God would likewise forgive them (Mk 11:26). In any event, Jesus was hardly alone in forgiving sins. Even before his ministry began, John the Baptist had been "proclaiming a baptism of repentance for the forgiveness of sins" (Mk 1:4). Indeed, Jesus' ministry did not even begin until Jesus *himself* had received John's baptism for the forgiveness of sin.

---

93 Two exceptions in which Jesus told *healthy* people that their sins were forgiven are discussed in chapter 11.

94 The Catholic Study Bible, 108.

Preaching to All Nations

Before his Ascension (the post-resurrection ascent to heaven), Jesus instructed his Disciples to preach his message "to all the nations." Christians have always understood this to mean that Jesus wanted his "new religion" (Christianity) to be taught throughout the world. But since Jesus always remained true to Judaism, this instruction was unquestionably a reiteration of the traditional Jewish belief that Israel was "a light unto the nations."[95] This is a common theme in many of the later prophets, especially in Isaiah:

> Thus says the Lord: ... Let not the foreigner say when he would join himself
> to the Lord, "The LORD will surely exclude me from his people." ...
> The foreigners who join themselves to the LORD, and become his servants—
> all who ... hold to my covenant ... I will bring to my holy mountain ... for my house
> shall be called a house of prayer for all peoples.
> (Isa 56:1–7, Masoretic translation)
> I come to gather nations of every language; they shall come and see my glory. I
> will set a sign among them ... to the distant coastlands that have never heard of
> my fame ... and they shall proclaim my glory among the nations.... They shall ...
> [come] to Jerusalem, my holy mountain.
> (Isa 66:18–20, Masoretic translation)

The "Last Shall Be First" Sayings

These famous sayings have long been regarded by Christians—who regard themselves as the "last"—as proof that they have inherited God's original covenant with the Jews. In actuality, however, these sayings merely reflect Jesus' oft-repeated message that even lifelong Jewish sinners who fully repented (the "last") would attain the Kingdom as readily as Jews who had always been righteous (the "first").

The Parable of the Vineyard Laborers is a fine example. A vineyard owner (God) hired some extra laborers late in the afternoon, to work alongside others who had been toiling since morning. The full-day laborers protested upon discovering that their wages were identical to that of the new arrivals. The owner retorted that he had cheated no one, for everyone had received a fair day's wages: "Take what belongs to you and go; I choose to give to this last one the same as I give to you.... So the last will be first, and the first shall be last" (Mt 20:14–16). All the laborers in this parable are similar in every regard, and all are Jewish.

---

95 It should be recognized that the Evangelists themselves undoubtedly interpreted "preaching Jesus' message to the nations" as meaning proselytizing (Judeo)-Christianity to all people. However, assuming that Jesus himself spoke these words in the early 30s CE, *he* would have meant them in the traditional Jewish sense.

(Gentiles appear infrequently enough in the Gospels to be identified as such.) But notice that despite the statement that "the last will be first," *everyone* received the same reward simultaneously. The moral is plain: even those who repent late (are late in toiling in God's vineyard, such as many of Jesus' followers) would attain heaven alongside those who have always been observant.

Further evidence of this meaning comes from the previously described pericope about the prosperous young man that Jesus "loved." Recall that this virtuous youth walked away disappointed because he could not steel himself to give everything to the poor. Peter, shocked at Jesus' harshness, nervously asked whether even the Disciples could be confident of gaining the Kingdom. Jesus reassured him by responding, "Everyone who has left houses or brothers or sisters or father or mother or children … for my name's sake, will … inherit eternal life. But many who are first will be last, and the last will be first" (Mt 19:29–30). Thus, God would handsomely reward the Disciples for their exceptional devotion to Jesus' ministry, even though all had been commoners (e.g., fishermen) and even sinners (the tax collector) until recently. But since everyone is this pericope was Jewish (the young man, the Disciples, and Jesus), both the "first" and the "last" applied to Jews. There are several other "last shall be first" stories, but the bottom line is that not one explicitly alludes to Gentiles or Christians.

***

Our examination of Jesus' message is now complete. It is now time to examine Jesus' behavior as a Messiah, and the Jewish response to his ministry. But having covered so much material in this chapter, a brief Interlude of additional Jewish devotional stories from the Gospels would be worth looking at.

INTERLUDE:
MORE JEWISH DEVOTIONAL
STORIES

Although an examination of Jesus' sayings has demonstrated his devotion to traditional Judaism, it is richly rewarding to explore some of the beautifully poetic parables that reaffirm this point. One of these, the Parable of the Rich Man and Lazarus, is printed opposite this book's cover page. Briefly, a rich, callous man died shortly after the death of a beggar who used to lie on his doorstep, named Lazarus. When the rich man awoke in the underworld and saw Lazarus far above him in Heaven, speaking with the patriarch Abraham, he realized the fruits of his selfishness. He thereupon entreated Abraham to send a messenger to warn his still-living brothers to change their ways: "Abraham replied, 'They have Moses and the prophets; they should listen to them.' He said, 'No, father Abraham, [but] if someone goes to them from the dead, they will repent.' He said to him, 'If they do not listen to Moses and the prophets, neither will they be convinced even if someone rises from the dead'" (Lk 16:29–31).

Each of the Synoptics also contains a brief "conflict story" in which a Pharisee asked Jesus why he willingly associated with sinners. Jesus answered, "Those who are well have no need of a physician, but those who are sick; I have come not to call the *righteous* but *sinners* to repentance" (Lk 5:31–32). Thus, righteous Jews needed no ministration from him. Interestingly, Luke also provides a variant of this same passage, in which Jesus then illustrates his point with a string of touching parables. The first was the famous Parable of the Lost Sheep, where Jesus says, "Which of you ... having a hundred sheep and losing one of them, does not leave the ninety-nine ... and go after the one that is lost.... And when he has found it ... he calls together his friends and neighbors, saying to them, 'Rejoice with me, because I have found my sheep that was lost.' I tell you, there will be more joy in heaven over one sinner who repents than over ninety-nine righteous people who need no repentance" (Lk 15: 4–7). Jesus thereby reiterated that his mission was not to the faithful majority of Jews (and certainly not to Christians, who did not exist during Jesus' life), but only to the minority who had strayed from Israel.

Luke follows this parable with the similar Parable of the Lost Coin (Lk 15:8–10), and then tops it off with arguably the most thrilling parable of all: The Prodigal Son. A father (God) had two sons, and the thriftless younger one asked for his share of the inheritance so he could squander it on dissipation. After sinking so low that he had to hire himself out to the meanest possible job for a Jew—tending swine—he swallowed his pride and returned home:

> While he was still a long way off, his father saw him
> and was filled with compassion; he ran and put his arms around him
> and kissed him. Then the son said … "Father, I have sinned … I am
> no longer worthy to be called your son."
> But the father said to his slaves, "Quickly … get the fatted calf and let us
> eat and celebrate…." Now his elder son was in the field; and when he approached
> the house, he … heard music…. He called one of the slaves and asked what was
> going on. He replied, "Your brother has come back and your father has killed the
> fattened calf…." Then he became angry and refused to go in. His father came out
> and began to plead with him. But he answered his father, "Listen! For all these
> years I have been working like a slave for you, and I have never disobeyed your
> command; yet you have never given me even
> a young goat that I might celebrate with my friends. But when this son
> of yours came back, who has devoured your property with prostitutes,
> you killed the fattened calf for him!"
> Then the father said to him, "Son, you are here with me,
> and everything that I have is yours.
> But we had to celebrate and rejoice, because this brother of yours was dead and
> has come to life again; he was lost and has been found." (Lk 15:20–32)

The same point is made anew: Jesus loved the faithful more than the sinners but viewed his special mission as returning lost Jews to their people.[96]

---

96   Only one other Evangelist (Matthew) mentions any of these stories (The Lost Sheep). Not surprisingly, Matthew places his Lost Sheep parable in the "Church Order Discourse" (Mt 18:1–35), so called because experts agree that this chapter consists of the rules of conduct for Matthew's *own* late-first-century church/synagogue. In this historically impossible context, this parable seems to refer exclusively to Christians and Judeo-Christians.

CHAPTER 10

JESUS AS (HIDDEN) MESSIAH (?)

If the Day of the Lord was imminent, most Jews would have expected a Messiah (Christ, in Greek) who would reunite his people, free them from foreign bondage, restore the Temple, and rule in perfect righteousness. It was noted earlier that some people began questioning this traditional concept after the idea spread that God himself might choose to defeat all evil, without human participation. Some Jews in first-century Palestine accordingly believed that no Messiah would appear, while the ultra-pious Essenes expected two of them (a king and a priest), although both would merely witness God's triumph. But most people retained their belief in a Davidic Messiah.

Regarding Jesus, there are two main questions. First, did he believe he was the Messiah, given the obvious ways in which he differed from people's expectations of a Messiah? Second, even if *he* believed he was, would anyone else have recognized him as such? These questions can be answered by examining his use of the word *Messiah*, the significance of his miracles, and his aura of "authority."

Claims of Messiahship
Pre-Ministry Pronouncements
Inasmuch as the Nativity stories have been shown to be nonhistorical, the first pronouncement of Jesus' Messiahship seems to have been made by John the Baptist (but see chapter 12). The Gospels describe John as a pious ascetic so revered that many viewed him as a prophet, possibly even the reincarnated Elijah (who Jewish tradition expects to return to earth to announce the Messiah's coming). And John the Baptist seemed to publicly announce Jesus' identity in the pericope that literally begins Mark's Gospel:

> As it is written in the prophet Isaiah,
> "See ... the voice of one crying out in the wilderness:
> 'Prepare the way of the Lord ...'"
> John the Baptist appeared in the wilderness, proclaiming a baptism
> of repentance and forgiveness of sin ... And people from the whole
> Judean countryside and all the people of Jerusalem were going out to him....
> He proclaimed: "The one who is more powerful than I is coming after me.... I have
> baptized you with water, but he will baptize you with the Holy Spirit." ... In those
> days, Jesus came from Nazareth ... and was baptized by John in the Jordan.
> And just as he was coming up out of the water, he saw the heavens torn apart,
> and the [Holy] Spirit ... descending like a dove on him. And a voice came from
> heaven, "You are my Son, the Beloved, with you I am well pleased."[97]
> (Mk 1:3–11, brackets added)

Yet no one in Palestine seems to have known of these dramatic events. Indeed, when Jesus initiated his ministry two months later, no one appeared to know anything about him, let alone to accept him as Messiah. It is easy to understand why the baptismal miracle itself was unknown, because it seems clear that Jesus was the only person who witnessed it. But John's words should have been heard by everyone. Had anyone remembered these words, few would have dared challenge Jesus' preaching, for even the Temple Sadducees feared the Baptist's renown (Mk 11:32).

Pronouncements during the Ministry

Instead, the first explicit revelation of Jesus' identity occurred midway through each Gospel—but only in *private*. While traveling, Jesus asked his Disciples who the people thought he was. After hearing that people believed he was the reincarnation of John the Baptist (who had recently been killed by Galilee's ruler, Herod Antipas) or of an ancient Jewish prophet, he asked what the Disciples themselves thought.

---

97 These words are derived from Psalm 2:7, where God tells King David, "Thou art My son, this day have I begotten thee" (Masoretic translation). Interestingly, these are Gods only words in the Synoptics, except for God's later command to the Disciples, "This is my beloved Son; listen to him!" (Mk 9:7). Because Jesus and the Disciples apparently kept these revelations secret, no one else in Palestine was aware of any pronouncements from God about Jesus.

Simon Peter [i.e., Peter] answered, "You are the Messiah,
the Son of the Living God."[98]
And Jesus answered him, "Blessed are you … for flesh and blood has not
revealed this to you, but my Father in heaven. And I tell you,
you are Peter, and on this rock I will build my church."
Then he sternly ordered the disciples not to tell anyone that
he was the Messiah. (Mt 16:16–20)

Jesus' conviction that only divine revelation could explain Peter's insight (called "Peter's confession [of faith]") clearly demonstrates that no one else had yet penetrated his secret. The Disciples apparently obeyed his command of silence, for even in his final days only a handful of people imagined that he might be the Messiah. One Gospel records that when he reached Jerusalem in the last week of his life, the crowds who greeted his entrance may have known who he was, for they cried "Hosanna" and called him the Son of David (Mt 21:9). However, the salutations in the other Synoptics are more ambiguous. (As an important addendum to the above passage, this chapter shall show that the CSB doubts that Peter called Jesus "the Son of God," because scholarship indicates that this title first appeared *after* Jesus' death, along with the title "Lord."[99])

Even in Jerusalem, Jesus never publicly admitted his identity. Whether he announced it even privately (to anyone beyond his Disciples) is unclear. One Gospel states that he revealed himself at the Sanhedrin's secret trial, the night before his death. (The full account of Jesus' last days in Jerusalem will be presented in chapter 13.) During the trial, the Temple high priest directly asked Jesus if he was the Messiah. In Mark's Gospel, he answered, "I am" (Mk 14:62–63). But he was far more equivocal in the other Synoptics. In Luke, for example, he replied, "You say that I am" (Lk 22:70). All three Synoptics agree that he subsequently died without any further claim of Messiahship. Indeed, his attempts to conceal

---

98   The Catholic Study Bible, 35, 107.

99   This passage is the most elaborate Synoptic version and is quoted here because it is the most famous, because Catholics have traditionally believed that Peter ultimately became the first Bishop (Pope) of Rome after Jesus' death (i.e., became the "rock" of the new Church). The other, simpler versions nevertheless confirm that only Peter knew his identity. In Mark's Gospel, for example, Peter answered Jesus' question by simply saying, "The Messiah" (Mk 8:27–30). (Incidentally, many scholars doubt the authenticity of Jesus' statement about "building my church." Jesus believed the Day of the Lord was too imminent to start establishing a "church," and in any case he believed only in Judaism.).

his identity from the people were so persistent, particularly in Mark's Gospel, that scholars call this phenomenon the "messianic secret."[100]

In sum, Jesus never publicly proclaimed himself Messiah, with the result that few people seemed to view him as anything more than a prophet/teacher/miracle worker. That said, many Christian scholars believe that Jesus disclosed himself through his use of two other Messiah-like appellations: "Son of Man" and "Son of God." There is no question that these terms have a divinelike ring. However, inasmuch as all early Gospel manuscripts lacked any capitalization, these terms can just as correctly be written as the far humbler "son of man" and "son of god."[101] Let us examine these in turn." Son of man," in the Tanakh, simply means "a person," or "people." Jesus often called himself the Son of Man/son of man. The key question is, how did his contemporaries interpret this term? Careful inspection of the Gospels reveals that no one in the Gospels seemed to pay any attention to this title. Moreover, Jesus had publicly called himself "son of man" many times before his amazement at Peter's insight ("confession"). These facts suggest that "son of man" was probably interpreted by listeners simply as a third-person form of "I." The CSB agrees, saying that "Jesus' use of the title in [the divine] sense is questionable. Of itself, this expression means simply a human being.... Its use in the New Testament is probably due to Jesus' speaking of himself in that way, 'a

---

100 Adding to the mystery is the Synoptics' assertion that Jesus also seemed to refer to a *different* Messiah. While describing to his Disciples the events of the forthcoming apocalypse, Jesus warned, "Then if anyone says to you, 'Look, Here is the Messiah!' or 'There he is!—do not believe it. For false messiahs ... will appear and produce great signs and omens, to lead astray ... even the elect" (Mt 24:23–24). Jesus seemed to be predicting a different Messiah here, because Jesus expected the Day of the Lord to be imminent, and the Disciples knew him too well to confuse him with someone else.

Because this warning is so difficult to understand, many scholars doubt it is authentic. Instead, since the Synoptics were written many decades after Jesus' death, when most people who had known Jesus were already dead, the Evangelists were probably warning their readers not to be misled by false prophets pretending to speak in Jesus' name.

101 It is difficult to overstate how much of Jesus' exalted stature in the Gospels results from the standard practice of capitalizing "Son of Man" and "Son of God." He would seem appreciably less significant if "son of man" and "son of god" were substituted. Likewise, the common word "lord" is always capitalized as "Lord" when referring to Jesus. (Recall too the CSB's doubts that Jesus was ever called "Son of God" or "Lord" until after his death.) If all the terms above were written in lower-case letters, the Jesus depicted in the Gospel of Mark would become entirely human.

human being.'"[102] It should be noted that Jesus also occasionally spoke of a Son of Man who would appear in the *future*, but never explicitly claimed to *be* this other Son of Man.[103]

---

102 The Catholic Study Bible, RG 341, 81. Incidentally, chapter 6 showed (with the CSB's assistance) that Jesus was not abrogating the Sabbath when he said, "The sabbath was made for humankind, and not humankind for the sabbath. So the Son of Man is lord even of the Sabbath" (Mk 2:27–28). We can now interpret these verses directly. If "Son of Man" simply means "a person, or people," then the second sentence becomes a restatement of the first: that God made the Sabbath for the people, for their spiritual and physical renewal.

103 In Mark's version of the Sanhedrin trial (above), Jesus followed his admission of Messiahship by declaring to the Sanhedrin that "'you will see the Son of Man seated at the right hand of the Power, and coming with the clouds of heaven'" (Mk 14:62). *This* Son of Man was no mortal, but rather a symbolic figure that the Book of Daniel prophesied would appear on the Day of the Lord:

> I saw in ... visions ... there came with the clouds of heaven one like unto
> a son of man, and he came even to the Ancient of days [God] ... and there was
> given him dominion, glory, and a kingdom, that all the peoples,
> nations, and languages should serve him. (Dan 7:13–14, brackets added)

Many Christians interpret Jesus' statement that "you will see the Son of Man seated at the right hand of the Power" as a prophecy that he himself would return as this divinelike Son of Man. However, the Book of Daniel explicitly states that this Son of Man symbolizes "the saints [plural] of the Most High" (Daniel 7:18). On this basis, the CSB concurs that Jews interpreted Daniel's Son of Man as the symbol of the *righteous Jews of Israel*, who would be rewarded at the time of the Kingdom: "The Son of Man [is used] in Daniel ... as a symbol of ... the faithful Israelites who will receive the everlasting kingdom ... from God" (The Catholic Study Bible, 81). Thus, Jesus may have merely been warning the Sanhedrin members that whatever their power over him, they would soon face their own judgment on the Day of the Lord.

That said, the "Son of Man question" is the Great Black Hole of New Testament scholarship. The controversy will be succinctly outlined here, but this brief discussion will not change the earlier conclusion that very few people in the Synoptics believed Jesus was the Messiah, or claimed to be one. For those interested in the controversy, however, it must be noted that Jesus spoke not only of Daniel's "Son of Man coming on clouds/on the right hand of Power," but also of a celestial "Son of Man" (with no descriptive phrases) who would appear shortly before the Day of the Lord.

Who was this Son of Man? The simplest hypothesis is that he was simply Daniel's Son of Man, but with the descriptive phrases omitted. Evidence of this can be found in one of Jesus' prophecies, in which he initially spoke about the "Son of Man coming on clouds," but then referred to the self-same person/symbol as the "Son of Man"

"Son of God"/"son of God" is a simpler story, for, paradoxically, it had no divine connotations in Jesus' time. The Tanakh routinely calls the Jewish people the "children of God," and calls esteemed prophets, judges, or kings "sons of God." Thus, this common term would have messianic connotations only if it was linked to King David's name, since most Jews expected the Messiah to be David's scion. But Jesus never claimed Davidic descent and even derided the idea that the Messiah would spring from David (Mt 22:41–46).[104] (Although several Jews in the Gospels did call Jesus "son of David," he never confirmed this title.)[105] In short, "son of God" would be most commonly used by Jews to refer to any esteemed leader or prophet—which is how many viewed Jesus.[106]

Having said all this, it is very important to note that most lay Christians interpret *all* "Son of Man" and "Son of God" references as proof that Jesus was divine. They therefore believe—erroneously—that his divinity must have been obvious to his contemporaries. Much of the misunderstanding with regard to Son/son of

---

immediately thereafter (Mt 21:26–30). However, some scholars believe that Jesus did occasionally speak about yet another Son of Man—the one discussed in *1 Enoch*. This was a Messiah-like *individual*, who "is the Son of Man who hath righteousness. [who] will raise up the kings ... and break the teeth of the sinners" (*1 Enoch*, chapter 46ff). However, no one knows whether Jesus or his contemporaries even knew about this third Son of Man, because this section of *1 Enoch* was apparently written sometime between 5 and 60 CE—in other words, possibly after Jesus' death. (*1 Enoch* was composed over the course of centuries by multiple authors, and its famous Satan section had been written two hundred years earlier.) Yet even if this Son of Man was known during Jesus' life, there is nothing in Enoch's description to suggest that this might be Jesus. In brief, regardless of whether there were one or two celestial Sons of Man, there is no reason to think that Jews would have associated Jesus with either.

104 His derision resulted from his misinterpretation of Psalm 110 (The Catholic Study Bible, 49).

105 The Evangelists certainly believed Jesus was descended from King David, and Matthew and Luke present full genealogies of Jesus' lineage from David in their Nativity stories. However, the genealogies are not only contradictory but also technically flawed. For example, they occasionally include women in their genealogies, which is not accepted in Jewish tradition.

106 An unusual usage of "Son of God" occurs in Mk 3:11, which is the very first "Son of God" reference in the Synoptics. According to this verse, the demons that Jesus exorcised from the sick shouted out that he was the Son of God. The CSB doubts that these spirits knew who he was. However, they assumed he worked through God's powers, and they held the magical belief (very common at that time) that pronouncing the name of their enemy [i.e., God] would weaken its force over them (The Catholic Study Bible, 69, 72).

Man is simply that few people have ever been alerted to the complexity of this appellation. With regard to "Son of God," most of the confusion results from Paul's Letters, which declare that Jesus *was* literally the Son of God. These enormously influential Letters make it difficult for Christians to realize that Paul's terminology/theology cannot be automatically applied to the Gospels themselves. Only one of the Evangelists (Luke) seems to have ever heard of Paul, his teachings, or his definitions.

The Miracles: Evidence of Messiahship?

Would Jesus' miracles have convinced the people that he was the Messiah? The Synoptics' pericopes describe details of twenty healings, six nature miracles (e.g., walking on water), and two resurrections. (Many additional "narrative" verses report mass healings, but without pericope-type details that allow assessment.)

The answer is no. Miracle workers and magicians were commonplace in the superstitious Roman Empire, particularly in Palestine.[107] Jesus himself knew of other Jewish exorcists, for he rebutted accusations that he used satanic power for his cures by saying, "If I cast out demons by Beelzebul [Satan], by whom do your own exorcists cast them out?" (Mt 12:27). One of his Disciples complained, "Master, we saw someone casting out demons in your name and we tried to prevent him because he does not follow our company" (Lk 9:49). In Luke's Acts of the Disciples, the magician Simon "amazed the people of Samaria.... All of them, from the least to the greatest, listened to him eagerly, saying 'This man is the power of God that is called Great'" (Acts 8: 9–10). When Paul converted some Gentiles in Ephesus (Turkey), those who had practiced magic "collected their books and burned them publicly.... The value of these books was ... fifty thousand silver coins" (Acts 19: 18–19). Considering Judas Iscariot's satisfaction with only thirty silver coins for betraying Jesus, an astonishing number of magic books must have been consumed in that fire. All these examples of miracles and magic come from the Synoptics and Acts, but many more are documented in contemporary non-New Testament writings.[108]

---

107 Sanders, *The Historical Figure of Jesus*, 138.

108 The historian Josephus described Honi the Circle Drawer, renowned for ending a great drought. His powers were considered so great that a mob killed him in 65 BCE for refusing to use his powers against their political enemies. His rainmaking ability was described in a story (which may or may not have been historical) in the Mishnah (c. 200 CE). The Mishnah relates that when Honi was asked to pray for rain during a drought, nothing initially happened. He then drew a circle on the ground and stood in it, saying, "Lord of the world ... I swear by thy great name that I will not move from here until Thou hast mercy on Thy children." When it began sprinkling,

We have lumped miracle workers and magicians together, even though scholars typically differentiate them. Miracle workers are defined as people who perform extraordinary deeds by using the powers provided by God, whereas magicians use incantations and potions to force supernatural spirits to do their will. We have nevertheless combined these terms because Jesus may have been both. He cured a deaf man by putting "his finger into his ears, and he spat and touched his [the deaf man's] tongue. Then looking up to heaven, he sighed and said to him, 'Ephphatha,' that is, 'Be opened'" (Mk 7:33–34, brackets added). This sounds like ordinary magic. He also rubbed his spittle into a blind man's eyes, but too sparingly, for all the patient could see were "people looking like trees" (Mk 8:24). So Jesus repeated the treatment, and succeeded. Similarly, Jesus felt "that power had gone forth from him" while healing one woman (Mk 5:30), and he was unable to cure the skeptical people of his hometown of Nazareth (Mk 6:5). True miracle healing through God's powers should presumably not sap a healer's strength, nor fail due to lack of human faith. All of these magical elements are from Mark's Gospel. Matthew and Luke seemed to have found them embarrassing enough to delete them from their own Gospels.

This discussion has focused so far on healings, but faith healing has been common in many societies even to our own time. What about Jesus' more spectacular miracles? There were three significant nature miracles. In the "multiplication of the loaves," Jesus used a few bread loaves and fish to feed one crowd of five thousand listeners, and another crowd of four thousand. However, these miracles seemed to make little impression, because everyone simply ate the food without comment. The other two miracles occurred on the Lake of Galilee: Jesus' walk on water, and his stilling of a storm threatening to overturn his boat. But both miracles occurred at night, far from shore, and were probably unseen by anyone except his Disciples. Regarding his famous walking on water, it is curious that the Disciples "worshiped" Jesus for his ability to walk on water in one Gospel (Mt 14:33), but inexplicably "hardened their hearts" against him in the other (Mk 6:52).

The two resurrections did elicit amazement. After all, Elijah and Elisha were the only Tanakh figures who had ever accomplished this. However, it is not entirely clear whether the first one, which is described in all Synoptics, was really

---

he protested, "I have not asked for this, but for rain to fill the cisterns." After this came such a heavy deluge that he had to pray again for it to moderate. A contemporary rabbi supposedly commented that Honi deserved excommunication for acting so petulantly, but that God obviously loved him as a son. The greatest of all miracle workers described in the Mishnah was Hanina ben Dosa, who may have lived in Jesus' time just north of Nazareth. Unlike Honi, Hanina's existence has not been independently confirmed by Josephus or others (Vermes, *The Changing Faces of Jesus*, 255ff).

a resurrection. According to Mark and Luke, a synagogue leader rushed into the street to beg Jesus to heal his "dying" daughter. When Jesus entered the house and saw her family wailing over her death, his first words were "The child is not dead but asleep" (Mk 5:38). The girl then revived when he told her to awake. This event is generally considered a resurrection, but Jesus' words, coupled with the fact that the girl had been alive minutes previously, raise the possibility that she had never died, and that Jesus was the first to notice continued signs of life. However, the third Synoptic account (Matthew's) states that the girl was already dead when her father reached Jesus, which, if true, makes a resurrection more likely. Jesus' one unquestioned resurrection, reported only in Luke, was his restoration to life of the Widow's Son, whose corpse was already being carried to the grave for burial (Lk 7:12–15).

There is a sound reason for the cautious tone above in describing the nature miracles and resurrections: no one in Palestine seems to have heard of them. They are *never* alluded to by anyone (even Jesus) after they happened. Conversely, his healing skills were apparently universally known. All Synoptics agree that people begged him for cures wherever he went. Hence, it seems that Jesus was famous only as a healer.[109] Was he superior to other healers or miracle workers of the time? We do not know, because the Evangelists never compared him to anyone, with the exception of Simon the Magician, who was less powerful (Acts 8:13). Moreover, the Evangelists differed as to Jesus' achievements. We have noted Mark's report that Jesus' miraculous powers largely deserted him while he was in his skeptical hometown of Nazareth, but Matthew instead states that "he did not do many deeds of mighty power there, because of their unbelief" (Mt 13:58), implying that he *chose* not to perform many miracles. Luke went further by stating that Jesus refused to perform any miracles at all. In another disparity, Mark states that Jesus cured "many" people one night in Capernaum (Mk 1:34), whereas the other

---

109 This seems to be supported by the Q-source, the Gospels' earliest component. The only miracles specifically reported are two healings. No nature miracles are mentioned. Nor are any resurrections specifically described. (It is true that upon being asked for proof that he was the Messiah, Jesus said: "The blind receive their sight, the lame walk, the lepers are cleansed, the deaf hear, [and] the *dead are raised*" [Mt 11:5]. However, this is a quotation from Isaiah [actually, an amalgamation from three chapters of Isaiah]. This makes it difficult to know whether Jesus was actually claiming a resurrection, or merely quoting the Tanakh.) Meanwhile, Paul's Letters, the New Testament's oldest writings, shed no light on these matters. Remarkably, they mention no miracles at all. However, it will be seen that although Paul may never have heard of any, it is also true that his Letters are so focused on Jesus' resurrection that his life is virtually ignored.

Evangelists reported "all" were cured (Mt 8:16).[110] Even Mark, the only Evangelist willing to admit Jesus' failures, clearly wished to downplay them, for he recorded only Jesus' successes in his pericopes.

In brief, Jesus' miracles generated excitement, but they are not claimed by the Gospels to have been unique. Yet if Jesus had wanted to convince people of his messianic identity through his miracles, he could have, by performing a "sign." The Jewish people were familiar with miracles primarily through the Tanakh stories. Interestingly, there is no word meaning "miracles" in the Tanakh.[111] The word "wonders" is usually used, but this term also includes extraordinary natural events. However, the Tanakh employs "sign" to signify any special miracle through which God reveals his Will. Signs could range from modest (e.g., the transformation of Moses' staff into a serpent, to reveal God's Will to Pharaoh) or stupendous (the Ten Plagues of Egypt). But as direct proof of *God's Will*, signs were more significant than healing people or walking on water. This is why all the Synoptics concur that the religious authorities, who were already familiar with Jesus' healing skills, came to ask him for a sign. But he rebuked them, saying:

> This generation is an evil generation; it asks for a sign, but no sign
> will be given to it except the sign of Jonah. For just as Jonah became a sign
> to the people of Nineveh, so the Son of Man will be to this generation.
> The people of Nineveh will rise up at the judgment with this generation
> and condemn it, because they repented at the proclamation of Jonah,
> and see, something greater than Jonah is here![112] (Lk 11:29–32)

It is safe to assume that his refusal and rebuke not only strengthened the authorities' suspicions of him, but also increased their irritation at his abrasiveness.

Jesus' Authority: Evidence of Messiahship?

Thus far, it seems clear that Jesus neither publicly declared himself the Messiah nor performed miracles that would demonstrate it. Instead, the clearest visible manifestation of his belief in his Messiahship was his "authority": his conviction that he was in intimate communion with God and had been chosen for a critical role in the coming of the Kingdom. This authority was evinced in everything he did. His contemptuous rebuke of the religious authorities requesting a sign was a

---

110 Incidentally, some cured people may have relapsed, because Jesus often felt compelled to order exorcised demons not to return.

111 *Encyclopedia Judaica*, s.v. "Miracles," 12:74–6.

112 There are several variants of this pericope, but Jesus refused to perform a sign in all of them.

perfect example. So was the Sermon on the Mount. Whereas the Jewish prophets had proclaimed, "Thus saith the Lord," Jesus said, "But I say to you." Whereas Pharisees and other contemporaries carefully quoted the Tanakh as the basis of their opinions and teachings, Jesus spoke as if he was God's conduit, rendering references to the Tanakh superfluous. Only forty scriptural quotations or allusions can be found in all three Synoptics—compared to nearly eighty in Paul's Letter to the Romans.[113] No wonder the people who heard his teachings were routinely "astounded at his teaching, because he spoke with authority" (Lk 4:32).

Jesus' authority was similarly manifested in the remarkable fact that only once did he pray for God's assistance in performing miracles. This occurred late in his ministry, after he had taught the Disciples how to heal on their own. When they shamefacedly admitted their failure to exorcise a Boy with a Demon, Jesus replied that only prayer could heal him (Mk 9:29). The fact that Jesus had apparently never previously used prayer in their presence is extraordinary, for prayer is assumed to have been an important tool of other Jewish miracle workers.[114] But Jesus seemed to believe that verbal prayer was unnecessary, for he apparently believed that God was privy to his thoughts. He certainly prayed to God at important moments, but this was usually on mountains and other private places when he was alone or only with his Disciples. For this reason, most Jews probably never saw him pray. Thus, many must have wondered whether his powers came from God or from evil spirits. Indeed, the religious authorities (or "the people," in one version) accused him of the latter, saying, "It is only by Beelzebul, the ruler of the demons, that this fellow casts out the demons" (Mt 12:24). They were wrong. Jesus was merely supremely self-confident that he was God's instrument. He even believed God was using him to broadcast the initial signs of the incoming of the Kingdom. This was illustrated earlier by such statements as "If it is by the finger of God that I drive out demons, then the Kingdom of God has come upon you."

His authority was also visible in other spheres. He occasionally called God "Abba" ("Father" in Aramaic, in the sense of "Dad"), an astonishingly informal term that had never previously been used in this way in the recorded history of the Jewish people.[115] He rejoiced to his Disciples that "All things have been handed

---

113 Vermes, *The Authentic Gospel of Jesus*, 212.

114 Actually, the dearth of contemporary records about other Jewish miracle workers makes it unclear how often prayers were used (Meier, *A Marginal Jew*, 2:536, 2:581ff). They may not have been typical in exorcisms (where commanding the demon to depart often sufficed) or in magic (where incantations and potions worked). However, prayers appear to have been necessary for nature miracles, resurrections, and many faith-healings.

115 Meier, *A Marginal Jew*, 2:299.

over to me by my Father; and no one knows who the Son is except for the Father, or who the Father is except the Son"[116] (Lk 10:22). Since Judaism has traditionally been an open religion free of cultlike "mysteries," this statement is jarring (and will be revisited in the final chapter). But it dramatizes his certainty that he was closer to God than a prophet, and perhaps even than a Messiah. He chose twelve Disciples so that when the Kingdom came, "You ... will ... sit on twelve thrones, judging the twelve tribes of Israel" (Mt 19:28). His conviction that he could appoint judges over Israel, and presumably occupy an even mightier position himself, was awesome.

***

In sum, Jesus seemed to consider himself some kind of Messiah, although a highly unconventional one. At the least, he envisioned himself as an eschatological prophet (i.e., a prophet of the End of Days) entrusted with a special divine mission. But, as noted earlier, few people other than his Disciples could have imagined this. He never publicly claimed to be the Messiah. His miracles did not constitute proof. His authority was a strong clue, but he reserved his most explicit sayings (e.g., "All things have been handed over to me ...") for his own Disciples. Instead, his supreme confidence in himself was the primary manifestation of his self-perception as Messiah. As we have seen from his reception in Nazareth, however, this extreme self-confidence was often considered merely odd, if not downright sacrilegious. Who was this woodworker who seemed to believe he knew God's wishes, and treated even learned scholars with contempt? Jews were expecting an unmistakable Messiah who would overwhelm the mighty Romans and help establish the Kingdom. Jesus was nothing like this. He was an itinerant Galilean who taught in rural villages, far from Jerusalem, without actually doing anything to bring independence to his people. It is easy to see why so few people in the Gospels considered him a Messiah ... especially since, as will be shown in the next chapter, *he hid even his message from the people.*

---

116 Such a highly Christological verse is very atypical for the Synoptics, although very common in John's Gospel. The fact that it is a Q-saying proves, at the least, that as early as 50 CE, Jesus was believed to have said this.

CHAPTER 11

DID THE JEWS REJECT JESUS, AND WHY? PART I: THE PEOPLE

That the vast majority of Jews ultimately rejected Jesus is well known. But is it possible that he was highly influential *during his life*, and that his impact faded from memory simply because of his premature death? Or was he rejected during his ministry, and if so, why? Because virtually everyone around him was Jewish, many people must be considered: his family and his neighbors, the common people, the religious authorities, and so forth. Jesus' family and neighbors were discussed in chapter 5, so we begin here with his Disciples.

The Twelve Disciples

Jesus' Disciples are named but barely described in the Gospels, except for Peter. They were ordinary men—at least four were fishermen and one was a tax collector—who lived in the Capernaum area. They responded to Jesus' call to become his Disciples even though they seem not to have known who he was. Luke may have considered this odd, for he introduced a miracle story to explain why the original group joined him. In any case, although Jesus' family and neighbors may have wondered about Jesus, one would imagine that the Disciples who accompanied him everywhere must have been solid in their faith. They had seen him raise the dead, walk on water, heal the sick, and feed thousands with some fish and loaves. And they were more than mere witnesses, for Jesus gave them the power to *personally* perform healing miracles. Their powers apparently rivaled those of Jesus, judging from their surprise at their failure to cure the Boy with a Demon.

Indeed, they were faithful in their acceptance of Jesus as teacher/prophet/Messiah … overall. But one of the Twelve, Judas Iscariot, actually betrayed Jesus to the Temple authorities.[117] In Mark's original version, Judas did it without even asking for a reward. (The famous request for thirty pieces of silver appears only in Matthew's Gospel.) We are so familiar with this story that conscious effort is required to recognize its staggering import. Judas had not only witnessed Jesus' miracles, but had also been personally empowered to perform his own. He had followed and obeyed, for more than a year, a man who claimed to be the Messiah (or a Messiah-like eschatological prophet). How could anyone even *think* of condemning himself to eternal damnation for no reward whatever, or a few coins? Uniquely, Luke tried to explain this mind-boggling event by stating that Satan compelled him to do it (Lk 22:3).

The other eleven disciples were loyal to Jesus, but with two major caveats. The first is that despite their assiduous efforts on his behalf, they often seemed *unaware of who Jesus was or what he was saying*. Their confusion, particularly in the Gospel of Mark, is so pervasive that it is best conveyed through the CSB's commentaries: "One of the intriguing features of Mark's portrayal is the disciples have a hard time understanding Jesus." "The disciples ... understood Jesus' message dimly at best ... the disciples are blind in a sense far more disabling than that of physical blindness; they have a deep-seated block to understanding Jesus and his message." "The Disciples ... try to discourage the children from coming to Jesus ... and continued to be baffled by Jesus' teaching." "As the Galilean ministry ... comes to a close, the disciples' difficulty in understanding Jesus only seems to increase. They are completely baffled at his mysterious power in calming the storm, and walking on the sea. They are out of sympathy with Jesus' compassion for the crowds. And the section ends with their complete confusion about Jesus' words and deeds."[118]

The Disciples are less obtuse in the other Synoptics. In both Luke's and Mark's, however, they were totally uncomprehending when Jesus told them—three separate times—that he would ultimately be killed and resurrected. Perhaps the Disciples could be forgiven their shock, for the concept of a dying Messiah was completely alien to both Jews and Gentiles of the Roman Empire. The first time, when Jesus revealed that he would suffer, die, and be resurrected in Jerusalem: "Peter ... began to rebuke him, saying, 'God forbid, Lord! This must never happen to you.' But he turned and said to Peter, 'Get behind me, Satan! You are a stumbling block to me'" (Mt 16:21–23). The second time, the Disciples "did not

---

117 It is perplexing that some Christians consider Judas the "Jewish Disciple," when all twelve were as Jewish as Jesus himself. The sole reason for selecting exactly twelve Disciples was so they could ultimately help judge the twelve tribes of Israel, as previously noted.

118 The Catholic Study Bible, RG 406, RG 412–16.

understand what he was saying" when he repeated his prophecy (Mk 9:30–32). The last time, on the road to Jerusalem: "they understood nothing … in fact, what he said was hidden from them, and they did not grasp what was being said" (Lk 18:31–34).

The second caveat about the Disciples' faith is that it evaporated during their first *real* test, in Jerusalem. Prior to Jerusalem, they had worked indefatigably for Jesus, but had never encountered physical danger. No one had ever lifted a finger against them. Moreover, the Galilean Jews had always provided them (and Jesus) with all the necessities of life, since none of them worked during the ministry. Jesus was confident enough of this support that when he asked the Disciples to briefly missionize on their own, he instructed them to travel without food or supplies. As expected, they all returned sound and healthy.[119] But when the acid test came, they all failed. When we discuss Jesus' last week in Jerusalem, we will see that they instantly fled upon his arrest—even though they themselves were never threatened. Peter did sit outside the Sanhedrin building during Jesus' trial for several hours, but he repeatedly denied knowing Jesus to bystanders. After that, he apparently joined the other Disciples in hiding, for none of them were in the crowd that Pontius Pilate later asked to determine Jesus' fate. They were absent from the public crucifixion, and the removal of Jesus' corpse from the cross. They never even visited the tomb to await his predicted resurrection. And when he appeared to them (since they made no effort to find him), they were so amazed, they thought him a ghost. How could the Disciples have been so obtuse in understanding Jesus, and so faithless as to desert a man they believed was God's Messiah? The Synoptics are silent about this mystery, so we will reserve this discussion until the final chapter, "Who Was Jesus?"

Despite their flaws, the Disciples redeemed themselves after the resurrection, by establishing the Mother Synagogue that ultimately ensured his memory. It is often overlooked that Jesus' Disciples were the first itinerant Jewish disciples in seven hundred years, since the time of Elijah and Elisha.[120] Countless other disciples during that interval studied at the homes of their masters and occasionally

---

119 One Gospel reports that Jesus warned his Disciples, before sending them on this mission, "See, I am sending you out like sheep in the midst of wolves.… Beware [of people], for they will hand you over to the councils and flog you in their synagogues … you will be hated by all because of my name" (Mt 10:16–23, brackets added). However, the CSB doubts the authenticity of these words (from Matthew, predictably), because the other two Synoptics instead place this warning just before Jesus' death, when he alerted his Disciples to the possible dangers of proselytizing *outside* of Palestine (The Catholic Study Bible, 23).

120 Meier, *A Marginal Jew,* 3:42.

joined them on trips, but only Jesus' Disciples abandoned home and family to follow him everywhere.

The Common People (and the Disciples, continued)

Did the Jewish masses accept or reject Jesus during his lifetime? This question is surprisingly complex. To begin with, it must be recognized that except for his last twenty-four hours of life, Jesus was always surrounded by adulatory crowds. With the single exception of his neighbors' rejection in Nazareth, not a single group of ordinary Jews ever argued, ignored, or threatened him. Quite the opposite, they flocked to him:

> Jesus departed with his disciples to the sea, and a great multitude
> from Galilee followed him; hearing all that he
> was doing, they came to him in great numbers from Judea, Jerusalem, Idumea,
> beyond the Jordan, and the regions around Tyre and Sidon. He told
> his disciples to have a boat ready for him because of the crowd, so they
> would not crush him.[121] (Mk 3:7–9)

And during his only trip to Jerusalem, the only non-Galilean journey described in detail by the Synoptics:

> A very large crowd spread their cloaks on the road ... shouting, "Hosanna to
> the Son of David! Blessed is the one who comes in the name of the Lord! ..."
> When he entered Jerusalem the whole city was in turmoil, asking, "Who is this?"
> The crowds were saying, "This is the prophet Jesus." (Mt 21:8–11)

So the Jewish masses unquestionably adored Jesus. But for what? Certainly for his miracles. But miracles could not have been the only reason, since the crowds that followed him must have contained many healthy people. Did they also follow him because he was the Messiah? That is doubtful, since he never revealed himself publicly. Did they follow him for his eloquence and teachings? Quite likely, for Jesus certainly was a masterful speaker who captivated the crowds with his vivid, poetic, and hyperbolic rhetoric, as well as his magnetic authority. They probably also perceived him as "one of their own"—someone from humble circumstances who shared their familiarity with powerlessness and poverty, and placed a welcome emphasis on ethical precepts. The Gospels (especially Luke's) contrast Jesus'

---

121 Idumea was part of Palestine, and "beyond the Jordan" may have referred to Palestine's Perea district, which was ruled by Herod Antipas (who also governed Galilee). Tyre and Sidon were in southern Syria, with primarily Gentile populations.

compassion for the poor, widows, and downtrodden with the alleged insensitivity of the religious authorities. This portrayal probably contains some truth, but does not necessarily suggest that Jesus was exceptionally compassionate for someone of his background. As a commoner himself, he knew firsthand about the concerns and worries of ordinary people.

But Jesus' mission was to spread his message of repentance for the approaching Day of the Lord. How did the people respond to *this*, the real focus of his ministry? The Synoptics are surprisingly silent on this issue. The pericopes focus so tightly on Jesus that his audiences' reactions are never mentioned beyond their momentary awe or gratitude for being cured. What they did thereafter is never mentioned. We have seen that a handful of people were sufficiently impressed to seek permission to join him. But they apparently were exceptions, for apart from the Disciples, *no Synoptic ever identifies any group of people that responded to his message.* He sometimes praised other individuals for their virtue, but many of these had already been pious for many years. In sum, excluding the Disciples, *there is no evidence that he transformed even one individual during his ministry* (with the possible exception noted in the upcoming footnote). He certainly commended the "faith" of many who approached him for cures, but this referred merely to their faith in his curative powers. But the Gospels never explicitly state that any of them repented or were transformed. Many of these people never spoke a word, and all of them completely disappeared from the Gospels following their brief healing encounters. Given that Jesus was not an infallible judge of people (consider his fatal misjudgment of Judas Iscariot, and his amazement at being rebuffed by family and neighbors), we cannot really know what happened to these people.

But whereas no Synoptic provides solid evidence of his successes, all of them document his failures. They all agree that Jesus:

> *… began to reproach the cities in which most*
> *of his deeds of power had been done, because they did not repent.*
> "Woe to you, Chorazin! Woe to you, Bethsaida! …
> And you, *Capernaum,*
> Will you be exalted to heaven? No, *you will be brought down to Hades.*
> For if the deeds of power done in you had been done
> in Sodom, it would have remained until this day. But I tell you that on the day of
> judgment it will be more tolerable for the land of Sodom than for you."
> (Mt 11:20–24, italics added)

This passage is revelatory, because Jesus' response to his rejection at Nazareth was to move to the fishing village of Capernaum. This remained the center of his ministry for the rest of his life. The fact that Jesus was rejected not only by

Nazareth but also by Capernaum and the other Galilean towns that knew him best, and had witnessed his "deeds of power," proves that his ministry *was a failure even during his lifetime.* It also raises, once again, the question of whether the Gospels may have exaggerated his miracles. Similarly, insofar as both Chorazin and Bethsaida were within four miles of Capernaum,[122] it raises questions of how extensive Jesus' ministry really was.

Why was Jesus rejected? Part of the reason must be that most Jews were skeptical about his prediction of an imminent Day of the Lord, or about their ability to adhere to his radical Jewish morality. This has already been discussed. But Jesus' often subversive morality must have been equally damaging. Calling Jesus' morality "subversive" may at first sound shocking, but we have already witnessed it. When he told the grieving son to leave his father's corpse unburied and let the "dead bury the dead," Jesus was demanding that he break the Ten Commandments' injunction to honor one's parents. The same is true of his declaration that he had come not to bring peace, but to tear families apart. Jesus certainly revered the Ten Commandments, and he knew that God's Final Judgment would take into account how people had treated their parents and siblings. But he felt that the imminent Day of the Lord superseded all conventional social norms. Each person had to devote himself or herself entirely to repentance, without regard for anyone unwilling to do the same. But for most Jews, who did not share or comprehend his thinking, these incidents would have sent shockwaves through everyone who heard of them. And considering his own Disciples' astonishment at his statement that even the righteous young man who refused to become a pauper was unworthy of the Kingdom, one can only imagine the reaction of outsiders.

Jesus' subversive morality manifested itself in other ways as well. One was his habit of feasting with "tax collectors and sinners," mentioned in all Synoptics. Let us first focus on the tax collectors (actually toll collectors). Tax collectors were justifiably hated in first-century Palestine, because they were often extortionists. They purchased their positions from the government so they could amass profits by squeezing excessive money from the powerless. They thereby impoverished the very people—the poor—for whom Jesus claimed special compassion. The people should have acclaimed Jesus a hero if he made these tax collectors honest. Therefore, their persistent resentment at his association with tax collectors suggests that he *failed* to do so (with one possible exception[123]).

---

122 Reed, *Archeology and the Galilean Jesus,* 184–85.

123 When Jesus was passing through an adulatory crowd in Jericho, he saw a wealthy tax collector, Zacchaeus, and asked to rest at his house. The crowd immediately began grumbling at Jesus' choice, for they knew Zacchaeus to be an extortionist. Zacchaeus thereupon declared that he would compensate anyone he had defrauded, and donate

Also provocative was Jesus' parable about a tax collector and a Pharisee wor-shiping at the Temple:

> The Pharisee ... was praying thus, "God, I thank you that I am not
> like other people: thieves, rogues, adulterers, or even like this tax collector.
> I fast twice a week; I give a tenth of all my income [to the Temple and charity]."
> But the tax collector ... would not even look up to heaven,
> but was beating his breast and saying, "God,
> be merciful to me, a sinner!" [Jesus said] "I tell you, this man went down
> to his home justified rather than the other; for all who exalt themselves will be
> humbled, but all who humble themselves will be exalted."
> (Lk 18:11–14, brackets added)

The tax collector in this parable obviously feared God's judgment but gave no indication that he had ever tried to reform or intended to do so. The Pharisee, conversely, was a pious man who merely thought to himself—as would all decent people—that he considered himself morally superior to adulterers or extortion-ists. That Jesus would acclaim the tax collector's "humility" while excoriating the Pharisee's "arrogance" must have left his audiences aghast.

His attitude toward sinners was equally inflammatory. When a Pharisee invited Jesus to dine at his home, a woman known to be a prostitute to the host, but not to Jesus, walked in unannounced. She began anointing Jesus with ointment, while weeping and kissing his feet. The Pharisee must have been visibly surprised, for Jesus discerned his thoughts ... and proceeded to lambaste him for his discomfort, and for not having anointing Jesus personally! Jesus then informed the prostitute that her sins were forgiven (Lk 7:36–50).[124] This event would have scandalized every Galilean Jew. The Pharisee had hospitably invited Jesus to dine and remained

---

half his wealth to the poor. The delighted Jesus announced: "Today salvation has come to this house, because this man too is a descendant of Abraham. For the Son of Man came to seek out and save the lost" (Lk 19:9–10). But Zacchaeus disappears after this pericope. Because he had made his promises largely to pacify the angry crowd, we cannot know whether he fulfilled his pledges following Jesus' departure.

124 Chapter 9 noted that nearly all of Jesus' "your sins are forgiven" assertions were mere factual observations when sick people recovered, stating that God *must* have forgiven their sins. This pericope about the (healthy) prostitute, found only in Luke, is a rare exception to the rule. How can such exceptions be explained? Jesus believed he could look into people's hearts, and that whoever seemed repentant to him must seem equally repentant to God. He apparently regarded the prostitute's behavior as proof of her permanent repentance, and so felt comfortable in assuming that God had for-given her sins.

quiet when a prostitute barged into his house. Yet he ended up being upbraided by his guest for his "moral failings." In the ancient Middle East, where inviting someone to break bread obligated the guest to show respect for the host, this was unthinkable. It might be added that Christians interpret this story, correctly, as meaning that the prostitute accepted Jesus' Messiahship, whereas the Pharisee did not. ("Messiah" literally means "one anointed with precious oil," such as kings and prophets.) However, since we have already seen that very few of Jesus' contemporaries imagined him to be the Messiah, his elevation of the prostitute over his host would have been widely condemned. Speaking of prostitutes, another scandalous element of Jesus' ministry was that he and his Disciples occasionally traveled with some (mostly unidentified) women. In this period—and even in parts of today's Middle East—women traveling without family chaperones were considered harlots. That Jesus himself was an unmarried man (a real rarity at that time) would have loosened tongues yet further.

All the above problems must ultimately be understood as facets of a much broader problem—his "authority." Here was a man who routinely disparaged the religious authorities and many traditional societal values, while embracing extortionists and prostitutes. He preached as if he was in direct communion with God, but rarely prayed (publicly) or invoked the Tanakh, the unquestioned font of God's Words. This raised troubling questions about whether he truly came in God's name. First-century Jews were deeply conservative, particularly rural

---

The only other real exception, which is recorded in all Synoptics, occurred when he told a paralytic man, shortly *before* curing him, "Son, your sins are forgiven" (Mk 2:5). This was presumptuous, because he was implying an ability to predict God's Will. The scandalized onlooking scribes thought to themselves, "Why does this fellow speak in this way? ... Who can forgive sins but God alone?" (Mk 2:7). Yet John the Baptist had never been criticized for practicing his "baptism of repentance for the forgiveness of sin." The reason was that the Baptist was regarded as God's agent, for he was a pious ascetic who spoke in God's name and sought evidence of repentance before conferring his baptism. What made Jesus different was that he often seemed (erroneously) to act independently of God. Incidentally, shocked as the scribes were in this pericope, the other Jews who witnessed this miracle had no question about the true source of Jesus' forgiveness, for "they were all astounded and glorified God"(Mk 2:12), who "had given such authority to *human beings*" (Mt 9:8).

(There is one final instance in which Jesus forgave the sins of someone who was not sick. Luke states that while Jesus was being crucified, he told a criminal who spoke kindly to him from the adjacent crucifix that "today you will be with me in Paradise" (Lk 23:43). However, the other Synoptics insist that this criminal mocked Jesus instead. In any case, Jesus would have been in such intense pain that overanalyzing anything he said on the cross would be risky.)

ones. God was their provider of health, fertility, wealth, and even their identity as a people. They may have been briefly awed by Jesus' pyrotechnical teaching, but afterwards they were probably gnawed by doubts. Who exactly was he? His miracles and many of his teachings made him seem virtuous, but what about his often problematical ethics? Counterculture permissiveness was unknown in first-century Palestine. Life was hard. Starvation and illness were constant threats. Governments and soldiers were rapacious, and legal recourse nonexistent. The only bulwark against privation and assault was the extended family/clan, which remains so powerful even today in the Middle East. "Thou shalt honor they father and thy mother" was no sentimental bromide. It guaranteed the cohesion needed for survival in a dangerous world. And family life was undergirded by religion and strict moral codes. Any ordinary Jew who did not believe that Jesus was the Messiah (meaning nearly all of them) would have been offended by Jesus' unorthodox behavior.[125]

There is one final reason for Jesus' apparent failure to win the people's allegiance: all Synoptics agree that he *intentionally confused them!* This mind-boggling behavior began early during his ministry, when he "taught" a huge crowd with a parable that sounds straightforward to modern ears. A sower was spreading seeds (ethical teachings), some of which landed on a hard path (the unreceptive) and

---

125 A renowned Christian scholar Raymond Brown, offers his view of Jesus' persona (presented in a discussion of Jesus' trial and crucifixion): "Christians think of Jesus as an ideally noble figure, caring for the sick, reaching out to the poor ... and preaching love. How then could Jewish authorities have handed Jesus over to the Romans to be crucified? A traditional Christian answer has been that these authorities were not truly religious but were hypocrites ... or intolerant ultra-legalists.... That answer is not satisfactory.... Rather than blaming the authorities, one must reflect more carefully on the reaction produced by Jesus, a sharply challenging figure who could not always have been received sympathetically even by the truly religious. On the one hand, Jesus is portrayed as consorting frequently and pleasantly with public sinners.... On the other hand, he criticizes scathingly a religious ... Pharisee who has taken care not to break the commandments, who observes pious practices and prays, and who is generous to religious causes. To ... his era Jesus at times offers a sovereign challenge, the sole authority for which seems to be his claim that he can speak for God. *If one takes the Gospels at face value ... there emerges a Jesus capable of generating intense dislike* [italics added].... Christians ... fail to grasp that ... he would be offensive on any religious scene if he told people that God wants something different from what they know ... [and] if he challenged established sacred teaching on his own authority as self-designated spokesman for God.... More than likely ... were Jesus to appear in our time ... and be arrested and tried again, most of those finding him guilty would identify themselves as Christians and think they were rejecting an impostor" (Raymond Brown, *The Death of the Messiah* [New York: Doubleday, 1975], 1:392–93).

died, whereas some landed on fertile soil and flourished. But even the Disciples did not understand the story and asked him why he used parables. He answered:

> "To you has been given the secret of the kingdom of God, but
> for those outside, everything comes in parables; in order that,
> *'they may indeed look, but not perceive, and may indeed listen,*
> *but not understand; so that*
> *They may not turn again and be forgiven.'"*
> With many such parables he spoke the word to them [the people] …
> *he did not speak to them except in parables,* but he explained everything in
> private to his disciples. (Mk 4:10–12, 33–34, italics added)
> "The reason I speak to them in parable is that …
> 'this people's heart has grown dull …
> and they have shut their eyes; so that they might not look … and understand …
> and turn [reform].'" (Mt 13:13–15; brackets added)

Jesus continued using parables throughout his entire ministry; they were in fact his most characteristic form of expression. Jesus even exalted in the people's confusion, for he said, "I give praise to you, Father, Lord of heaven and earth, for … you have hidden these things from the wise and the learned…. Yes, Father, such has been your gracious will" (Mt 11:25–26). He did state elsewhere in this prayer that the "childlike" would understand him. But Jesus generally defined the "childlike" in a last-will-be-first manner—any people, whatever their past, willing to accept his authority without question.

Jesus' rationale for using parables seems incredible. Why would he travel ceaselessly to disseminate a deliberately obscure message?[126] The passages above actually contain two answers. One is that God, in his inscrutable will, had decided to withhold Jesus' revelations from the people. As the CSB notes, "To understand is a gift of God, granted to the disciples but not to the crowds … both the disciples' understanding and the crowd's obtuseness are attributed to God. The question of human responsibility for the obtuseness is not dealt with [i.e., is not explained]."[127]

---

126 Remarkably, shortly after quoting Jesus as saying he used parables to confuse the people, Matthew quotes Jesus as saying that he spoke in parables "to fulfill what had been spoken through the prophets: 'I will open my mouth to speak in parables, I will proclaim what has been hidden from the foundation of the world'" (Mt 13:34–35). This internal contradiction probably resulted from Matthew's attempt to prove that Jesus had fulfilled as many Tanakh prophecies as possible.

127 The Catholic Study Bible, 29.

The second answer is more obvious: the people were too wicked to deserve a chance to repent. But this is puzzling. God had forced Jonah to give the wicked city of Nineveh a chance to repent, and Abraham had pleaded with God to save wicked Sodom and Gomorrah for the sake of ten righteous inhabitants. Is it possible that a similar opportunity was to be denied to the people who had literally invented religious martyrdom and suffered two thousand crucifixions during their "No King but God" anti-Roman revolt during Jesus' own youth? If Jesus believed that Jews were so irredeemably wicked, why race from place to place to spread his gospel?

In the end, the Gospels provide no convincing explanation of this jaw-dropping mystery: a Messiah who would neither reveal himself nor his full message. Equally unfathomable was his inability to explain himself even when he tried, to his Disciples (particularly in Mark's Gospel). Because the Synoptics are largely silent on these issues, we will defer discussing them until the final chapter. (Impatient readers can read the nutshell comment below.[128]) For now, we will wrap up the original question of whether ordinary Jews accepted Jesus' core message during his lifetime. It seems that the great majority did not, and many of those who did probably melted away after he never returned from Jerusalem.

---

128 Scholars agree that the Evangelists were on a tightrope. Because they were trying to spread their new Christian religion, they had to depict Jesus as a wise, holy miracle worker followed at every step by awed crowds. However, they also had to cope with the well-known fact that nearly all the Jews who personally saw Jesus remained Jewish after his death, including his Disciples. The only possible explanation was that the Disciples were too dim-witted to really understand Jesus, and that the Jewish people were too foolish and/or wicked to accept and/or deserve his words.

CHAPTER 12

DID THE JEWS REJECT JESUS, AND WHY? PART II: THE RELIGIOUS AUTHORITIES

There were three major Jewish sects in first-century Palestine. Of these, the Essenes require no discussion, since they are never mentioned in the Gospels.[129] The focus will instead be on the two groups that are: the Sadducees and the Pharisees. However, the fact that no Sadducees or Pharisees are ever named in the Gospels (except Caiaphas, the high priest) makes it impossible to know whether

---

129 The Essenes were ultra-pious Jews who largely lived in monastic-like desert communities, such as Qumran (c. 150 BCE–68 CE), the site of the Dead Sea Scrolls. Their monastic isolation stemmed from their conviction that the Temple priests—along with virtually everyone else—were utterly corrupt, making it their responsibility to become the "true priests" of Israel. Although their isolation explains their absence from the Gospels, their ritual immersion ceremonies (mikvas/baptisms) may have influenced John the Baptist. More significantly, the 1947 discovery of the Dead Sea Scrolls opened scholars' eyes for the first time to Judaism's extraordinary diversity in the early first century, revealing that Jesus himself was comfortably within the spectrum of contemporary Judaism.

(Josephus mentioned a "fourth" Jewish sect, the Zealots, which was not a true religious sect. The Zealots first appeared during the revolt of 6 CE as a group of religious zealots dedicated to overthrowing Roman rule. They disappeared from history during the first decades after their defeat, so nothing is known about them during Jesus' life. They reemerged after 40 CE and played an important but disastrous role in the First Jewish Revolt, during which they were exterminated. Their last stronghold, the desert mountain of Masada, fell in 73 CE, three years after Jerusalem's destruction.)

any of them knew Jesus well. We will therefore begin with John the Baptist, who unquestionably did.

John the Baptist

John the Baptist was a revered Jewish figure who was, according to Josephus, "a good man" who "had exhorted the Jews to righteous lives, to practice justice towards their fellows and piety towards God, and so doing join in baptism."[130] It is widely believed that John pronounced Jesus the Messiah, when Jesus came to receive his baptism. In fact, only Matthew's Gospel explicitly makes this claim. The other two Synoptics do not, but they are artfully written to create that impression. We have already seen Mark's version of the baptism (beginning of chapter 10), in which John proclaimed, "The one who is more powerful than I is coming after me.... I have baptized you with water; but he will baptize you with the Holy Spirit." Mark goes on to say, "In those days Jesus came from Nazareth in Galilee and was baptized by John" (Mk 1:7–8). However, John never stated here that Jesus was "the one." Instead, Mark created this impression by following the prophecy that "one mightier than I is coming" with the statement that Jesus arrived thereafter. But so did unknown thousands of other Jews. In writing his own account, Luke borrowed Mark's technique by implying, but never stating, that John identified Jesus as the Messiah.[131]

That the Baptist was not convinced that Jesus was the Messiah is supported by subsequent events. Shortly after Jesus' baptism, John was arrested and imprisoned by Herod Antipas for criticizing Herod's illegal marriage. When Jesus began his own ministry shortly thereafter, John's disciples somehow managed to stay near John, and they kept their imprisoned master informed of Jesus' activities—healings, preaching, and so on. Hearing of these, John sent his disciples to Jesus to ask: "Are you the one who is to come, or are we to wait for another?" Jesus replied indirectly, saying, "Go and tell John what you have seen and heard: the blind receive their sight, the lame walk ... the poor have good news brought to them" (Lk 7:20–22). John's reaction to Jesus' reply is unknown, for he was soon beheaded by Herod's soldiers. Nevertheless, he clearly died convinced that Jesus was no Messiah. How is this known? The decision of John's disciples to remain with their imprisoned master while Jesus' ministry was in full swing could be ascribed to personal loyalty. However, not one of them is reported to have joined Jesus even *after* the Baptist's death. Instead, they continued as a separate sect. This is shown in the Gospels themselves, for we read that "the Disciples of John came

---

130 Josephus, *Antiquities*, 18:117–19.

131 John might have been convinced if he saw the baptismal vision that Jesus did (chapter 10), but Jesus' vision was a personal one.

to him [Jesus], saying, "Why do we and the Pharisees fast often ..., but your disciples do not fast?" (Mt 9:14). If the Baptist had believed that Jesus was the Messiah, he assuredly would have instructed his disciples to follow Jesus. Yet it is a well-established historical fact that John's sect persisted for nearly a hundred years, into the early second century.[132]

The CSB concurs that John apparently died convinced Jesus was no Messiah, and speculates why: Jesus' ministry had "not been one of fiery judgment, as John had expected."[133] In short, the Baptist expected the same sort of Messiah as most other Jews. Jesus was not a King David-like hero preparing to defeat the Roman legions. It's true that he was prophesying about the Day of the Lord and the coming Kingdom, but he seemed content to preach and perform small-scale miracles in backwater Galilee. Why wasn't he calling on God's power to destroy the Romans as Moses had destroyed the Egyptians? Where was the apocalypse?

The Baptist's well-known rejection of Jesus embarrassed early followers of Jesus. Equally humiliating was that Jesus had sought John's "baptism for the forgiveness of sins." This implied that Jesus had been sinful, and needed John's absolution. These problems may explain why, following Mark's original account, the later Synoptics downplayed the Baptist's importance. Matthew's Gospel—the only one in which the Baptist explicitly proclaimed Jesus the Messiah—agreed that Jesus asked John to be baptized, but that John was so startled by the request that he said, "I need to be baptized by you, and do you come to me?" To which Jesus replied in the affirmative (Mt 3:14–15). Jesus was then baptized. Luke's revision was more radical. His story begins in the usual way, with John's prophecy and Jesus' arrival. But the Baptist is immediately arrested (in this account) by Herod Antipas' troops, preventing the baptism from happening (Lk 3:16–21).[134]

The Sadducees
The Sadducees dominated the upper ranks of the Temple priesthood, and particularly the coveted position of high priest. They were also overrepresented in the

---

132 If the Baptist never proclaimed Jesus the Messiah, why did he later ask, "Are you the one who is to come, or should we look for another?" This question sounds authentic, for it is too embarrassing for the Evangelists to have created. It does reveal that John had at least entertained the notion that Jesus might be the Messiah. Perhaps the simplest speculation is that following his baptismal vision, Jesus told John that he believed God had chosen him for a messianic/eschatological mission.

133 The Catholic Study Bible, 24.

134 The Gospel of John goes one step further, by eliminating the baptism altogether. The Baptist's sole role is to prophecy Jesus' coming, after which he states that his role is finished.

ruling elite. As such, they were the Romans' chief collaborators and comprised much of the Jewish aristocracy.[135] Although the Temple's exalted status conferred the Sadducees with great religious esteem, they were probably disliked personally by most Jews on nationalistic and socioeconomic grounds. Their religious tenets were also unpopular. Their intense Temple focus persuaded them that Temple worship was essentially synonymous with Judaism (as had been relatively true during First Temple times). They scrupulously observed the voluminous Temple regulations of the Mosaic Law, but had little interest in the ethical Psalms and Prophetic books that were so meaningful to ordinary Jews. They also rejected the notion of resurrection that brought comfort to struggling commoners; their own privileged positions convinced them that God's rewards were conferred in this world. They also rejected the Pharisees' oral law, which allowed commoners to become more active participants in their religion (see below).

This background made their opposition to Jesus, as chronicled in the Gospels, historically plausible. They would have been indifferent to him while he remained in far-off Galilee, and the Gospels never even mention them until Jesus arrived in Jerusalem. But when he entered the Temple, font of their prestige and livelihood, his attacks against them and their Temple practices probably made him a marked man. The Romans needed Sadducee assistance in controlling the Jews, and so would have been quite willing to accommodate their allies in such minor matters as liquidating an obscure Galilean preacher. This said, the next chapter will suggest that the Sadducees' role in Jesus' death may have been exaggerated by the Gospels.

The Pharisees

Jews have always regarded the Pharisees as the heroes of first-century Judaism because they were the only Jewish sect to survive the First Jewish Revolt. Over time, they evolved into the early sage/rabbis who ultimately created the Mishnah, the Talmud, and modern Judaism. Yet surprisingly little is really known about them. The problem is that our only written sources are the Gospels (the earliest but most hostile of all sources), Josephus (who skewed his description in an attempt to portray the Pharisees as a "philosophical school" to his mostly Hellenistic readership), and the Mishnah (which provides little detail about the Pharisees, and in any event was written too late to be of great historical value).

---

135 Cohen, *From the Maccabees to the Mishnah*, 143–64; *Anchor Bible Dictionary*, s.v. Sadducees, 5:892ff; *Encyclopedia Judaica*, 14:620–22.

The key misconception about the Pharisees is that they were "religious authorities" at all.[136] They were *not* like modern rabbis who earn their livelihood by heading synagogues or communal organizations. Not until c. 700 CE did modern, professional rabbis arise. Instead, the Pharisees earned their livings in secular occupations. Most appear to have been literate, well-off, predominantly urban people who worked as minor government functionaries, teachers, merchants, and small landowners. They therefore had the money and education to become religious scholars in their spare time. They were few in number, perhaps totaling one or two percent of the population.[137] They had no power over anyone else, except by the force of their personal example. Sadly, Christians have (until recently) cartoonishly misrepresented them as harsh taskmasters of the common people, making their lives miserable by forcing them to comply with endless petty laws, and castigating them when they inevitably failed.

Although the Pharisees had no power over the common people, they were the religious sect most attuned to them. Like the people—and unlike the Sadducees—they highly valued the Prophetic books, and believed in resurrection. Moreover, their oral law democratized Judaism by asserting that anyone could become as holy as even the Temple priests, if they adopted the Temple laws regarding food preparation and ritual cleanliness. In practice, however, most commoners were too poor to have time for anything beyond supporting their families, and too illiterate to study and punctiliously follow all the laws. Because first-century Palestine was as highly stratified as every other country in the Roman Empire, the Pharisees viewed themselves as a pious, literate elite, and preferred to congregate among themselves. Indeed, many held quite unflattering opinions of anyone lacking the wherewithal or inclination to become strictly religious.[138] They probably did not

---

136 The main references for this section are as follows: Cohen, *From the Maccabees to the Mishnah*, 111–15, 143–64, 214–31; *Anchor Bible Dictionary*, s.v. Pharisees, 5:289ff; White, *From Jesus to Christianity*, 78–80, 243–46; *Encyclopedia Judaica*, 13:263–64.

137 This rough approximation is based on our only available statistic, from Josephus, that there were only six thousand Pharisees during Herod the Great's reign (which ended when Jesus was an infant). The approximation is rough because it relies on assumptions about what proportion of Palestine's two million (or so) Jews were males old enough to be Pharisees.

138 In return, commoners undoubtedly harbored the same human resentment found in any stratified society between commoners and the elite—however pious those elites may be. Nothing captures the tension between them as colorfully as the comments, several generations later, of the renowned sage/rabbi Akiva (c. 50–135CE), as recorded in the Mishnah:

mingle much with ordinary people even at synagogues, because contemporary synagogues were simply rooms in the homes of anyone, literate or not, willing to invite neighbors in on the Sabbath. Instead, the Pharisees' major contact with commoners was probably limited to selling goods or scribal/legal services.

(Returning momentarily to ordinary Jews: if their contact with the Pharisees was so limited, the obvious question is, which sect did they belong to? The answer is *none*. The large majority of Jews were "unaffiliated." That is, they simply adhered to the ancient Judaism of their forebears, which revolved around the Sabbath, the Festival Days, eating kosher and other basic precepts, and occasional pilgrimages to the Temple. They often assembled in their tiny synagogue-rooms to hear and discuss the Tanakh, but without a "rabbi" present. None was needed, because their society was so steeped in Jewish practice that infants learned their religion at their parent's knees. They were aware of the religious authorities, but infrequently met any of them, particularly in Galilee. They regarded the few Pharisees they knew with respect as religious exemplars, but most Jews lived too humbly to think of emulating them. The Sadducees had enormous status as the descendants of the hallowed ancient priests of Israel, but they were distant figures with little personal appeal. The Essenes were probably regarded with awe for their ascetic purity, but were seen rarely if at all.)

With this understanding of the Pharisees, we can now ask how they reacted to Jesus.[139] The Gospels reveal that some individual Pharisees were drawn to Jesus, and even tried to become disciples. Most Pharisees, however, probably paid no attention to him, if only because relatively few Pharisees in that era seem to have lived or traveled in rural Galilee. Those who did probably paid as little attention to him as possible. To begin with, he was a commoner—respectable enough, but hardly a scholar. It is not certain he could even read. Although one Gospel

---

Rabbi Akiva said: When I was an am-ha-aretz [commoner]
I said: If only I had a scholar [before me], I would maul him like as ass.
Said his disciples to him: Rabbi, you mean like a dog.
Rabbi Akiva answered: No, the former bites and breaks the bones,
while the latter bites but does not break the bones. (Pesachim 49b)

139 Several Jewish scholars have claimed that Jesus was himself a Pharisee. Jesus' "Woes" (chapter 6) provide the strongest evidence for this viewpoint, for Jesus proclaimed here that the Pharisees now occupied the seat of Moses, and that Jews must obey all of their teachings. The Gospels also contain stories of Pharisees who are drawn to Jesus' teachings, speak to him respectfully, or invite him into their homes. Nevertheless, the overall tone in the Synoptics of Jesus' relationship with the Pharisees is one of mild and occasionally strong antagonism. Therefore, it appears most likely that Jesus was not a Pharisee, or that, if he was, he belonged to a very liberal group that was at the fringes of the sect's mainstream.

portrays Jesus reading from a Tanakh scroll in synagogue (Lk 4:16–19), the three verses he recited were so far apart (Isaiah 58:6 and 61:1–2) that it is physically impossible to unroll such a length of scroll. When Jesus quoted the Tanakh in his oral teachings—which was suspiciously infrequent—he occasionally misattributed his quotes to the wrong book, or misquoted the verses. (Curiously, the misquoted verses were often taken word-for-word from the Septuagint [the Greek translation of the Tanakh], which was used by the Evangelists, but not by Palestinian Jews.) He could utter outrageous things, as when he angrily told one scholar that he and his generation would "be charged with the blood of all the prophets shed since the foundation of the world, from the blood of Abel to the blood of Zechariah" (Lk 11:50–51). Even uneducated Jews knew that Abel was no prophet, that "this generation" of Jews could not possibly have been guilty of a murder that predated Judaism, and that no prophet named Zechariah had ever been killed.[140] Jesus' statement may have simply reflected his penchant for hyperbole, but Pharisees would not have found this any more endearing.

Far more disturbing than his lack of erudition was his "authority." This has been discussed at length. He infrequently referred to the Tanakh, seemed to believe he was in direct communion with God, and occasionally forgave sin in an unorthodox manner. Most seriously, he sometimes claimed the authority to modify the Mosaic Law, even if only to stiffen it. All Synoptics (and even Paul's Letters) attest to his declaration that divorce was henceforth illegal (except, perhaps, in cases of adultery). And if Matthew's Sermon on the Mount is to be believed, he tightened many other laws as well. Altering the Mosaic Law in any way was unheard of. Because not even his family or neighbors believed he was special, it was inevitable that the religious authorities would sometimes question his actions. But, as we have seen, Jesus was irascible with anyone unwilling to accept him unconditionally. He believed he knew God's Will and that whoever questioned him was a fool or an evildoer. Although we have already reviewed many stories of his verbal clashes with the Pharisees, yet another pericope explicitly reveals how upsetting his behavior could be. (This pericope is where Luke placed many of the "Woes" sayings that Matthew used in Jesus' Jerusalem tirade [see chapter 6]). When Jesus was invited into a Pharisee's house to eat:

---

140 Uriah was the only prophet reported to be killed in the Tanakh. Jesus often accused the Jews of murdering their prophets, but Zechariah was the only one he ever named. A minor priest (not prophet) named Zechariah was killed in c. 800 BCE, but Jesus' denunciation clearly referred to some recent figure (Vermes, *The Authentic Gospel of Jesus*, 202). However, the apocryphal *Martyrdom of Isaiah* (second century BCE) claimed that Isaiah had been killed, and *The Lives of the Prophets* (late first century CE, which the Evangelists might have seen) added Zechariah, Jeremiah, Ezekiel, Micah, and Amos (Meier, *A Marginal Jew*, 2:175).

> The Pharisee was amazed to see that he did not first wash before dinner.
> Then the Lord said to him, "Now you Pharisees cleanse the outside of
> the cup ... but inside you are filled with greed and wickedness. You fools! ...
> One of the lawyers answered him, "Teacher, when you say these things, you are
> insulting us too." And he said, "Woe also to you lawyers! For you load people with
> burdens hard to bear, and you yourselves do not lift a finger to ease them. Woe
> to you! For you build the tombs of the prophets whom your ancestors killed. So
> you ... are witnesses and approve of the deeds of your ancestors ...
> [All the blood] from ... Abel to ... Zechariah
> will be charged against this generation." (Lk 11:38–51, brackets added)

Understanding the significance of this incident hinges on the fact that Jesus must have realized that, because his host was a Pharisee, guests might be expected to wash their hands before eating. To refuse to do so, even as a courtesy, was a deliberate affront. To magnify this insult by spewing invective against everyone at the table must have left them aghast. It is hardly surprising that upon Jesus' departure, "The scribes and Pharisees began to be very hostile toward him and to cross-examine him about many things, lying in wait for him, to catch him in something he might say" (Lk 11:53–54).

Small wonder that the Pharisees often seem to be lurking in the background in the Gospels, waiting to pounce on Jesus for even the smallest infraction of the oral law. What better way to prove to others that such a man could not possibly be God's messenger? Yet it must be reiterated that even if some (or many) Pharisees rejected Jesus, they were toothless enemies. They had moral stature, but no temporal power. The Romans recognized only the Sadducees as the religious and civil authorities of Palestine. The Pharisees had no power to coerce or punish anyone. The Sanhedrin did contain Pharisees, but was always headed by a Sadducean high priest loyal to Rome. The Synoptics lack even a single example of any Pharisee physically touching either Jesus or any Disciple, and agree that the Pharisees were not involved in Jesus' trial and death. On the contrary, Luke's Gospel contains two pericopes involving Pharisees who tried to protect Jesus from possible danger from the Romans and Herod Antipas (Lk 13:31–33; Lk 20:39).

Postscript: Elders, Scribes, Scholars, & Lawyers

The identities of these people are unclear, except possibly for the elders. Because the elders always appear in Jerusalem, they were probably the aristocratic lay elite, such as the nonpriestly Sadducees or the powerful Herodian family. The scribes are more mysterious, for "scribes" has two meanings. One is the modern one:

people literate enough to write or copy documents. There were many such scribes in Palestine, including civil scribes who wrote marriage contracts and business documents. The other definition of scribes is "scholars." But whether scribes and scholars were different or the same, the key point is that such people might be Pharisees or Sadducees (or neither). Both sects had religious scholars and scribe-copyists. If one sect had been substantially larger than the other, we might be able to assume that it contained most of the scribes and/or scholars. Unfortunately, the only statistics available are Josephus' outdated estimates that shortly before Jesus' birth there were six thousand Pharisees and four thousand Sadducees. Yet even if the Sadducees remained the smaller group, they controlled the world's largest Jewish institution, the Temple. This was not only the premiere religious site, but it also served as the national Treasury. Large numbers of scribe-copyists would have been needed to keep track of tithes paid, Temple expenditures, Sanhedrin rulings, and so forth.

In short, it is rarely clear which religious sect these individuals belonged to. Indeed, it is questionable whether such terms as "scholar," "scribe," or "lawyer" have any real meaning, because the Evangelists tended to conflate them. A "scribe" in one version of a pericope is often called a "scholar" or even "person" in another. (Note that in this chapter's pericope about Jesus dining with the authorities, Jesus initially castigated the Pharisees and the "scholars," but the latter suddenly became "scribes" in the final verse.) Perhaps the only useful rule of thumb is that most scribes and scholars located in far-off Galilee were probably Pharisees (unless they were visiting from Jerusalem), whereas those at the Jerusalem Temple could be either Pharisees or Sadducees. There are no definitive answers.

CHAPTER 13

JESUS' END, PART I:
THE LAST DAYS IN JERUSALEM

Jesus' final days in Jerusalem constitute the only true narrative section in the Synoptics, with events following one another in a logical order. It is also the longest section, as befits the centrality of these events in Christian thought and doctrine. This chapter will review the pre-resurrection phase of this period, in two passes. The first will summarize his few days of teachings, the Last Supper, and his Passion (Greek for suffering—the arrest, trial, and crucifixion). Because Gospel details vary, the "consensus" narrative (at least two of the three Synoptics) will be provided. Minimal commentary will be made on the narrative. The second pass will focus on the trial itself—why he was killed and who was responsible—with substantial commentary.

The Narrative
After Jesus' rapturous acclaim by a Jewish crowd during his entrance to Jerusalem,[141] his first action was to "cleanse" the Temple by driving out the moneychangers and sacrifice-sellers, crying:

> "Is it not written, 'My house shall be called a house of prayer for all nations'?
> But you have made it a den of robbers." And when the chief

---

141 Matthew's Gospel contains the famous interpretive error of depicting Jesus riding into Jerusalem simultaneously straddling an ass and a colt, which is physically impossible. Matthew was trying to prove that Jesus was fulfilling the Tanakh's prophecy, "your king shall come to you … riding on an ass, on a colt" (Zechariah 9:9). As noted by the CSB, Matthew did not realize that "the ass and the colt are the same animal, mentioned twice … the common Hebrew device of poetic parallelism" (The Catholic Study Bible, 21).

> priest and the scribes heard it, they kept looking for a way to kill him;
> for they were afraid of him, because the whole crowd was
> spellbound ["astonished," in the CSB translation] by his teaching."
> (Mk 11:17–18)

This was a seminal moment, for both this account (Mark's) and Luke's suggest that it triggered the authorities' decision to kill Jesus. However the authorities feared doing anything publicly, since his continued popularity with the Jewish masses might cause "a riot among the people" (Mt 26:5). It is worth noting once again that Jesus' fury at the Temple's operation, which inspired him to recite Isaiah and Jeremiah in the passage above, testifies to his devotion to the sanctity of the Temple, Judaism's core institution.[142]

When Jesus and his Disciples returned to the Temple the next day to preach to the crowds, he was quickly confronted by some religious figures demanding that he justify the basis for his teachings and actions. When he refused, they tried to trap him into saying something foolish or seditious. ("The Greatest Commandment" was one question.) The interrogators were primarily the chief priests, scribes, and elders, with Pharisees playing a lesser role. This was Jesus' first ever confrontation with the chief priests (the high priest's highest-ranking associates) or any other known Sadducees. The episode ended with Jesus' "Woe to you" rebuke of the authorities (chapter 6).

Now alone with his Disciples, Jesus began prophesying the upcoming events of the apocalypse, which would begin with the destruction of Jerusalem and the Temple.[143] He also warned them against heeding "false Messiahs." Pointing to the massive Temple walls, he said, "Do you see these great buildings? Not one stone will be left here upon another; all will be thrown down" (Mk 13:2). He concluded on a more joyous note, by reminding the Disciples that "This generation will not pass away" before witnessing the coming of the Kingdom.

---

142 Jesus' rationale for his "cleansing" was unclear, since these merchants were required for proper Temple function. The moneychangers were needed to exchange the foreign currencies brought by pilgrims coming from across the Roman world, while the sacrifice-sellers allowed the required animals to be conveniently purchased. Jesus may have believed that the merchants were profiteering. Alternately, considering his conviction that money was worthless in a world approaching the apocalypse, he may have been offended by the thought of any profit at all.

143 Jerusalem's destruction was Jesus' only accurate apocalyptic prophecy. His accuracy is not surprising, inasmuch as the Synoptics were all written either during Jerusalem's siege or after its final destruction in 70 CE. Of course, the Temple was not completely razed, as its Western Wall survives to this day.

The conspiracy of the chief priests, scribes, and elders now commenced. The Pharisees disappear entirely from the story at this point. The conspirators' earlier fear that taking action during the Passover pilgrimage might provoke a riot was eliminated when Judas Iscariot suddenly appeared and informed them as to how Jesus could be secretly arrested. Shortly after, Jesus commenced his Passover seder (the Last Supper) at a local residence, with Judas in attendance. Jesus immediately revealed Judas' betrayal, causing deep distress among the other Disciples.[144] The Last Supper concluded with the "Lord's Supper," which later evolved into the Roman Catholics' Eucharist ceremony (consuming wine and a wafer). Jesus blessed bread (presumably matzo) and distributed the pieces to his Disciples, saying:

> "Take, eat; this is my body." Then he took a cup, and after giving thanks,
> he gave it to them, saying, "Drink from it, all of you,
> for this is my blood of the covenant,
> which is poured out for many for the forgiveness of sins." (Mt 26:26–28)

This is the most famous version of the Last Supper, and the most Christological. (All versions are among the most Christological passages in the Synoptics.) However, the CSB believes that these words originated in the liturgical services of the *post*-Jesus synagogues/churches, since they "show the influence of Christian liturgical usage," and contain the Evangelists' own "theological insights."[145]

---

144 In Luke's odd version, the Disciples not only appeared relatively unperturbed, but also seemed to begin arguing about who should assume leadership if Jesus was arrested. "A dispute … arose among them as to which one of them was to be regarded as the greatest" (Lk 22:24). Luke made an infelicitous editorial decision here; the other Evangelists placed this debate during Jesus' peaceful Galilean ministry, making it far more innocuous.

145 The Catholic Study Bible, 56, 58. The belief that the Evangelists incorporated their own theology into their Last Supper account is due to the fact that the oldest and presumably most accurate version of the Supper is actually found in Paul's First Letter to the Corinthians (c. 56 CE). Here, Jesus' words sound mostly commemorative, not Christological. According to Paul, Jesus distributed the bread saying, "This is my body that is for you. Do this in remembrance of me." Later, after dinner was finished, he took the wine cup, saying, "This cup is the new covenant in my blood. Do this, as often as you drink it, in remembrance of me. For as often as you eat this bread and drink this cup, you proclaim the Lord's death until he comes" (1 Cor 11:24–26). Note that Paul says nothing about the wine/blood being poured out for the forgiveness of sins. Neither do the Gospels of Mark or Luke; only Matthew's (above) does.

Everyone now walked outside onto the Mount of Olives, where Jesus accurately predicted his Disciples' imminent unfaithfulness to him. Frightened for the first time in his ministry, he prostrated himself and said, "My Father, if it is possible, let this cup pass from me; yet not what I want but what you want" (Mt 26:39). Judas now appeared with the armed crowd sent to arrest Jesus.

Events now accelerated with astonishing speed. In the next twelve hours or so, Jesus would be tried before the Sanhedrin, Pontius Pilate, and (according to one Gospel) Herod Antipas, and be affixed to the cross. In the first step, Jesus was brought to the Sanhedrin[146] for a night trial before the high priest, the chief priests, and their allies. They initially could find no witnesses able to provide any credible evidence of Jesus' "guilt." None of them, for example, could recall Jesus ever having called himself the Messiah. Some witnesses distorted his prophecy of the Temple's destruction by claiming that he intended to personally destroy it, but they lacked proof for this absurd charge. Frustrated, Caiaphas, the high priest, confronted Jesus directly by asking whether he was the Messiah. As discussed earlier, Jesus responded, "I am" in Mark's Gospel, but ambiguously in the other Synoptics. Whatever happened, all sources agree that the high priest interpreted Jesus' response as affirmative, and declared him guilty of blasphemy. With this criminal charge now in hand, the Sanhedrin brought him early the next morning to Pontius Pilate, the Roman procurator of Judea. Although the Synoptics diverge slightly on what then happened (as shall be seen), Pilate asked Jesus:

"Are you the king of the Jews?"
He answered him, "You say so." Then the chief priests accused
him of many things. Pilate asked him again, "Have you no answer?"
But Jesus made no further reply. (Mk 15:2–5)
Then Pilate said to the chief priests ... "I find no basis for
an accusation against this man." But they were insistent. (Lk 23: 4–5)

Despite Pilate's own belief that Jesus should be freed, the chief priests urged Pilate to ask the crowd, which had assembled for the Passover prisoner-release

---

146 The Sanhedrin was a council that the high priest called into session on an ad hoc basis, whenever he desired advice or a judgment on important matters. These included religious questions, administrative issues involving Jerusalem, and political problems with the Romans. The members of the Sanhedrin numbered approximately seventy-one, although it probably functioned with as many members as were available at the time. The membership was composed of equal numbers of Sadducees, elders (aristocrats), and scribes (including some Pharisees).

ceremony, which prisoner should be freed: Jesus or Barabbas. Barabbas was an anti-Roman insurrectionist who had apparently been arrested some weeks earlier.

> Now the chief priests and the elders persuaded the crowds to ask for Barabbas.... Pilate said to them, "Then what shall I do with Jesus who is called the Messiah?" All of them said, "Let him be crucified!" Then he asked, "Why? What evil has he done?" ... When Pilate saw that he could do nothing, but that a riot was beginning, he took some water and washed his hands ... saying, "I am innocent of this man's blood." ... Then the people as a whole answered, "His blood be on us and on our children." (Mt 27:20–25)

Unfortunately for Jews of the last two millennia, this is the favored version of the trial scene. The two other Gospels omit the horrific-sounding cry, "His blood be on us and on our children." Actually, this was merely the traditional statement during first-century capital offense trials whereby judges and witnesses publicly accepted responsibility for their verdict.[147] In any case, Pilate thereupon ordered Jesus flogged in his presence, and then turned him over to Roman soldiers who mocked him and crowned him with thorns. He was taken to nearby Golgotha and crucified by 9 AM, with the legal verdict of "King of the Jews" affixed to the top of the cross. He was mocked by the chief priests, a crowd of ordinary Jews, and the two revolutionaries being crucified near him. At noon, a three-hour solar eclipse began. As the sky brightened at 3 PM, he spoke his only words on the cross, in his native Aramaic. Agonizingly, in apparent incomprehension of his unexpected fate, he cried out, "Eli, Eli, lema sabachthani?" ("My God, my God, why have you forsaken me?")[148] (Mt 27: 46). With this he died,[149] and the "curtain of the Temple" (the curtain before the innermost chamber, which only high priests could enter) was miraculously torn in two. One Gospel adds that a great earthquake rocked

---

147 Brown, *An Introduction to the New Testament*, 201.

148 Some scholars question whether these words (from Psalm 22) were indicative of despair, because the Psalm ends on a triumphant note.

149 Luke diverges from the other Evangelists in his characteristically irenic way, by portraying a more loving, serene Jesus. Thus, Jesus says, "Father, forgive them; for they do not know what they are doing" (Lk 23:34) in his early hours on the cross. (The New Revised Standard translation brackets this quote to indicate that it was probably added to the original text by a later scribe.) Similarly, the mocking Jewish crowd instead watches in subdued silence. One of the co-crucified revolutionaries declares his faith in Jesus, who responds, "Truly I tell you, today you will be with me in Paradise" (Lk 23:43). Finally, Jesus' anguished last cry is transmuted into the tranquil, "Father, into your hands I commend my spirit" (Lk 23:46).

Jerusalem, resurrecting the bodies of ancient Jewish holy men who "appeared to many" on the city's streets (Mt 27:52–53). Thus ended Jesus' earthly life.

***

Commentary on the Trial
For both Christians and Jews, the main questions arising from this narrative are these: who was responsible for Jesus' death, and why did they do it? At a rational level, the answer is irrelevant insofar as no sensible person could seriously believe that Jews of later centuries and millennia could bear guilt for something that happened in a 30 CE Jerusalem courtyard. Emotionally, however, the issue still resonates.

The answer is simple if we abide by our rule of accepting the Gospels except in the face of strong counterevidence. Jesus was killed by the Romans, under strong pressure from the Sadducees, who apparently saw him as a threat to Temple worship and their own religious and political standing. The Jewish crowd at Pilate's trial was also complicit. The Pharisees were not involved. The pertinent parties—the Sadducees, the crowd, and the Romans—will now be discussed in turn.

The Sadducees
The Sadducees' probable involvement is considered credible by most historians. The Sadducees were highly respected in their role of Temple custodians, but they were personally disliked by most Jews. They were Roman collaborators and wealthy aristocrats who considered themselves the Jewish elite and were supercilious toward ordinary Jews and even the pious Pharisees. They could easily have resented a Galilean preacher who was stirring up the crowd, railing against their colleagues, and generally disrupting Temple operations. When they were later wiped out in the First Jewish Revolt, they received no eulogies.

That said, many questions persist about the Synoptics' account of the Sadducees and the trial. (Because the Sanhedrin was dominated by the Sadducees, this section will, for simplicity's sake, use "Sadducees" to refer to both.) Why, for example, did Jesus' Passion (arrest, trial, and execution) occur at such breakneck speed? For the Sadducees, Passover represented the most hectic, exhausting time of their year.[150] The prior week had required their supervision of the elaborate Temple purifications, and Jerusalem's preparations for receiving up to several hundred thousand pilgrims. (The Sanhedrin controlled the city's civic administration.) On the day of Jesus' nighttime arrest, they would have overseen the slaughter of tens

---

150 Paula Fredriksen, *Jesus of Nazareth, King of the Jews* (New York: Alfred A. Knopf, 1999), 221.

of thousands of ritual animals shortly before sunset, followed by the rewashing and repurification of the Temple. As mandated by the Tanakh, they would have then had to observe their own Passover seder, presumably at home. With such an exhausting schedule, only the most urgent emergency could have induced them to hurriedly assemble a Passover night Sanhedrin meeting, and return early the next morning (unless the meeting lasted all night, which is possible) to beg Pilate for Jesus' death … in time to rush back to the Temple for Passover day services.

That this *was* an emergency seems obvious to many believing Christians. The Messiah Jesus, with his immense influence over the people, had confronted the Sadducees with an existential challenge to their status and religion. However, the previous chapter has demonstrated that however popular Jesus was for his healing, he had little overall impact on the people of Galilee, the center of his mission. He never claimed he was the Messiah or the bearer of a new religion. Few people seemed to regard him as more than an apocalyptic prophet and faith healer. He had threatened no one, and in turn was never threatened (except in Luke's Nazareth story). Moreover, the Gospels do not record, during his entire Galilean ministry, even one encounter between Jesus and any Sadducee, or any other Temple figure. And had the Sadducees nevertheless heard of Jesus during this time and been concerned about him, they may have been able to silence him before he ever reached Jerusalem. Galilee and Jerusalem had different rulers (Herod Antipas and Pontius Pilate, respectively), but both were responsible to Rome for maintaining public order and might well have cooperated in arresting anyone who seemed really dangerous.

So why should the Sadducees have become so frenetic about plotting Jesus' death within twenty-four hours of his arrival in Jerusalem? We have seen that two Synoptics specify his cleansing of the Temple as the trigger, and they dramatize this incident as a sovereign challenge that could not be ignored. According to one Gospel, Jesus' actions were so encompassing that he "would not allow anyone to carry anything through the Temple" (Mk 11:16). In reality, this sounds unlikely. The Temple was enormous. Occupying 170,000 square feet (the size of twelve soccer fields), and capable of holding over three hundred thousand people on a crowded festival day, it is probable that relatively few people would even have noticed his overturning of the tables. Moreover, the cleansing occurred in the enormous Outer Temple courts, an unsanctified area open even to Gentile sight-seers. The same pragmatic observations apply to Jesus' teachings to the crowds, which also reportedly disturbed the authorities. The Temple was commonly filled with so many pilgrims prior to Passover that a dozen preachers could have spoken to as many crowds without noticing the others.

The trial itself, rather than clarifying these issues, clouds them even further. Unexpectedly, neither the witnesses nor the Sadducees said a word about either the cleansing or his teachings. Also unmentioned was anything he did in Galilee. Instead, the witnesses' only accusation was that he intended to destroy the Temple, a fallacious charge that was quickly dismissed. It was then that the frustrated High Priest asked Jesus if he was the Messiah. This seems odd. Jesus had taken great pains to conceal his identity, and, moreover, bore no resemblance to any Messiah expected by the Jews. Only a very small number of people seem to have discerned his identity. So why would the high priest have thought to ask, as his one and only question, whether Jesus was the Messiah? And why, assuming Jesus answered affirmatively (as reported by only one Synoptic), would he then be charged with blasphemy? Judaism has always strictly defined blasphemy as pronouncing or cursing God's holy name (YHWH), which Jesus never did. None of the many messianic claims in Jewish history was ever considered blasphemous. More to the point, Messianic claims were not punishable offenses. If the high priest had simply wanted to frame Jesus with a bogus crime, what was the need for witnesses and a full Sanhedrin meeting?[151]

Many other aspects of the trial have been questioned. For example, the Mishnah (c. 200 CE) states that the Sanhedrin could not hold trials on a Feast Day, or on any night. Nor could it not pronounce a verdict on the same day as the testimony. Unfortunately, no one knows whether these regulations were in force at the time of Jesus' trial. Nevertheless, the cumulative weight of all the questions above creates serious reservations about the Gospels' accuracy. Not surprisingly, the scholarly consensus is that these accounts are broadly historical, but highly unreliable in their details. The CSB itself, in its commentary on Luke's Gospel, states, "*The Passion Narrative [i.e., arrest, trial, and crucifixion] is not a report of what happened, but a narrative shaped by the conviction that Jesus was the suffering servant ...* "[152]

The Jewish Crowd

All Synoptics agree that the crowd at Jesus' trial bore some guilt for his death. But who was in this crowd? We have repeatedly seen that the Jewish masses flocked eagerly to Jesus, whether for his miracles, his message, or his charisma. He was thronged by crowds throughout Palestine, including Jerusalem. He entered Jerusalem to the excited acclamation of people shouting, "Hosanna." Large crowds

---

151 It is true that by the first century, Jewish authors writing in Greek, such as Josephus, used "blasphemy" in the broader sense of insulting any important person or institution. Since the Gospels were written in Greek, this might explain the high priest's accusation. In some cases, such blasphemy was a punishable offense. (Brown, *Death of the Messiah*, 1:522).

152 The Catholic Study Bible, RG 433. Italics and underlining added.

listened to his Temple teachings, and the Temple authorities were afraid to touch him for fear of causing a riot among the people.

So the crowd before Pilate was very atypical. In fact, it was the *only* physically threatening Jewish crowd in the entire Synoptics (except in Luke's Nazareth story). Instead of rioting against Jesus' arrest as originally feared, this crowd frightened Pilate into fearing a riot if Jesus was released! Since the Gospels never describe this crowd—not even its size, which may have been quite small—one can only speculate about its aberrant behavior. The Gospel passage above provides one explanation: that the chief priests and their allies "persuaded the crowds to ask for Barabbas" (Mt 27:20). The Sadducees certainly had the power to do so. They were the wealthiest and most powerful elite in Palestine (along with the Herodian family). It might have been easy to persuade commoners with bribes or threats, especially since most of them may never have heard of Jesus of Nazareth. This was Jesus' first trip to Jerusalem during his ministry, and he may well have been unknown to the vast number of pilgrims from outside of Galilee.

However, two other possibilities are worth consideration. One is immediately suggested by the fact that this crowd assembled quite early (apparently between 6 and 8 AM) the morning after the Passover seder. But for these pilgrims, the seder, which had begun only after sunset, was probably the most joyous, celebratory meal of the entire year. According to Josephus, the scene was unforgettable: Jerusalem, Palestine's largest city, with a permanent population of twenty-five thousand, was now swollen by an additional one hundred thousand pilgrims or more, scattered among innumerable houses and campsites. These pilgrims, many of whom had traveled days to reach Jerusalem, were happily consuming their feast of meat and other delicacies, surrounded by the festive hubbub of multitudes of celebrants from both Palestine and surrounding nations. This carnival-like celebration must have continued late into the night. So who would be motivated enough to arise early the following morning for the prisoner-release? The obvious answer: people intent on saving a favored prisoner.

But few Jesus supporters would have been expected to come, and indeed not one was present. In the first place, considering how quickly the panicked Disciples fled during Jesus' arrest, they and everyone who heard their tale were probably in a state of shock. Despite Jesus' thrice-told prophecy, the Disciples never expected such a calamity. They may even have begun questioning whether Jesus was the Messiah they had imagined. Moreover, they could hardly have guessed that Jesus would be before Pilate the very next morning. He had been arrested only the previous night. Who could have imagined that in the middle of the hectic Passover, he would have already been tried, convicted, and awaiting execution the very next morning?[153]

Barabbas' advocates, conversely, might have been there in force. Any anti-Roman activist was likely to command considerable sympathy among the nationalistic masses. And having been arrested a few weeks previously, he was likely to have already been tried, sentenced, and be present for the event. Furthermore, he would have benefited from other supporters: the Sadducees, who were the *only* people who actually knew that Jesus would be present. They would have had more than enough time to guarantee the outcome by packing the crowd with people who were partisans of Barabbas, or those who had never heard of Jesus. In short, the atypical crowd before Pilate may simply have been a selective group intent on freeing Barabbas and/or condemning Jesus.

The second possibility is that there was *no* Jewish "crowd" at all, but only a group of *the high priest's associates*. This speculation is prompted by Luke's failure to mention any Passover prisoner-release custom. According to Luke, the Sanhedrin trial occurred the morning after Jesus' arrest, rather than that evening. "When day came, the assembly of the elders of the people, both chief priests and scribes ... brought him to their council [presumably the Sanhedrin] (Lk 22:66)." After declaring him guilty:

> The *assembly rose as a body* and brought Jesus before Pilate.
> They began to accuse him, saying ... "We found this man ...
> saying that he himself is the Messiah, a king."
> Then Pilate asked him, "Are you the king of the Jews?" He answered,
> "You say so." Then Pilate said to the *chief priests and the crowds*, "I
> find no basis for an accusation against this man."
> (Lk 23:1–4; italics and brackets added)

Thus, these "crowds" were not a new group of people coming for a prisoner-release custom—which is unmentioned in Luke's—but rather the *very same Sanhedrin members who had already condemned Jesus*. Luke's narrative continues by stating that Pilate learned, seconds later, that Jesus was a Galilean. He therefore

---

153 In theory, Peter might have guessed, for after fleeing the arrest, he stopped and watched the arresting mob lead Jesus into the Sanhedrin building. Peter remained outside the building until the second "cock-crow." This would have occurred sometime between 12 and 4 AM (depending on whether the cock-crow referred to roosters, or to the "cock-crow" horn signals of Jerusalem's night watchmen [Brown, *Death of the Messiah*, 1:606]). However, Peter appears to have then gone into hiding until after the resurrection.

immediately sent Jesus for a new trial with Herod Antipas (Galilee's ruler), who was also in Jerusalem for Passover. When Herod returned Jesus to Pilate with an "innocent" verdict, Pilate immediately called together "the chief priest, the rulers, and the people" (Lk 23:13) to inform them of the verdict. Since this new session was merely a *continuation of Pilate's initial private meeting with the Sanhedrin* (to convey his verdict), the "people" must have been, once again, the Sanhedrin itself.

Luke's "minority view" may seem a weak reed with which to challenge the other Synoptic accounts, but is powerfully supported by the historical record. The CSB notes that "outside the gospels there is no direct attestation" of a Passover prisoner release custom.[154] This is an understatement. Generations of historians have failed to find unambiguous evidence of *any* prisoner-release custom, at *any* festival or other scheduled time, at any time in Palestine. For example, there is no mention of this custom in the detailed hour-by-hour description of the Passover Festival provided by Josephus, who was a member of a priestly Jerusalem family. Likewise, such a custom has never been unearthed from the ancient Greek world (which controlled Palestine from 332 to 167 BCE) or the Roman Empire (which controlled Palestine from 63 BCE on).[155] There were numerous instances of one-time amnesties, prisoner exchanges, and so on. But no annual prisoner-releases have ever been documented anywhere in or near Palestine, for centuries before or after this period. Thus, whether or not Luke's details are all accurate, the key point is that if there was no Passover prisoner-release, *a Jewish crowd calling for Jesus' crucifixion never existed.* Although most Christians will undoubtedly continue to believe in the Jewish crowd scene, the evidence of Luke and later historians raises the real possibility that this episode was a fabrication.[156]

---

154 The Catholic Study Bible, 61.

155 Brown, *The Death of the Messiah*, 1:814–20.

156 Some later scribes inserted a prisoner-release verse into their manuscripts of Luke's Gospel in order to "harmonize" his account with the other Synoptics, but modern Bibles omit this inauthentic addition (The Catholic Study Bible, 142). Incidentally, another provocative detail that casts doubt on the historicity of the story of Jesus and Barabbas is that Matthew states that the latter's full name was Jesus Barabbas (Mt 27:13). The Hebrew/Aramaic translation of Jesus Barabbas is "Jesus, son of the father/Father". It seems to be an extraordinary coincidence that the two prisoners in the courtyard were Jesus, son/Son of God (as some considered him), and Jesus, son of the Father/father.

The Romans

Pontius Pilate is portrayed in all Gospels as a sympathetic man forced against his will to send Jesus to his death. But several aspects of his behavior seem difficult to explain. One is that every Synoptic states that when Jesus refused to explicitly answer Pilate's question about whether he was the King of the Jews, Pilate immediately declared him innocent. The Roman legal system did not typically release suspects who refused to cooperate. Torture was more the norm. Additionally, Pilate's fright at the crowd's anger (in Mark's and Matthew's Gospels) rings false, for this event transpired in the "governor's headquarters" (Mk 15:16, Mt 27:27), which must have been either the Roman's Antonia Fortress or the fortress palace built by Herod the Great.[157] Both fortresses were too thick with Roman soldiers for Pilate to feel intimidated by an unarmed Jewish crowd.

The final oddity is more fundamental: how could Pilate be unconcerned with Jesus' (assumed) claim to be the Messiah, King of the Jews? Rome's unprecedented imperial success rested on its remarkable ability to retain control over its vassal nations. In the Roman Empire, the most serious of all crimes was sedition against the state. If Jesus represented a threat to the Sadducees, the civic pillars of Roman domination, he threatened Rome as well. As the Sadducees told Pontius Pilate, "He stirs up the people by teaching throughout all Judea, from Galilee where he began even to this place" (Lk 23:5).[158]

But the Romans didn't need to be warned about the potential danger of charismatic Jews. Having been involved in Palestine's affairs for nearly a century, they knew they were dealing with the nation that had mounted the only religious revolt in world history, the Maccabean Revolt. Just twenty years previously, they had had to crush Judah of Galilee's "No king but God!" insurrection. And Pilate certainly understood the meaning—and threat—of the title "Messiah." We have seen that when the chief priests brought Jesus before Pilate with the charge that he claimed to be Messiah, Pilate's first question to Jesus was, "Are you the king of the Jews?" Pilate had ruled Judea long enough to know that anyone claiming to be Messiah was also claiming to be the temporal king. This was a direct political challenge. In its discussion of the terms "Messiah" and "King of the Jews," the CSB remarks that "The normal political connotation of both titles would be of

---

157 Brown, *The Death of the Messiah*, 1:706.

158 Two Synoptics try to explain Pilate's willingness to release Jesus by stating that he "realized that it was out of jealousy that they [the Sadducees] had handed him over" (Mt 27:18). But the Sadducees would have been jealous of Jesus only if they believed he was more popular with the masses than they were; i.e., that he was a challenge to their control. If Jesus really threatened the Sadducees, whom Pilate relied upon to maintain order, Pilate's own control would also be at risk.

concern to the Roman governor."[159] In fact, "The residence of the Roman governor [Pilate] … was at Caesarea Maritima on the Mediterranean coast, but he went to Jerusalem during the great feasts, when the influx of pilgrims posed the danger of a nationalistic riot."[160] The Romans' Antonia Fortress towered above the Temple, and Roman soldiers patrolled the Temple's portico roofs during Festivals. And Passover was the most dangerous festival of all, for it celebrated the Israelites' attainment of sovereignty by overthrowing their foreign master (Egypt). Indeed, revolutionaries had apparently been active very recently, for Barabbas himself, and some fellow rebels, had been imprisoned shortly before for committing murder during an insurrection (Mk 15:7).[161]

Another recent reminder of the potential danger of Jewish charismatics was John the Baptist. John had been beheaded by Herod Antipas, ruler of Galilee, one or two years before Jesus' trial. The Synoptics state that Herod's anger was stoked by John's criticism of his illicit marriage and other misdeeds. But the historian Josephus provided additional insight, by writing, "When … the crowds around him [the Baptist] … were aroused to the highest degree by his sermons, Herod became alarmed. Eloquence that had so great an effect on mankind might lead to some form of revolt, for it looked as if they would be guided by John in everything they did. Herod decided therefore that it would be preferable to strike first and get rid of him before his work led to an uprising." [162]

If Herod thought it wisest to kill someone who might *potentially* incite a revolt, what would he or Pilate think of Jesus, who was so remarkably similar?

- Jesus had come to John to be baptized. He probably stayed with John for some time, for it was the Baptist who taught Jesus the Lord's Prayer (Lk 11:1–4). Jesus also seems to have learned his "gospel" from John, because Jesus' gospel ("Repent, for the kingdom of heaven has come near" [Mt 4:17]) was word-for-word identical with John's (Mt 3:2). Moreover, it was John's arrest that somehow triggered Jesus' own ministry, as if Jesus felt that John's mantle was now on him: "When Jesus heard that John had been arrested, he withdrew to Galilee … [and] from that time on, Jesus began to preach" (Mt 4:12, 17, brackets added).

---

159 The Catholic Study Bible, 61.

160 Ibid., 62, brackets added.

161 The Synoptics don't pinpoint the date of Barabbas' arrest, but inasmuch as Roman prisons were typically used for prisoners' short-term detention (until their trial and punishment), rather than for long-term incarceration, the rebellion must have been recent.

162 Josephus, *Antiquities*, 18:117–19, brackets added.

- Jesus was believed by many Jews and by Herod Antipas to be the reincarnation of John the Baptist (i.e., John resurrected in Jesus' body), as earlier noted.

- Jesus was as fearless as John in attacking powerful leaders capable of wreaking vengeance, albeit only in his last few days, in Jerusalem. (Luke's Gospel also claims that Jesus left Galilee partly to escape Herod Antipas' wrath, although the cause of Herod's anger is not explained. Interestingly, Jesus was warned of his danger by friendly Pharisees [Lk 13:31–33]).

Thus, there is good reason to think that Jesus would have been perceived by any Roman ruler as a potential revolutionary, just like John the Baptist. And Pilate's perception was presumably reinforced by his local network of spies and informants. We have heard about Jesus' clamorous reception upon entering Jerusalem. One Gospel even states that the crowd was so passionate that some Pharisees warned Jesus to "order your disciples to stop" (Lk 20:39), out of concern, according to the CSB, that the Roman authorities might "interpret the acclamation of Jesus as king as an uprising against them."[163] According to Luke, even his Disciples expected him to seize power, for in Acts of the Apostles, their very first words to the risen Jesus were, "Lord, is this the time you are going to restore the kingdom of Israel?" (Acts 1:6).

If Pontius Pilate had even a shred of concern about any of this, he would have acted forcefully. It was his imperial duty to maintain order and control, and he did not flinch from brutality. One Synoptic notes that during Jesus' journey to Jerusalem, he learned that Pilate had slaughtered some Galileans during their prayers (Lk 13:1). The CSB comments that "The slaughter of the Galileans by Pilate is unknown outside Luke; but from what is known about Pilate from the Jewish historian, Josephus, such a slaughter would be in keeping with the character of Pilate. Josephus reports that Pilate had disrupted a religious gathering of Samaritans on Mt. Gerizim with a slaughter of the participants ... and on another occasion Pilate had killed many Jews who had opposed him when he appropriated money from the temple treasury to build an aqueduct in Jerusalem."[164] Indeed, Pilate was recalled to Rome in 36 CE to answer charges of excessive brutality, and never returned. But his departure did not end Rome's policy of preemptive strikes against charismatic leaders. In c. 45 CE, the "prophet" Theudas was beheaded and his followers killed as he led them to the Jordan River to prove he

163 The Catholic Study Bible, 135.
164 Ibid., 125.

could miraculously part the river's waters. A decade later, the "Egyptian" (a Jewish "prophet" from Egypt) led the masses to the Mount of Olives, so they could watch him command Jerusalem's walls to collapse. Roman cavalry slaughtered many in the crowd, though the Egyptian managed to escape.

Thus, Pilate must have considered Jesus a potential revolutionary when Jesus refused to deny that he was the Messiah, King of Israel. That would explain also the choice of crucifixion, which was reserved primarily for political dissidents. Crucifixion was the most public, humiliating, ghastly way to die, and so fit the most serious of all crimes, sedition. The two men crucified alongside of Jesus were revolutionaries, as was Barabbas. And the specific charge against revolutionaries was always inscribed above the cross: in this case, "King of the Jews."

It is in fact the consensus of almost all modern historians that Jesus was crucified by Pilate as a potential revolutionary.[165] Why would the Gospels wish to

---

165 This conclusion demands a reconsideration of the Sadducees' guilt in Jesus' death. The Romans were in Palestine to stay, and they found it easiest to work through local collaborators. Despite the Jews' understandable distaste for the Sadducees' collaboration, it actually benefited everyone. The high priest's three thousand-strong Jewish Temple Guard could maintain order in Jerusalem and Judea with far less bloodshed than Pilate's Roman Legion (Sanders, *The Historical Figure of Jesus*, 23). Caiaphas and Pilate apparently worked well together, for they served unusually long and overlapping periods (18–36 CE and 26–36 CE, respectively), and kept Judea relatively peaceful. (Interestingly, Pilate was recalled to Rome for brutality in the very same year that Caiaphas stepped down.) Caiaphas' longevity was presumably due in part to his ability to nip problems in the bud before the Roman Legion was called from its barracks. It is therefore quite possible that Caiaphas had few personal concerns about Jesus, but feared that failure to act on his part might induce the Romans to intervene directly. Even scholars who use John's Gospel very sparingly believe there may be political truth in this passage:

> The chief priests … called a meeting of the council and said, "What are we
> to do? This man is performing many signs. If we let him go on like this,
> everyone will believe in him, and the Romans will come and destroy both
> our holy place and our nation." But … Caiaphas, who was high priest …
> said … "You know nothing at all! You do not understand that it is better … to have
> one man die for the people than to have the whole nation destroyed."
> … So from that day on they planned to put him to death." (Jn 11:47–53)

The importance of the Sadducean buffer is demonstrated by the fact that the catalyst for the First Jewish Revolt was the high priest's decision to halt sacrifices to the Roman Emperor in 62 CE, to protest the brutality of post-Pilate procurators. Once the traditional buffer was removed, and the Romans unleashed their own soldiers

conceal this fact? As the CSB's commentary on Luke states, "The Passion Narrative is *not a report of what happened*, but a narrative shaped by the conviction that Jesus was the suffering servant.... Luke is concerned with presenting Christianity as a *legitimate form of worship in the Roman world*. To this end, Luke depicts the Roman governor Pilate declaring Jesus innocent of any wrongdoing three times. At the same time Luke argues ... that Christianity is ... deserving of ... toleration and freedom ... by Rome."[166] The same argument applies to the other Evangelists too. Although they were purportedly describing Jesus' early-first-century life, their Gospels were written after the Jerusalem Mother Synagogue's destruction in the First Jewish Revolt. By this time, most Christians lived in Gentile congregations in Syria, Turkey, Greece, Rome, and so on. They were few in number—probably only several thousand adherents (see chapter 3 footnote)—and desperately wished to avoid persecution by local Roman authorities. Any Gospel admission that their leader/founder had been executed for sedition in Palestine would have been suicidal. It was far safer to lay the blame on the Sadducees (who no longer existed in the Evangelists' day) and Jews generally (who were scattered and demoralized by their homeland's destruction). Blaming the Jews also helped the early Christian Church explain why the Jews had refused to accept Jesus—they had been too evil and too blind to understand who Jesus was.

Postscript: Was Jesus an Actual Revolutionary?

Pontius Pilate must have considered Jesus a potential revolutionary, because Jewish tradition expected the Messiah to destroy all foreign occupiers. But was Jesus really an insurrectionist? During the 1960s and 1970s, "Liberation Theology"—the notion that oppressed people were justified in overthrowing their governments, because Jesus himself had been a revolutionary—became widely popular in Latin America and the Third World.

The Gospels certainly portray Jesus as a purely spiritual/ethical figure (which is why John the Baptist doubted his identity). But is it possible that Jesus was actually a rebel whose political/military goals were bowdlerized by Evangelists fearing a Roman backlash? It is impossible to guess, but if he was, the Evangelists were pretty thorough in eliminating the evidence. However, a few scattered "clues"

---

to maintain order, the momentum towards a final confrontation was unstoppable. Thus, the Sadducees played a useful, if distasteful, role. It is possible that much of their current black image stems from their failure to write any literature of their own. They are therefore known entirely through the hostile writings of the Evangelists, Josephus, and the pro-Pharisaic sage/rabbis of the Mishnah.

166 The Catholic Study Bible, RG 433, 95.

remain. One of Jesus' Disciples was Simon the Zealot (also called the Cananean, which is a transliteration of the Greek word for Zealot). Simon's words or actions are never mentioned, but the Zealots were bloodthirsty anti-Roman insurrectionists. When Jesus asked the armed mob that arrested him in Jerusalem why they were treating him like a "bandit" (Mk 14:48), his word "bandit" is more accurately translated as "revolutionary." Also, one of the "trap questions" Jesus was asked in Jerusalem was whether Jews should pay taxes to the Romans ("render unto Caesar what belongs to Caesar"). The authorities might not have asked that question unless they thought he was rebellious, because, according to the CSB, they hoped "to force Jesus to take sides on one of the sensitive political issues of first-century Palestine. The issue of nonpayment of taxes to Rome becomes one of the focal points of the First Jewish Revolt [66–70 CE] that resulted in the Roman destruction of Jerusalem and the temple."[167]

The most provocative bit of evidence is a speech from the early post-Jesus years, recorded in Acts. Gamaliel, a highly respected Pharisee,[168] saved Peter's life during a Sanhedrin debate about whether to kill him, by cautioning the assembly against hasty action:

> "For some time ago Theudas rose up, claiming to be somebody, and a number of men, about four hundred, joined him, but he was killed, and all who followed him were dispersed and disappeared. After him came Judas the Galilean.[169] ... He also perished, and all who followed him were scattered. So in the present case, I tell you, keep away from these men, and let them alone; because if this ... undertaking is of human origin, it will fail." (Acts 5:35–38)

Overall, however, the case for Jesus as an insurrectionist is weak.

---

167 Ibid., 136

168 Identified in Acts as Paul's early teacher, although Paul's Letters make no such claim. (He is called Gamaliel the Elder in the Mishnah.)

169 Judas the Galilean in fact preceded Theudas by half a century.

CHAPTER 14

JESUS' END, PART II: THE RESURRECTION

All the Synoptic Gospels agree on the early post-resurrection events. Jesus' corpse was removed from the cross and laid in an empty rock-hewn tomb by Joseph of Arimathea, who is variously described as a compassionate Jew or a disciple of Jesus. Joseph sealed the tomb with a heavy rock. Following him to the tomb were several women who had watched the crucifixion from afar, including a woman Jesus had healed in Galilee, named Mary Magdalene.[170] The women quickly returned home because of the approaching Sabbath, for they wanted to rest, "according to the commandment" (Lk 25:56). The Gospels begin diverging after the women returned, and so merit separate treatment.

Mark
The returning women were surprised to find the stone rolled away, and upon entering the tomb:

---

170 Despite her prominence in *The Da Vinci Code*, this is the sum total of Synoptic information about Mary Magdalene, other than the fact that she had contributed to Jesus' support in Galilee, possibly in gratitude for her cure.

Parenthetically, one woman absent from Jesus' tomb was his own mother, Mary. Chapter 5 noted that after Jesus' departure from Nazareth, no one in his family seems to have bothered to ever see him again. This may have distressed Luke, because Luke states in his Acts of the Apostles that Jesus' family was actually in Jerusalem during Jesus' last week, lodging with the Disciples. Luke did not try to explain why, if this was the case, they failed to attend Jesus' teachings, Last Supper, trial, crucifixion, and resurrection.

> They saw a young man ... dressed in
> a white robe ... and they were alarmed. But he said to them,
> "Do not be alarmed! You are seeking Jesus of Nazareth, who was crucified.
> He has been raised; he is not here.... But go; tell his disciples and Peter that
> he is going ahead of you to Galilee;
> there you will see him, just as he told you." So they went out and fled from
> the tomb, for terror and amazement had seized them; and they said nothing
> to anyone, for they were afraid. (Mk 16: 5–8)

This *concludes* the Gospel of Mark, on an astonishing note: there is no true resurrection scene, because *Jesus never reappears.* The young man's statement that "He [Jesus] is going before you to Galilee" is not proof of a resurrection, especially as he never claimed to have witnessed Jesus' rising. The CSB admits: "What precise meeting with Jesus does Mark have in mind—resurrection appearances? Or the final meeting with the Risen Christ at the end of the world [i.e., at the Parousia (Second Coming)]? Or does he mean that the Risen Christ would be with his disciples as they take up their mission? Mark leaves the question unanswered." Interestingly, many modern Christians are probably unaware of the absence of a resurrection story. This is because all modern Bibles contain a resurrection scene (actually two, the "Short" and "Long" Endings) which anonymous scribes later appended to the Gospel. But the CSB, speaking of the more important Long End (twelve verses, compared to only one for the Short Ending), agrees that "an author later than Mark added [this] ending." The New Revised Standard Bible concurs that the Longer Ending "cannot have been part of the original text.... [it] may have been compiled early in the second century as a didactic summary of grounds for belief in Jesus' resurrection."[171]

This omission is arguably the greatest of all Synoptic enigmas, because the resurrection is Christianity's core event, more important than anything Jesus did during life. (Its equivalent in Judaism is the Exodus, including God's appearance on Mount Sinai.) Many scholars believe that the Gospel's concluding page(s) was simply lost. However, the CSB disagrees, saying, "This story of the empty tomb was probably the original conclusion to Mark's story."[172] No rationale for this conclusion is provided, but some reasons seem apparent. First, every "uncorrupted" early manuscript ends at this point. Second, Mark was no hermit hiding in a

---

171 The Catholic Study Bible, RG 416, brackets added; New Oxford Annotated Bible, 74NT. A fuller, more academic discussion of this matter can be found in Bruce Metzger and Bart Ehrman, *The Text of the New Testament* (New York: Oxford University Press, 2005).

172 The Catholic Study Bible, RG 416.

Judean cave. He was an educated man with access to money and goods, because composing and completing such a lengthy document would have required large amounts of expensive papyrus (paper did not yet exist), and probably scribal assistance. Further, any man so religiously committed presumably lived among other Christians, who would have known of his effort to compose the first ever story of their leader. His community presence is also indicated by the speed with which copies of his Gospels began circulating, to Matthew, Luke, and many others. Hence, if Mark had still been alive when the last page disappeared, he would have rewritten it. But even if he was dead or incapacitated, its loss would probably have been quickly noted by others, who would have recreated it from memory as best they could. After all, Mark's Gospel was not composed to achieve personal fame, but as a faith-document to disseminate his new religion.[173] Mark's co-religionists should therefore have had little compunction about adding the story's necessary climax. Finally, it is not obvious how the Gospel's last page could have been lost in the first place, because the original Gospel was almost certainly a scroll. (The book ["codex"] was not yet in use.) Whereas a *book's* last page can easily tear off, a *scroll's* last "page" is generally on the inside, protected by the manuscript's full thickness.

In short, the resurrection story was far too important to have accidentally disappeared for decades. So is it possible that the reason for the omission was that Mark had never heard about any resurrection? Shocking as this sounds, the fact is that no mention of Jesus' physical resurrection can be found in the two pre-Marcan sources in the New Testament: the Q-source and Paul's Letters. The absence of post-resurrection sayings or stories from the Q-source is noteworthy. If its compilers knew of a resurrection, it is difficult to imagine why they would have ignored Jesus' triumphant sayings to his Disciples. The situation with Paul is different. For him, the resurrection was the unquestioned centerpiece of his Letters. But we shall see that his Letters seem to imply that the resurrection had been *visionary*, rather than physical. Thus, amazingly enough, the first explicit testimony about Jesus' physical resurrection appeared a full fifty years after his death, in the Gospels of Matthew and Luke.

But if Mark was unaware of a resurrection, what could explain his bizarre ending? Or the apparent contradiction of a Gospel containing Jesus' thrice-told prophecy of his death and resurrection, but no resurrection scene? A speculative though ingenious explanation has in fact been suggested, based on three of this Gospel's most striking aspects: its date of composition, its portrayal of the Disciples' deep

---

173 Neither Mark nor the other Evangelists even included their names on their Gospels. Instead, the early Church named them for the men who were (erroneously) believed to be their authors.

befuddlement, and its near-frenetic depiction of Jesus' attempt to complete his mission before the apocalypse. The hypothesis is as follows: Perhaps, after Jesus' death, his tomb was found to be empty, but he himself was never seen. Many of Jesus' distraught followers might have abandoned the sect, while some remained faithful. But it is a historical fact that apocalyptic fever gripped Jews throughout the turbulent 60s CE, peaking during the final years of the First Jewish Revolt, when Jerusalem was besieged and assaulted. Surely God would rescue his people and Temple by crushing the Romans and introducing the Kingdom! Many Judeo-Christians and also some Christians shared in this expectation. Mark may have been such a man. Perhaps this explains what compelled him to write his Gospel precisely at this moment (c. 70 CE): to warn Christians to urgently prepare *now* for Jesus' resurrection, and the apocalypse. This explains, to proponents of this hypothesis, Mark's depiction of the breathless Jesus and the equally breathless fleeing women. No time remained; every Jesus-follower must immediately prepare with the same urgency as the Messiah himself, and of the terrified women who fled at the first sign of his rising. As for Jesus' thrice-told prophecy, perhaps the earlier expectations of an immediate resurrection had been misplaced. According to Mark's Gospel, the Disciples never really comprehended Jesus, and certainly not this specific prophecy (as the Gospel explicitly states). So perhaps Jesus had indeed forecast his return, but *this* was when he was coming.

Luke

This Gospel is far more elaborate than Mark's. When the women entered the tomb, surprised at the stone's removal, they encountered two men in "dazzling" clothes, who said: "Why do you look for the living one among the dead? He is not here, but has risen" (Luke 24:4–5). The women now rushed excitedly to the Disciples, who refused to believe their story until Peter examined the empty tomb himself. Later that day, Jesus appeared to the Disciples, saying:

> "These are my words that I spoke to you while I was still with you—that everything written about me in the law of Moses, the prophets, and the psalms must be fulfilled…. that the Messiah is to suffer and rise from the dead on the third day,[174] and that repentance and the forgiveness of sins is to be proclaimed in his name to all nations, beginning from Jerusalem…." While he was blessing them, he withdrew from them and was carried up to heaven. They … returned to Jerusalem with great joy; and were continually in the temple blessing God. (Lk 24:44–53)

---

174 The Tanakh contains no such prophecy.

And the Gospel of Luke ends there, with Jesus ascending to heaven. So Jesus definitely reappeared in this account, in Jerusalem, for one day.[175] Of special importance, the passage discloses that Jesus *provided no new teachings about Judaism* to his Disciples, and abrogated no laws. His statement about preaching "to all nations" would have referred to the traditional Jewish idea of being a light unto the nations (chapter 9). After all, the Disciples' "continual presence in the Temple" following the Ascension (above) confirmed yet again their continuing Jewishness, as Luke reaffirmed in his later Acts of the Apostles.

Matthew

This version is also longer than Mark's, and introduces an additional subplot. Before the women returned to the tomb, the Jewish authorities urged Pilate to post guards at Jesus' tomb, for fear that the Disciples would steal the body and claim it had been resurrected (Mt 27:62–65). Pilate complied. When the women returned to the tomb after the Sabbath, they were startled by a great earthquake:

> For an angel of the Lord ... came and rolled
> back the stone and sat on it.... The guards shook and became like dead men.
> But the angel said to the women, "Do not be afraid; I know that you are looking
> for Jesus who was crucified.
> He is not here; for he has been raised ... tell his disciples
> 'he is going ahead of you to Galilee; there you will see him.'" (Mt 28:2–7)

As the woman dashed joyously off, Jesus abruptly appeared to them to confirm that he would meet the Disciples in Galilee. Meanwhile, when the chief priests learned of this miracle, they bribed the guards to say that the Disciples had stolen the body away at night. In his own voice, Matthew adds, "And this story is still told among the Jews to this day" (Mt 28:15). Later, when the Disciples were assembled on a mountaintop in Galilee:

> Jesus approached and said to them, "All authority in heaven
> and on earth has been given to me. Go, therefore, and make
> disciples of all nations, baptizing them in the name of the Father
> and of the Son, and of the Holy Spirit, and teaching them to obey
> everything that I have commanded you. And remember, I am with
> you always, to the end of the age." (Mt 28: 18–20)

---

175 In Luke's Acts, he remained forty days. Luke presumably wished to use a time span associated with momentous biblical events ("forty days and nights").

Thus ends the Gospel of Matthew. The resurrection description differs from Luke's in many details. But *Matthew concurs with Luke that Jesus did not modify or abrogate the Law.* (Jesus' claim of "all authority" does not imply that this authority involved overturning Judaism, as underlined by the fact that Matthew's entire Gospel adheres more closely to the Torah than any of the other Synoptics.) Instead, the major novelty here is the highly Christological reference to the Trinity: the Father, the Son, and the Holy Spirit. Because this is the only such formulation in the Synoptics, the Catholic Church questions whether Jesus actually said this, for "it may have been the baptismal formula of Matthew's Church" in the late first century.[176] A late date is supported by the fact that this Trinitarian formulation is not found in any other Christian literature until the early-second-century Didache, a church-conduct manual.[177] The verse about "all authority" being given to Jesus may also be of post-Jesus origin.

***

What do these stories tell us? Beginning with the similarities, they all agree that Jesus was buried in a rock tomb sealed by a stone movable by one man. By the time the women returned, the body was gone—i.e., no one actually witnessed the resurrection of a corpse. The absence of witnesses reflects the fact no one expected Jesus' return, in accordance with the Disciples' inability to comprehend Jesus' prophecy. Finally, the two Gospels with resurrection stories record that Jesus appeared only to his Disciples (and a few commoners), for less than a day. During that brief time, he neither nullified nor modified the Mosaic Law. This is again consistent with Acts.

Beyond that, events become hazy. They become murkier still if the earliest of all resurrection accounts is considered: Paul's, in his First Letter to the Corinthians (c. 56). Despite its extreme brevity, scholars attach great weight to Paul's words. Paul's Letters are not only the earliest writings in the New Testament, but they appear to be quite accurate in describing historical events. According to Paul:

---

176 The Catholic Study Bible, 65.

177 Vermes, *The Authentic Gospel of Jesus*, 333. Recall too that all surviving manuscripts of the Synoptics are copies from the third and fourth century CE, making it impossible to date this phrase. It also bears mention that despite its Trinitarian ring, Matthew's verse neither states that the Father, the Son, and Holy Spirit are identical, nor that the Son/son (Jesus) is divine. Christianity's current formulation of the Trinity was developed only in the fourth century (chapter 17).

[Jesus] ... was buried ... and was raised on the third day ... [and] ...
appeared to Cephas [Peter], then to the Twelve. Then he appeared to
more than five hundred brothers and sisters
at one time.... Then he appeared to James, then to all the apostles. Last of all ...
he appeared also to me. (1 Cor 15:4–8, brackets added)

What is immediately striking is that Paul reports not only Jesus' appearance to
the Disciples, but also to the "five hundred" and "all the apostles" (including him).
These last appearances must have occurred months or years after Jesus' death, inasmuch as Jesus' only companions in the Synoptics were the twelve Disciples. (Other
than the Disciples, Jesus appears to have been occasionally accompanied by some
women, and, in Luke's Gospel's only, briefly by seventy other disciples.) Since the
Synoptics indicate that Jesus was never accompanied by more than perhaps one
hundred people at any time, who were the "five hundred" and the apostles? The
most likely answer is that they were the members of the Mother Synagogue, who
quickly numbered into the hundreds, according to Acts. If so, Jesus' appearance
to these people must have been *visionary*, since his physical presence lasted less
than a day, according to Matthew's and Luke's Gospels. Since Paul's account above
uses the same Greek word for "appeared" in every case, despite the availability of
Greek synonyms, was he implying that *all* the appearances, even to the Disciples,
were also visions? We cannot know,[178] but one additional detail may suggest that
he was. Paul states that Jesus appeared to "the Twelve," yet only eleven Disciples

---

178 Some scholars argue that Paul did believe in Jesus' physical resurrection, based on
his description of how the *human* dead would be resurrected on the Day of the
Lord. Paul declared that the dead would shuck their "earthly, physical" bodies for
new "heavenly, spiritual" bodies that would be imperishable (1 Cor 15:35–54). Some
scholars interpret "spiritual bodies" as being physical (albeit pure and indestructible),
and extrapolate from this that Paul likewise believed Jesus' resurrection had been
corporeal. However, Paul never stated whether "spiritual bodies" were physical or
not. In any case, Paul was describing the resurrection of ordinary humans, not Jesus.
In sum, Paul certainly believed in a celestial Jesus (such as he saw in his vision), but
there is no explicit evidence that he believed in, or had ever heard of, Jesus' physical
resurrection.

(Actually it can be argued that Paul's description of human resurrection makes it
unlikely that he thought Jesus' could have been similar. As noted above, Paul believed
that resurrection would elevate humans from a "base" form [physical body] to a higher
one [spiritual body]. But Paul taught that Jesus had originally been *divine* before his
brief earthly appearance. Hence, it seems contradictory to imagine that Paul would
expect God's Own Son to be resurrected into a *less* exalted [i.e., corporeal] form.)

remained following Judas' desertion. According to Acts, a replacement twelfth Disciple was chosen only later, in the early days of the Mother Synagogue.

***

This welter of information is summarized in Tables I and II. The first Table summarizes the full resurrection stories. It is immediately apparent that the Synoptics' details are consistent up to the end of Mark's Gospel. This suggests that Matthew and Luke were, as usual, following Mark's template. As soon as they reached the end of this template, however, their stories immediately diverge. Recall that Matthew and Luke are the same Evangelists who appended Nativity stories to Mark's original Gospel (which contains none). Because they were working separately, their Nativity stories ended up being entirely different. Is it possible that, once again, these Evangelists felt compelled to append resurrection scenes on their own, once again with irreconcilable results?

In fact, two disturbing discrepancies stand out. One is nominally trivial, but profoundly troubling: *How could the Disciples have forgotten where they met Jesus?* In our own age, most people who were alive during President Kennedy's assassination can vividly recall, over forty years later, where they were when the news arrived. Yet the Gospels recount an infinitely more staggering even—the pivotal event in Christianity. And the earliest Gospel was written slightly less than forty years after this event, a shorter interval than between Kennedy's death and today. Yet consider the two alternative scenarios:

- Reunion in Galilee

  If the Disciples had met Jesus in Galilee, they would have had to walk several days from Jerusalem to return there, since walking was their only mode of transportation. But the journey would have been electric with joyous anticipation, for they would soon be reunited with their master, in their familiar homeland. Then, after their thrilling mountaintop reunion with Jesus, they would have had to walk back to Jerusalem to establish the Mother Synagogue. (That Jerusalem did become their home is confirmed not only by Luke [both in his Gospel and Acts], but also by Paul's Letters [which speak of the Jerusalem Mother Synagogue, but never of any Galilean congregations] and by Josephus [who recorded that Jesus' brother James was murdered in Jerusalem in c. 62 CE for his Judeo-Christian activities]).

TABLE 1: Summary of Post-Resurrection Narratives

	MARK*	MATTHEW	LUKE	PAUL
	Events discussed in Mark's Gospel			
Man placing body in tomb	Joseph of Arimathea	Joseph of Arimathea	Joseph of Arimathea	n/a
Nature of the tomb	Rock-hewn, with rock cover	Rock-hewn, with rock cover	Rock-hewn, with rock cover	n/a
Women visiting the tomb	Mary Magdalene and one other woman	Mary Magdalene and one other woman	Mary Magdalene and several other women	n/a
Figure within the tomb	Young man	Angel	Two men/ angels	n/a
	Events __following__ conclusion of Mark's Gospel			
Location of Jesus' appearance to Disciples	None, but predicted to be Galilee	Physical appearance on mountain in Galilee, for less than a day	Physical appearance in Jerusalem, for less than a day	Physical and/ or visionary appearances (locations unknown), over several years
Jesus' Appearances	n/a	To three women in Jerusalem, then the (eleven) Disciples in Galilee	To two disciples in Jerusalem; then the (eleven) Disciples and their colleagues in Jerusalem	To Peter; then to all twelve Disciples; then to the five hundred brothers; then to James; then all the apostles; finally to Paul

	MARK*	MATTHEW	LUKE	PAUL
Jesus' days on earth	n/a	One	One	Unclear
Jesus' sayings to Disciples	n/a	Says he has received all powers on heaven and earth; tells Disciples to preach to all nations	Convinces Disciples he is not a ghost by eating fish; convinces them that Tanakh foretold a resurrected Messiah; tells them to preach to all nations	Unknown; only Jesus' message to Paul himself is disclosed (in Acts, but not in Paul's own Letters.)

*Mark's Two Resurrection Endings:

(1) "Short Ending"—Women leave tomb and alert Disciples; afterwards, "Jesus himself, through them" begins proselytizing mission; (2) "Long Ending—Jesus appears to Mary Magdalene, who tells disbelieving Disciples. Jesus then appears to two Disciples (who cannot convince the others), and finally to all Eleven, rebuking their disbelief. Tells them to preach to "whole world," and says believers will be able to exorcize demons, speak in tongues, and be immune to poisons and snakes.

- Reunion in Jerusalem.

  If the Disciples had met Jesus in Jerusalem, it would have been after hiding out in Jerusalem for several days in shock and deep mourning. Their distress would have been redoubled by their presence in a huge (by their standards) semibarren hilltop city that was largely unfamiliar to them. They would have been (and were, according to Luke) so astounded by Jesus' abrupt appearance that they would not have believed their eyes at first. Based on Jesus' order, they would have remained thereafter in Jerusalem, far from their birthplace.

We should remember that there were eleven Disciples, enough to remind one another of details even if several Disciples' memories began fading. So how could they have forgotten where they met Jesus, while *perfectly* recalling many trivial facts? For example, none of the Disciples ever seems to have met Joseph of Arimathea (who removed Jesus from the cross), who is unmentioned anywhere else in the Synoptics. Is it possible that they remembered such a minor detail, without being able to recall their epiphanous reunion with Jesus?

The other puzzle is more fundamental: that Jesus' sayings to his Disciples are so brief and so different (Table 2, arranged in synoptic [side by side] fashion). In Matthew's Gospel, Jesus speaks a mere *three* verses. In comparison, this Gospel's Sermon on the Mount is thirty-five times longer. Even the pericope of the centurion with the dying slave contains more Jesus sayings. Luke's account is slightly longer, but is wholly divergent, with one exception: Jesus' command to missionize all nations. Considering that missionization had begun decades before the Evangelists wrote their Gospels, and that the Gospels were probably written in part to stimulate this enterprise yet further, this single point of consensus is hardly surprising. What is surprising is the extent of the differences. How could the Disciples have forgotten Jesus' words in the unforgettable hours of his return from the dead?

TABLE 2. Jesus' Complete Post-Resurrection Sayings[179]

MATTHEW (28:16–20)	LUKE (24:36–48)
When they [the Disciples, in Galilee]	When they [the Disciples, in Jerusalem] were talking …
saw him	Jesus himself stood among them and said to them, "Peace be with you." They were startled…. He said to them, "Why are you frightened, and why do
they worshiped him; but some doubted.	doubts arise in your hearts? Look at my hands and my feet; see that it is I myself. Touch me and see; for a ghost does not have flesh and bones as you see that I have." … While in their joy they were disbelieving … he said to them, "Have you anything here to eat?" They gave him a piece of boiled fish, and he … ate in their presence.
And Jesus … said to them, "All authority in heaven and on earth has been given to me.	Then he said to them,
	"These are my words that I spoke to you while I was still with you—that everything written about me in the law of Moses, the prophets, and the psalms must be fulfilled. Then he opened their minds to understand the scriptures, and he said to them, "Thus it is written, the Messiah is to suffer and to rise from the dead on the third day,[177] and that repentance and forgiveness of sins is to
Go therefore and make disciples of all nations, Baptizing them in the name of the Father and of the Son and of the Holy Spirit, and teaching them everything that I have commanded you. And remember, I am with you always, to the end of the age."	be proclaimed in his name to all nations,

179 No such prophecy exists in the Tanakh.

MATTHEW (28:16–20)	LUKE (24:36–48)
	beginning from Jerusalem. You are my witnesses of these things. And see, I am sending upon you what my Father promised; so stay here in the city until you have been clothed with power from on high."

In short, the New Testament accounts of the resurrection, as summarized in Tables I and II, are extremely difficult to reconcile. Agreement does exist on one fundamental point, however: whatever transpired after Jesus' death, it did not satisfy the Disciples or other Jesus followers. They were seeking something even more important, as the next chapter shows.

CHAPTER 15

AFTER THE ASCENSION—
THE WAIT FOR THE KINGDOM
OF GOD CONTINUES

As stupendous as Jesus' resurrection was to his early followers, they desired much more. The resurrection was only a sign; what they really yearned for was the *arrival of the Kingdom*. In Acts, the Disciples' first question to the resurrected Jesus was, "Lord, is this the time that you will restore the kingdom to Israel?" (Acts 1:6). The CSB notes that the Disciples' question "implies that ... they had expected him to ... restore self-rule to Israel during his ministry. When this had not taken place, they ask if it is to take place at this time."[180] Jesus demurred, but the countdown for the Parousia—the Second Coming, which Jesus followers were confident would herald the Kingdom—had begun.[181]

How could it be otherwise? The most cursory reading of the Synoptics shows that Jesus' core message—his gospel—was the imminence of the Kingdom. This was the subject of endless sayings, parables, and teachings, from the beginning to the end of his ministry. Conversely, the resurrection was first mentioned only in the middle of the ministry, only to his Disciples, and never disclosed publicly. Jesus crisscrossed Palestine to tell everyone to expect the Kingdom, *not* his resurrection (see chapter 18). Thus, if the latter had any real significance, it was only as a presage of the Kingdom's arrival into the world. *This* is what kept Jesus' followers tense with joyous expectation.

---

180 The Catholic Study Bible, 185.

181 The Synoptics themselves make no mention of a Parousia, and the Gospel of John states that Jesus would always remain in heaven.

As indicated by the Disciples' question, the countdown probably began immediately after Jesus' Ascension. This feverish anticipation was in fact the subject of the *very earliest* writing in the New Testament, Paul's First Letter to the Thessalonians (c. 51 CE). Paul had previously visited this Greek church and apparently convinced everyone that the Parousia was so close that they would all personally witness the Kingdom. But they became traumatized when some of their members died after his visit. Had the deceased lost their chance to enter the Kingdom? Had their religious devotion been in vain? This precipitated a great crisis. "*Paul and other early Christians believed that the Parousia ... was very near,*" states the CSB.[182] "The death of Christians before the second coming seemed to prove a problem for their faith.... Paul fears that the death ... will so shake the Thessalonians' faith that their grief will give way to doubt, discouragement, and even apostasy." So Paul consoled them by pledging that Jesus would soon return, and immediately resurrect the dead so they too would receive their reward:

> For since we believe that Jesus died and rose again, even so, through Jesus,
> God will bring with him
> those who have died.... The dead ... will rise first. Then we who are alive ...
> will be caught up[183] in the clouds together with them ... to meet the Lord....
> You yourselves know very well
> that the day of the Lord will come like a thief in the night.... So then, let us not
> fall asleep as others do, but let us keep awake. (1 Thes 4:14–17, 5:2–6)

Paul's anticipation of an imminent Parousia was reiterated in c. 56 CE, in his First Letter to the Corinthians (Greece). It was so imminent that making long-term earthly plans was foolish:

> Listen, I will tell you a mystery!
> We will not all die, but we will all be changed,
> in a moment, in the twinkling of an eye ... (1 Cor 15:51–52)
> I think ... it is well for you to remain as you are.
> Are you bound to a wife? Do not seek to be free.
> Are you free from a wife? Do not seek a wife ...
> I mean, brothers and sisters, the appointed time has grown short.... For the
> present form of this world is passing away. (1 Cor 7:26–31)

---

182 Ibid., RG 526 (original italics).

183 Literally, "snatched up." This Latin verb (*rapiemur*) is the origin of the Christian concept of the "rapture": that God will lift the righteous to heaven immediately before the apocalypse, to save them from its horrors.

As the CSB notes, "Paul expected that the *end was imminent.*"[184] But when it failed to materialize, the early Jesus followers became increasingly disquieted, especially when Paul, Peter, and James all died in c. 62–64 CE. During this period, the Thessalonians panicked anew when word arrived that Jesus *had* returned, but without appearing to them. The Second Letter to the Thessalonians (written by a disciple of Paul, in c. 62) reassured them that the Parousia had not come, and explained its temporary delay in obscure terms:

> As to the coming of our Lord Jesus Christ ... we beg you ... not to be
> quickly shaken in mind ["shaken out of your minds," in the CSB translation]
> or alarmed ... to the effect that the day of the Lord is
> already here ... for that day will not come unless the
> rebellion comes first and the lawless one is revealed,
> the one destined for destruction....
> [But it will soon come when] the one who now restrains it is removed.
> (2 Thes 2:1–8, brackets added)

The concern of the Jesus sect (and Jews) everywhere soared several years later, when Rome's destruction of the Jerusalem Temple in 70 CE failed to trigger the Day of the Lord. Surely God would not allow this abomination to go unpunished. As previously noted, many scholars believe that the Gospels began to appear at this time precisely to reassure bewildered believers that Jesus' prophecies had been correct, but that the apocalypse had been delayed to *their* lifetime.

Then in c. 95 CE appeared the New Testament apocalyptic book *par excellence*: Revelation ("The Revelation to John"). This book was written by an anonymous author claiming it recounted an angel's revelation to Jesus' Disciple, John. (According to Church tradition, John died in that same year, and was the last Disciple to die.) Revelation promised a very rapid Parousia:

> Blessed is the one who reads aloud the words of the prophecy,
> And blessed are those who hear and who keep what is written in it;
> for the time is near. (Rev 1:3)
> And he [the angel prophesying to John] said to me, "These words are trustworthy
> and true, and ... show ... what must soon take place. See, I am coming soon!" ...
> And he said to me, "Do not seal up the words of the prophecy of this book,
> for the time is near.... See, I am coming soon.... It is I, Jesus,
> that sent my angel to you with this testimony...."

---

184 The Catholic Study Bible, 523, italicization in original.

The Spirit and the bride say, "Come." And let everyone who hears say, "Come...."
The one who testifies to these things says, "Surely I am coming soon.
Amen. Come, Lord Jesus!" (Rev 22:6–20)

He didn't, of course, causing further anguish with each passing year. A full century after the crucifixion, in c. 125 CE, an unknown author wrote the so-called Second Letter of Peter to counteract the many skeptics who were saying: "Where is the promise of his coming? For ... all things continue as they were from the beginning of creation!" (2 Peter 3:4, exclamation point in original). Here was his answer:

Do not ignore this one fact, beloved, that with the Lord one day is
like a thousand years, and a thousand years are like one day. The Lord is not slow
about his promise, as some think ... but is patient with you, not wanting any
to perish, but all to come to repentance. But the day of the Lord will come
like a thief, and then the heavens will pass away with a loud noise,
and the elements will be dissolved with fire. (2 Peter 3:8–10)

This argument was hardly airtight, because Jesus had dated the Kingdom's coming in terms of human lifetimes, not God's days or years. Nor was it obvious why, after a hundred years, people needed yet more time to repent. But the early Church's inclusion of this Letter into the New Testament reaffirms that despite the resurrection, many Christians continued to struggle with the question of why "all things continue as they were." Nothing had changed. Hunger, corruption, and the death of innocents continued as before. Why hadn't the Kingdom appeared? And it was their inability to answer this question that gradually induced Christians, as time progressed, to increasingly affirm that the *resurrection* itself was the pivotal event of their faith, rather than the Kingdom that was Jesus' true gospel. And we shall now see that it was Paul himself who unwittingly laid the foundation for this reinterpretation.

CHAPTER 16

DID PAUL REJECT JESUS, AND WHY?

With the resurrection, Jesus arose. But another man arose shortly thereafter, Paul, whose unique concept of Jesus is credited by most historians with transforming a Jewish sect into a wholly new religion.[185] *"Christianity might have remained as a sect within Judaism had it revolved only around belief that Jesus was the Messiah,"* according to the CSB.[186] *"Early Christianity, however, was almost immediately open to the conversion of the Gentiles."* And it was Paul, as we saw in Acts of the Apostles, who opened the floodgate to non-Jewish Gentiles, with his own unique interpretation of Jesus' "gospel." This gospel was expounded in his New Testament Letters, particularly the Letter to the Romans (c. 57 CE). The CSB notes that "it would be hard to overestimate the influence of Romans in the development of Christian doctrine."[187]

We have already examined *Jesus'* gospel: Rejoice, for the Kingdom approaches, and we must cleave as never before to our Judaism. Paul accepted this message, but completely redefined "Judaism" and "Messiah." Paul believed that Eve's sin in eating the forbidden fruit had tainted all humans with original sin. Before Jesus, God had allowed people to escape sin by following the Mosaic Law, which had been granted to the Jews as a sign of his special covenant with Israel. But the Law had never been perfect, and was difficult to follow. So in his mercy, God had finally sent Jesus, his own son, to earth. (Recall that Paul believed Jesus was literally the divine "Son of God.") Jesus was the Messiah: not the redeemer of

---

185 Strictly speaking, Paul built on the efforts of earlier, anonymous missionaries, but it was his titanic efforts that allowed Christianity to succeed.

186 The Catholic Study Bible, RG 503, italics added.

187 Ibid., RG 484.

the Jewish nation, but the one who, like a cosmic scapegoat, took upon himself the sins of the world, to redeem humanity through his suffering. But he had been resurrected to glory and now sat in heaven at God's right hand. Therefore, God no longer had to be approached indirectly through the Law. He could now be approached directly through worship of Jesus the Christ. And Christ would reward believers by granting them the same gift of deliverance and eternal life that he had introduced to earth. So the old covenant with Israel, based on the Law, had been superseded by this New Covenant. Through baptism and faith in Jesus, everyone could be saved. This path was now the *true* Judaism, the culmination of God's original Covenant with Israel.

If Paul's message sounds familiar, it should: it is the core creed of Christianity. Yet it sounds nothing like Jesus'. Paul had rejected Jesus' gospel, in the name of Jesus.

***

Who was Paul, and what was his justification for radically transforming Jesus' gospel? We met Paul earlier, in our discussion of the Acts of the Apostles.[188] Acts is our major source of information about Paul, along with Paul's own Letters. Scholars consider the Letters more factual. Aside from predating Acts by 30–40 years and containing no mention of miracles, they are clearly the writings of a very mortal man, filled with joy and despair, strength and weakness.

So what do we know about Paul? Our two sources frequently clash, but they do agree on some points. One is that Paul was born into a Jewish family in Hellenistic Cilicia (southern Turkey, c. 5 CE, perhaps in the town of Tarsus), with the Hebrew name Saul. He *never* saw Jesus. In fact, as a youth he was so outraged by Judeo-Christianity that he zealously persecuted its members (whether in Cilicia or Judea is unclear). However, he was transformed by a vision of the heavenly Jesus, c. 33 CE (i.e., several years after Jesus' death). He immediately became a Jesus missionary who unflaggingly traversed much of the Roman Empire. He finally gained official approval at the Counsel of Jerusalem (c. 48 CE) for his Christianized mission to the Gentiles, which he pursued with astonishing tenacity until his death in 62–64 CE.

Beyond this skeletal outline, the two sources diverge. The key discrepancy is that Acts portrays him as working in concert with the Mother Synagogue, whereas

---

188 Readers might wish to reacquaint themselves with chapter 4, because the current chapter will refer to Peter's visit to Cornelius, the early Antioch church, the Council of Jerusalem, and Paul's final argument with Peter.

Paul's own writings show he was following his own agenda, with minimal guidance from anyone.

Even though Paul's Letters are considered more accurate, we will begin with Acts' far more famous account of his life. According to Acts, Paul had been living in Jerusalem before his conversion, persecuting local Judeo-Christians, when he decided to extend his campaign to Damascus:

> As he was ... approaching Damascus, suddenly a
> light from the sky flashed around him. He fell to the ground
> and heard a voice saying ... "Saul, Saul, why do you persecute me?"
> He asked, "Who are you, Lord ["sir," according to the CSB translation]."
> The reply came, "I am Jesus, whom you are
> persecuting. But get up and go to the city, and you will be told what you
> are to do." The men who were traveling with him stood speechless because they
> heard the voice but saw no one. Saul got up ... and though his eyes were open,
> he could see nothing; so they led him by the hand ... into Damascus.
> (Acts 9:3–8)

In Damascus, Paul's sight was miraculously restored by a Judeo-Christian whom God had visited in a vision, saying that Paul had been selected to carry his name "before Gentiles and kings and before the people of Israel" (Acts 9:15). This concludes the story of Paul's "conversion on the road to Damascus."[189] There is obviously nothing here about radically redefining Judaism. It is also worth noting that this conversion *preceded* Peter's encounter with Cornelius, which is Acts' first explicit indication that (very exceptional) Gentiles could also follow Jesus. In any event, Acts reports that Paul returned to Jerusalem after some time, where he was gratefully accepted into the Mother Synagogue. He then began missionizing in Palestine and then in Syria, although the nature of his message at this time is unclear. It was during his Syrian travels that Paul joined Barnabas at the mostly Gentile Antioch synagogue/church, after which the pair was instructed to appear at the Council of Jerusalem.

This is Acts' depiction of Paul's early- to mid-stage ministry. It shows Paul working in tandem with the Mother Synagogue. But when we examine Paul's own Letters, we find a man marching to his own drummer. Paul's brief but pregnant account of this seminal period is found almost entirely in his Letter to the Galatians:

---

189 Acts repeats the conversion story in two later chapters. The first repetition is very similar, whereas the second contains significant differences.

I want you to know ... that the gospel that was proclaimed by me
is not of human origin; for I did not receive it from a human source, nor was
I taught it, but I received it through *a revelation of Jesus Christ.*
You have heard, no doubt, of my earlier life in Judaism. I was violently
persecuting the church of God [the Jesus sect] and was trying to destroy it....
But when God ... was pleased to reveal his Son to
me, so that I might proclaim him among the Gentiles, *I did not confer with any*
human being, nor did I go up to Jerusalem to those
who were already apostles before me
[i.e., the Disciples] but I went away at once
into Arabia and ... Damascus.
Then after *three years* I went up to Jerusalem to visit Cephas [Peter]
and stayed with him fifteen days; but I did not see any other
apostle except James the Lord's brother.... Then
I went into the regions of Syria and Cilicia, and I was still unknown
by sight to the churches of *Judea* that are in Christ.
(Gal 1: 11–22, brackets added)

This is a very different story. There is no indication here (or in his other writings) that, at the time of his conversion, Paul had ever been in Jerusalem or knew any Disciples. Nor does he reveal any details whatsoever about his revelation—not even what the celestial Jesus said. Of equal importance, he discloses that following his conversion he immediately began preaching his message in Syria and Arabia for three full years *without the knowledge or authorization of the Jerusalem synagogue.* As noted earlier, the specifics of his message in these early years are not clear: for example, whether he believed that only Jews could follow Jesus. Nor is it clear, when Paul finally went to Jerusalem after three years to "visit" privately with Peter and James (a meeting unmentioned in Acts) whether he informed them of his activities. The CSB comments that to "visit" with Cephas may mean simply "to get information from him about Jesus."[190]

Paul did not return to Jerusalem for another *fourteen* years, to attend the Council of Jerusalem. Based on Paul's Letters (as well as Acts), this seems to have been the *first time that Paul revealed his gospel to the Mother Synagogue leaders.* We already saw an abridged version of his account of the Council (chapter 4), but here is a fuller account:

Then after fourteen years I again went up to Jerusalem with
Barnabas ... in response to a revelation. When I laid before them

---

190 The Catholic Study Bible, 295.

(though only in a private meeting with the acknowledged leaders) the gospel
that I proclaim among the Gentiles ... those who were *supposed* to be
acknowledged leaders (*what they actually were makes no difference to me* ...)—
those leaders contributed nothing to me. On the contrary, when they
saw that I had been entrusted with the gospel for the uncircumcised, just as Peter
had been entrusted with the gospel to the circumcised ... when ... James
and Cephas [Peter] ... recognized the grace
that had been given to me, they gave to Barnabas and me their
right hand of fellowship, agreeing that we should go to the Gentiles
and they to the circumcised. (Gal 2:1–9, parenthesis in original,
italics and brackets added)

Some of the details of Paul's version of the Council differ from Acts.[191] But the
key difference is that Paul appears to have been a lone wolf so wedded to his own
conversion vision that he scarcely seemed to care what Peter and James thought
(although he needed their imprimatur for his success.) They were "supposed to
be acknowledged leaders," but "what they actually were makes no difference to
me." Recall too that after Paul's return to Antioch, when Peter visited and began
withdrawing from the non-Jewish congregants, Paul publicly upbraided him for
"ignoring" Jesus' teachings.

So Paul was a man who believed absolutely in his own conception of Jesus. No
one else's opinion mattered. As he declared to the congregations of Galatia and
Corinth:

"Even if ... an angel from heaven should proclaim to you a gospel
contrary to what we [Paul and his associates] proclaimed to you,
let that one be accursed! ...
I repeat ... let that one be accursed!" (Gal 1:8–9, brackets added)
"If someone comes and proclaims another Jesus than the one we proclaimed,
or a different gospel ... such boasters are false apostles, deceitful workers,
disguising themselves as apostles of Christ. And no wonder! Even
Satan disguises himself as an angel of light." (2 Cor 11:4, 13–14)

And as a waspish jab against those insisting on the necessity of full Jewish conversion to become a Jesus-follower, he prayed the circumcision knife might slip: "I
wish those who unsettle you would castrate themselves!" (Gal 5:12).

---

191 For example, Paul describes a relatively small meeting, claims he came on his own
initiative following a "revelation," and does not mention James's final conditions on
Gentile behavior.

This was Paul, according to his own words. He had never seen Jesus, rarely visited Jerusalem, and considered anyone who disputed his gospel, even Peter, a "false apostle."[192] Indeed, how much Paul actually knew about the living Jesus is a matter of debate. Paul's Letters are remarkable for their dearth of information about Jesus. Astoundingly, there is no mention whatsoever of any miracle, any saying (except the Last Supper ceremony, and the prohibition of divorce), any parable, or any event of Jesus' life except the crucifixion and resurrection. The latter are endlessly recalled, but as theological symbols, shorn of detail. This is surprising. Some of these Letters (including his epochal Romans) were written to congregations that had never seen Paul and might have possessed incomplete knowledge about Jesus, as no Gospel yet existed. Relating Jesus' miracles and sayings would presumably have been very useful. Did Paul even know who Jesus was, and what he had preached? Did he care? Scholars debate this endlessly, for he wrote, "even though we once knew Christ from a human point of view ["according to the flesh," in the CSB translation], we know him no longer in that way ... everything old has passed away; see, everything has become new!" (2 Cor 5:16–17). Yet even if Paul was convinced his revelation had superseded everything, one wonders whether he questioned why the celestial Jesus had never bothered to reveal this revolutionary new gospel to Peter, James, or anyone else.

Thus, Paul rejected the teachings of the living Jesus and his companion Disciples, in favor of his own solitary vision. Why did he do this, and how did he arrive at his understanding of the "gospel"? Perhaps this new gospel was conveyed full-blown to him in his vision, though neither Acts nor the Letters report the celestial Jesus saying anything whatsoever about a new gospel or a new religion. Scholars have long debated the origin of Paul's gospel. One possible answer is that Paul, like all people, was the product of his environment and his own life. Starting with the former, Paul lived in a Greek Hellenistic society that was very different from Jewish Palestine. Many contemporary Hellenists were deeply influenced by Plato's ancient dichotomy between the perfect "ideal" and imperfect "reality." Whereas Palestinian Jews believed that everything in God's world was good and intended for people's appropriate enjoyment, many Hellenistic philosophers taught that material objects—including the human body—were inherently base. Life's goal was to escape this earthly corruption by nourishing one's spirit and

---

192 Despite the bravado of Paul's Letters, the "false prophets" seem to have bested him. Paul never returned to the Galatian congregation following his argument with Peter, and Barnabus deserted him. Apparently upset by competitive missionaries, he ultimately decided to work in virgin territory, in Spain. But he was imprisoned on his way there in Rome, where he died in c. 63 CE. In the end, however, his Letters triumphed.

seeking union with the perfect "One" (God). This thinking influenced even the greatest Jewish philosopher of his age, Philo of Alexandria (Egypt, c. 25 BCE–43 CE). He too agreed that the Torah was merely an imperfect reflection of the "true" celestial Law, although he averred that it was earth's most perfect law. In short, Paul grew up in a culture with its own version of "original sin" and "salvation." Its spiritual thirst accounted for the popularity of the "mystery cults" of the day (e.g., the Elysian mysteries, and the Isis cult), which promised personal communion with the divine.[193]

To this background must be added the impact of Paul's own early life. He had been an ordinary artisan (a tentmaker), but zealously Jewish enough to persecute the Jesus sect. What must he have felt when Jesus revealed himself from the heavens and, rather than striking him dead for wickedness, had glorified him with a great life-giving mission? Undoubtedly he was awestruck, and filled with supernal love and gratitude that Jesus had "saved him" and "washed away his sins." Only a divine being would be capable of such loving kindness, and Jesus' celestial abode further established his divinity. He was not God, of course, for God had not directly revealed himself to the Jewish people since the age of the great prophets, several centuries earlier. Instead, he was obviously the Son of God, who had briefly been incarnate on earth as a mortal. And since Paul had communed directly with the Son of God—and thus God himself—of what further value was the Jewish Law? If other Jews—or Gentiles—approached Jesus as he had, everyone would be saved together in Christ, the font of eternal life. Yet Paul never perceived himself as abandoning Judaism, because his God was still the Jewish God of Abraham, Isaac, and Jacob. He had simply learned to commune with God directly, rather than through the Law.

---

193 The dichotomy between heavenly and earthly was carried to extremes by Marcion (c. 135 CE), the first Christian to try to establish an official canon. He rejected the entire Tanakh and even the Jewish God, arguing that a God who had created a material world must be inferior to the *real* God. He further believed that Jesus had been a nonmaterial "hologram" during his earthly appearance, since no Son of God would befoul himself by entering the impure world. (The early Church considered the concept of a nonphysical Jesus ["docetism"] heretical. Its struggle to suppress this heresy was a major reason for its qualms about accepting the Gospel of John, which skirted docetism.) Based on his thinking, Marcion proposed that the Christian Scriptures should omit the Tanakh (Old Testament), and contain only Paul's Letters and part of Luke. He did not include John's Gospel, probably because he was unaware of it. This proposal was vehemently rejected by the Church, but served as a major impetus for Bishop Irenaeus' later efforts to create a "correct" canon, c. 180 CE (White, *From Jesus to Christianity*, 445ff).

Whether Paul's unique gospel emerged gradually or all at once is unclear, although his message seems to evolve throughout his Letters. But when his message was rebuffed by most Jews but accepted by some Gentiles (mostly the powerless—women, slaves, and the poor—who resonated to the concept of a suffering savior who could bestow eternal life), he may have seen this as a sign of God's decision to create a new covenant with any people willing to believe in Jesus.

Postscript: Why did the Mother Synagogue authorize Paul's Mission?

Why did the Mother Synagogue's leaders agree to Paul's Christianized ministry? They must have been gratified by the Gentiles' acceptance of Jesus. And considering their (and Paul's) belief in an imminent Parousia, they probably assumed his mission would be brief in any case. But there was another reason. In Paul's summary of the Council of Jerusalem, he reveals something unmentioned in Acts: that Peter and James had insisted that Paul "remember the poor" (Gal 2:10).

The meaning of this obscure phrase becomes clear from Paul's other Letters. The Jerusalem Synagogue was struggling to support its many impoverished members and was willing to grant Paul's wishes if he promised to collect donations from the Gentiles. Paul was very diligent in this mission, as he explained in the Letter to the Romans: "At present ... I am going to Jerusalem in a ministry to the saints ["holy ones," in the CSB translation]; for [some Gentile churches] have been pleased to share their resources with the poor among the saints in Jerusalem ... and indeed they owe it to them; for if the Gentiles have come to share in their spiritual blessings, they ought also to be of service to them in material things" (Rom 15:25–27, brackets added).

Paul was true to his word and arrived in Jerusalem in c. 58 CE. Whether the money was delivered is unknown, because Acts records a huge riot erupting when Jerusalemites learned of the renegade's presence in the Temple. What *is* clear is that the authorization of Paul's mission for the sake of charity changed the course of Western history.

CHAPTER 17

HOW JESUS BECAME GOD

Even in the Synoptics, where Jesus is wholly human, his stature grows progressively. Mark's shocking verse about Jesus being "out of his mind" (Mk 3:21) was omitted by the later Evangelists. On the day he was rejected at the Nazareth synagogue, Mark notes that "he could do no deed of power there, except that he laid his hands on a few sick people" (Mk 6:5). Luke omitted this verse, while Matthew softened it by saying that Jesus decided not to cure anyone (Mt 13:58). In Capernaum, Mark reports that Jesus cured "many" of the sick people brought to him one evening (Mk 1:34), whereas "all" were cured in the other Gospels. When a woman suffering from heavy menstrual bleeding touched his cloak from behind in the hope of being cured, Mark records that Jesus was "immediately aware that power had gone forth from him" (Mk 5:30). He wheeled around, but was unable to determine who in the crowd had touched him. The other Synoptics excised the sapping of his power, and Matthew further claimed that Jesus managed to identify her instantly. (Parenthetically, both Matthew and Luke reported that she touched the "fringe" of his cloak, which the CSB assumes refers to the tzezit prescribed for men's clothing by the Mosaic Law.)[194] The later Gospels also omitted Mark's remarkably crude and unflattering description of Jesus' struggle to cure a blind man with his spittle, and his similar spittle-cure of a deaf man.

Strong human emotions are also progressively censured. In the Healing of the Withered Hand, Mark reports that Jesus looked at the synagogue congregation with anger and grieved at their hardness of heart (Mk 3:5). Luke and Matthew omitted both emotions. Jesus was "amazed" by his rejection in Nazareth in Mark's Gospel [Mk 6:6], but this was again deleted by Luke and Matthew, who may have been embarrassed by their savior's inability to predict even his family's reaction. While awaiting his arrest in Jerusalem, Mark records Jesus telling his Disciples, "My soul is sorrowful even to death" (Mk 15:34), which Luke omitted. Jesus'

---

194 The Catholic Study Bible, 21.

final cry on the cross in Mark is an anguished "Eloi, eloi, lema sabachthani?" ("My God, my God, why have you forsaken me?") (Mk 15:34). Matthew retained this, but Luke replaced it with the far more serene, "Father, into your hands I commend my spirit" (Lk 23:46). Luke further spiritualized Jesus on the cross by uniquely having him say, "Father, forgive them; for they know not what they are doing" (Lk 23:34).

Beyond such individual alterations, broader themes are reworked. We have already examined two examples. One is the shrinking importance of John the Baptist in Jesus' life. The other is the recasting of the Rejection at Nazareth to enhance Jesus' image, especially in Luke's drastic revision of Mark's original account of why the Nazareth congregants rejected Jesus. In Luke, the congregants were actually awed by Jesus and became hostile only when he preemptively declared them to be unworthy of his miracles. Luke thereby managed to highlight both Jesus' reverential reception and the Jews' underlying "selfishness."

Still, Jesus is always human in the Synoptics. So how and when did he become God? Since this is a historical question that does not involve Jesus' Synoptic portrait, we will rely on solid historical information for an answer (rather than accepting the veracity of individual New Testament verses). The answer is twofold: this transmutation occurred quite early among ordinary Christians, but received the Roman Catholic Church's official imprimatur only much later, in the fourth century. (Protestantism originated only in the sixteenth century.) The Church's delay is unsurprising, because the Church began to take form only in the early second century and tried to avoid contentious issues until its hand was forced by dangerous "heresies" among the people.

Starting with ordinary worshipers, Jesus' apotheosis was already far advanced among at least some Jesus followers even *before* the earliest Gospel. We have seen that Paul's Letters (c. 51–60 CE) rarely refer to Jesus' human life, for "even if we once knew Christ from a human point of view, we know him no longer in that way." Instead, Paul taught that Jesus was literally the Son of God, sitting at the right hand of God the Father. So, for Paul, Jesus was already inseparable from God, although not God himself. However, no one knows how widespread this notion was at this early time. Surprising as it might seem, Paul became truly influential only in the early second century, fifty years after his death. In his own life, he was merely one of many missionaries traversing the nations surrounding Palestine. (Recall his frustration with Peter and other "false prophets.") There is no way to know whether the contemporary Mother Synagogue, or any other congregation unaffiliated with Paul, viewed Jesus as the Son of God.[195] Two posthumous events

---

195 Some passages in Acts state that they did. However, since we are no longer discussing Jesus' life, we are relying on well-accepted historical information in this section,

were necessary for Paul's theology to become the cornerstone of Christianity. First, the Mother Synagogue, the headquarters of the Jesus sect, had to be destroyed, as it was by 70 CE. The destruction of this Jewish Synagogue, along with smaller Palestinian synagogues, allowed leadership of the Jesus sect to pass to the Gentile nations of the Roman Empire. Second, Paul's Letters to the various churches had to be collected, copied, and distributed widely. This happened in c. 100 CE. As earlier noted, there is no evidence that even Mark and Matthew, who wrote years after Paul's death, had ever heard of him. (Luke did, as evidenced by Paul's prominence in Acts.) Having said that, the belief that Jesus was the Son of God had certainly spread by 70 to 95 CE, because all three Synoptic Evangelists expressed this belief, at least implicitly, in their Gospels.

The next giant step was taken by the Gospel of John (c. 95–110 CE), which began blurring the distinction between Jesus (Son of God) and God the Father. The Gospel begins with the famous, slightly opaque introduction of Jesus as the "Word." ("Word" ["Logos" in Greek], is better translated as the aspect of God's mind understandable to humans). In John's theology, this Logos briefly descended to earth as Jesus, so God's Will could be apparent to all.

> In the beginning was the Word, and the Word was with God,
> and the Word was God. He was in the beginning with God.
> All things came into being through him,
> and without him not one thing came into being....
> And the Word became flesh and lived among us,
> and we have seen his glory, the glory as of a Father's only son. (Jn 1:1–14)

Note that the Word/Logos was not only "with God," but simultaneously *was* God. And Jesus is portrayed as God in many passages so starkly alien to his Synoptic portrait that the early Church's confusion about how to treat this extraordinary Gospel is easy to understand. Speaking to "the Jews" in one of his famous "I AM" passages, Jesus said:

> You are from below, I am from above; you are of this world,
> I am not of this world. I told you that you would die in your sins ...
> unless you believe that I am he ["I AM," in the CSB
> translation].[196] ... When you have lifted up the Son of Man, then you

---

rather than accepting the veracity of quotations from Acts unsupported by any other source.

196 *The Catholic Study Bible*, 162, states that "I AM" is "understood as Yahweh's own self-designation (Isaiah 43:10) ... Jesus is here placed on a par with Yahweh."

will realize that I am he ["I AM"], and that I do nothing on my own,
but I speak these things as the Father instructed me. And the one who
sent me is with me.... If God
were your Father, you would love me, for I came from God and now I am
here. Why do you not understand what I say? It is because you cannot
accept my word. You are from your father the devil, and ... he was
a murderer from the beginning and does not stand in the truth,
because there is no truth in him.... If I tell the truth, why do you
not believe me? Whoever is from God hears the words of God. The reason you
do not hear them is that you are not from God.... If I glorify myself,
my glory is nothing. It is my Father who glorifies me. (Jn 8:23–54)

Unsurprisingly, Jesus' vicious battles with the Jews in this Gospel go far beyond picayune disputes about oral law. They center instead on his startling affirmation of Godhood:

So the Jews gathered around him and said ... "If you are the Messiah,
tell us plainly." ... Jesus answered, "I told you.... The Father and I are one."
The Jews took up stones to stone him. Jesus replied,
"I have shown you many good works from the Father. For which ...
are you trying to stone me?" The Jews answered, "It is not for a good work
that we are going to stone you, but for blasphemy, because you, although only
a human being, are making yourself God." Jesus answered ... "Believe in the
works, so that you may know and understand that the Father is in me
and I am in the Father." (Jn 10:24–38)[197]

Jesus' oneness with God is less explicit elsewhere in John, but these passages demonstrate that at the "popular" level, the concept of Jesus as God was virtually complete by c. 100 CE, at least in John's own congregation. By 200 CE, after

197 The Gospel of John is the only anti-Semitic Gospel. Unlike the Synoptics, which distinguish between commoners, Pharisees, and so on, John's Gospel typically lumps everyone together as "the Jews," who are forever plotting to kill Jesus. The CSB recognizes this Gospel's contribution to anti-Semitism by noting that "We must acknowledge that in the past people [Christians] have not distinguished between John's use of 'the Jews' as characters [in this Gospel] and the Jewish people. Today, we must be very careful not to continue that misreading. In some contexts [for teaching this Gospel], it might be appropriate to substitute another phrase like 'Jesus' enemies' or ... 'the Judeans.' ... Such substitutions are particularly important when working with young children who cannot make the distinction easily between 'the Jews' ... and their Jewish classmates and neighbors" (The Catholic Study Bible, RG 438).

Bishop Irenaeus' decisive endorsement of this fourth Gospel, Jesus' identity with God was widely accepted.

Thus, Jesus' apotheosis was a spontaneous event that initially occurred at the popular level.[198] And although we have focused thus far on the powerful influence of Paul and the Evangelists, conditions in the early Christian world were ripe in any case. Hellenistic Gentiles were polytheists, unaccustomed to worshipping only one God. Worse, the one Jewish God was literally faceless. In Jesus they already had a Savior so concrete, approachable, and authoritative that it was easy for them to transform him into a multiplicity of divinities, including God the Father. Greek mythology was filled with gods who temporarily turned themselves into human or animal form on earth, so the concept of a god with multiple manifestations was familiar. The same dynamic also led to the unexpected elevation of Jesus' mother, Mary. (The later Protestant Church rejected this Adoration of the Virgin Mary.) All Synoptics depict Mary as upset by, and indifferent to, her son's ministry (except in Luke's Nativity story). John's Gospel even actively disparages her. But polytheistic Gentiles had always worshiped female goddesses (e.g., for fertility), and so yearned for a soft maternal figure in their new faith.

Turning from ordinary Christians to the official Catholic Church—which began to emerge only in the early second century—it obviously had to accept the prevailing beliefs of its members. Nevertheless, its leaders felt compelled to refine and systematize those beliefs. This was partly owing to the need to explain their new religion to government officials and the huge majority of still-pagan Gentiles. More important, the continual eruption of "heretical" Christian sects threatened to fragment the religion into feuding cliques. In particular, Jesus' precise identity and his relationship with God had to be clarified.

It would be overly tedious to trace the long, complex process through which the Church ultimately hammered out its solution, in the form of the doctrine of the Trinity. The key point is that the question of Jesus' nature—mortal? God? Lesser God?—was highly contentious for centuries, and required the suppression of many "heresies" that threatened to split the Church. To name only three, these included:

---

198 We have been discussing "popular" Christianity so far, as opposed to official Church teachings. It may seem odd to think of Paul and John as "popular" figures. But first-century Christianity was an unorganized, minuscule sect of a few thousand people. Just as Paul was a mere missionary who was so convinced of an imminent Parousia that he could never have imagined that an institutionalized Church would one day canonize his Letters, the Evangelist John was probably a local church notable who never dreamed that his writings would someday also become Scripture.

- Monarchianism. This popular early concept was a "monotheistic heresy" claiming that Jesus had been born an ordinary human. This notion was rooted in the fact that the Synoptics said nothing about his adult life until his baptism by John the Baptist, and that his death by a handful of Roman soldiers indicated he remained mortal to the end. According to this heresy, however, Jesus was "adopted" by God as his only Son ("adoptionalism") at the moment of either his baptism or resurrection. Another monotheistic heresy, Sabellianism, asserted there was only one God, who could alter himself into a true human. God had briefly descended to earth in the form of Jesus, and being true flesh, had literally suffered physically during the crucifixion.

- Gnosticism. The Gnostics believed they possessed special knowledge ("gnosis," in Greek) not contained in the Gospels: that the world had been created by a "foolish god," without the approval of the true God. When the true God discovered this calamity, he bestowed humans with a divine spark that could rescue them from the corrupt material world by inspiring them to live at a wholly spiritual level. This theology often led to docetism, which maintained that Jesus had descended to earth as a hologram, since no real God would debase himself by taking on earthly flesh and making contact with the befouled world. Docetism has already been mentioned, and was expressed in its purest form by Marcion, and more subtly by John's Gospel.

- Arianism. This extremely serious heresy nearly fractured the fourth-century Church, and was the direct impetus for the Church's decision that the time had finally come to formulate an official, orthodox theology for all time. Arius taught that God had first created the Logos (the "Word"), which then created Jesus. Jesus was therefore inferior to God. This belief, which was actually one formulation of a broader heresy (subordinationism), led to the convocation of the Councils of Nicæa (325 CE), Constantinople (381 CE), and Chalcedon (451 CE). These meetings formulated the basic doctrine of Jesus and the Trinity we have today, although refinements were made at subsequent convocations. The doctrine states that there is only one God, composed of God the Father, God the Son (Jesus Christ), and the Holy Spirit,[199] each of which is however a separate entity, with Jesus being both completely God and completely human. The full doctrine is such

---

199 As the least important entity of the Trinity, the Holy Spirit will not be discussed further. However, it is God's spirit that directly interacts with humans. It may be recalled

an elaborate philosophical/theological construct that the Catholic Church regards it as a "mystery" that worshippers must be accepted by faith, as it can scarcely be comprehended by the human mind.[200] (As an historical aside, the Roman emperor Constantine, who participated actively at the Council of Nicea, was himself an Arian heretic. However, he did not interfere with the Council's anti-Arian decision because his primary goal was to create a cohesive Christianity that could unite his heterogeneous peoples.)

However complex the details, the crux is that although the human Jesus of the Synoptics had became Son of God and then God by c. 100 CE or so in certain Christian communities, the Church itself required several more centuries to formulate an orthodox theology of Jesus and the Trinity. The Councils' outcomes were uncertain until the end, for they were riven by both impassioned theological disputes and age-old political maneuvering. Under different historical circumstances, Jesus might never have become God.

---

that the Holy Spirit appeared to Jesus as a dove at his baptism and inspired Cornelius to speak in tongues.

200 Parenthetically, one late heresy (1054 CE) did finally divide the Church into a Western (Roman) and an Eastern Orthodox (Constantinople) branch. The aforementioned Councils had promulgated that the Holy Spirit "proceeded from the Father (God)," but the Roman Church later infuriated the Eastern churches by unilaterally adding the "filioque" clause, stating that the Holy Sprit "proceeded from the Father *and* from the Son." The Eastern churches denounced this as heresy, along with Rome's broader claim of primacy over the worldwide Church. As a result, it split away from the Roman Catholic Church.

CHAPTER 18

WHO WAS JESUS?

This book has tried to adhere to its original goal of portraying Jesus by assuming that the Synoptic Gospels' accounts are true unless contradicted by internal discrepancies, the scholarship of the Roman Catholic Church, or well-established historical facts. However, because our final portrait contains some contradictory and incomprehensible elements, the author now wishes to bend this rule in an effort to resolve these enigmas. As part of the process, the author will provide his own interpretation of who Jesus was. This will necessarily be subjective. Surprising as it may sound, Christian scholars continue to disagree widely over Jesus' teachings and character, because any interpretation necessitates weighing the relative authenticity of discrepant Gospel passages, and trying to fill in the Gospels' many narrative gaps.

We will begin by highlighting a CSB commentary that was previously skipped over. Specifically, the Catholic Church doubts that Jesus actually told his Disciples that he would die and be resurrected. Commenting on the first of this thrice-told "prediction," the CSB states, "Neither this nor the two later passion predictions can be taken as sayings that, as they stand, go back to Jesus himself."[201] This commentary was omitted earlier because no rationale was provided for this conclusion. However, the reason seems apparent. For one thing, the Catholic Church teaches that Jesus was entirely human while on earth (although simultaneously God and Holy Spirit) and had very limited ability to predict the future. In addition, this assertion solves one major Gospel puzzle: why the Disciples could not "understand" this prediction, and so immediately abandoned Jesus during his arrest, and never visited his tomb to witness the resurrection. There had never been such a prophecy. Instead, the Disciples were stunned by the arrest, and believed their master was dead. Why didn't the Evangelists write an internally consistent story, by coupling Jesus' "prophecies" with an ending in which the Disciples displayed

---

201 The Catholic Study Bible, 38.

greater faith and resolve? The answer is that the Evangelists worked under serious constraints. The Disciples' panicked flight during the arrest was apparently common knowledge in the first century, and could not be denied. It was easier to create fictitious private sayings, since most of the Disciples who would have known of them were probably dead when the Gospels appeared.[202]

If the Evangelists (or the sources they drew on) sometimes used "private revelations" to enhance Jesus' image, two more episodes spring to mind. One is his claim of Messiahship. We have seen that Jesus privately revealed his identity only to the Disciples (and the Sanhedrin?), and swore them to secrecy. Consequently, hardly anyone in the Synoptics had any inkling that he was the Messiah. This seems contrived. Furthermore, using this appellation would simply have perplexed the people, who were anticipating a Davidic warrior-king. So what did he call himself? Despite the single Gospel description of him as "meek," Jesus was assertive enough to have told people exactly who he was. And what he often called himself publicly was a prophet. But he did believe he was an eschatological prophet—God's final prophet, whose actions somehow symbolized or even hastened the incoming of the Kingdom. Thus, although he probably never used the term Messiah, he did seem to regard his role in some kind of messianic light.

The greatest of all Synoptic puzzlers should be obvious: his private revelation that he spoke in parables to confuse the people, to prevent them from entering the Kingdom. This "private revelation" also includes two of the Synoptics' most startling passages. ("I give praise to you, Father … for … you have hidden these things from the wise and the learned," and "All things have been handed over to me by my Father. No one knows who the Son is except the Father, and who the Father is except the Son."). We have already emphasized the incongruity of a messianic prophet traveling indefatigably to spread an incomprehensible message. Few nonfundamentalist scholars accept this bizarre notion. Instead, it seems far likelier that this private "revelation" was created by later Jesus followers trying to prove that the Jews who saw and heard Jesus rejected him as their savior because they were too wicked and unworthy to understand him.[203]

---

202 If Jesus did not predict his resurrection, the "sign of Jonah" saying (chapter 10) would also be ahistorical.

203 A lesser private revelation that is probably nonhistorical is Jesus' prophecy that the Day of the Lord would be triggered by the Temple's desecration. Since Jesus' ministry occurred during a peaceful period in Palestine, it is hard to understand why he would have preached the Kingdom's imminence at a time when the Temple faced no threats. Similarly, Paul's First Letter to the Thessalonians proves that he too expected the Day's imminent arrival by 50–51 CE, despite Palestine's continued calm. This suggests that

If all this is true, what is the final portrait of Jesus that emerges? He was a Nazareth artisan of no special distinction who adopted the traditional rural Judaism of his period. His first thirty-one or thirty-two years were so mundane that the Synoptics record not a single event from this period. Then, suddenly, he fell under the sway of John the Baptist. The Baptist's enormous impact is obvious from the fact that every Synoptic begins Jesus' adult life with his baptism, during which he experienced his private revelation of being chosen by God. Most scholars believe, in fact, that Jesus then remained with John as a disciple. This would explain how Jesus learned John's gospel of the Day of the Lord and the Kingdom, and even the "Lord's Prayer" (chapter 12). It would also explain why Jesus began his ministry only after his master's arrest. John's influence remained strong even after his murder by Herod Antipas. This is evident from John's distinction of being the only person Jesus ever spoke about in the Synoptics. (Jesus used his Disciples' names only while speaking with them, whereas he spontaneously spoke about John to others.)

Interestingly, a close reading of the Synoptics suggests that the Baptist was always the more influential figure, as also implied by Josephus. We have already remarked that Jesus came to the Baptist for a "baptism of repentance for the forgiveness of sins," suggesting that Jesus had been sinful until then, and so was John's inferior. (The people believed John's own baptism had been divine [Mt 21:23–27]). John was the first to provide the precise boon—forgiveness of sins—that was supposed to be Jesus' unique gift to humanity.[204] Continuing the comparison, huge masses journeyed to John's remote desert location on the Jordan River, solely for his baptism and teachings. No one went hoping for miracles, for he performed none. Jesus, on the other hand, seems to have attracted people primarily for his miracles. Without them, it is questionable whether he would have been paid much heed. Moreover, his crowds seemed to be almost exclusively composed of "ordinary" Jews, for he did not impress the educated Pharisees. In contrast, John was so well regarded by everybody that even his murderer, Herod Antipas, respected him to the very end. After John's death, the belief rapidly spread among the masses that he had been reincarnated as Jesus. Far fewer people so quickly believed in Jesus' own resurrection. The Baptists' reputation remained so high after his death that

---

Paul had never heard any desecration prophecy from the Disciples. Consistent with this is the Q-source's silence about such a prediction.

204 Matthew "rectified" this problem in his Gospel by transferring "for the forgiveness of sins" from this passage to the Last Supper story. This is why only in Matthew's Gospel does Jesus say, over his cup of wine, "Drink … for this is my blood of the covenant, which will be shed on behalf of many for the forgiveness of sins" (Mt 26:28).

the same religious authorities who boldly challenged Jesus' authority in Jerusalem were afraid to publicly disparage the Baptist (Mt 21:23–28).

Returning to Jesus himself, he returned to Galilee after John's arrest, to begin his own mission. He soon arrived in Nazareth but had changed so radically that his family and neighbors could scarcely recognize him. The change was not physical, since there is no suggestion that he looked or sounded different. But his behavior was so odd that everyone around him was bewildered by his words and conduct. Jesus, startled in turn by this rejection, moved to Capernaum. Both Nazareth and Capernaum were small village/towns in southern Galilee, where he presumably felt most comfortable. The Synoptics probably exaggerate his travels outside Galilee. It has already been mentioned that the Synoptics disclose very few details about anything that happened outside of Galilee and Jerusalem.[205] Some of the non-Galilean travel routes described are so improbable that they seem to reflect the Evangelists' shaky grasp of Palestine's geography. Furthermore, Luke routinely tacked the words "and to Judea" to Mark's original accounts of Jesus' travels through Galilee.

Jesus' healing power was his calling card. One of the Synoptics' most consistent themes is that everyone knew him for his cures. Not even his Jewish opponents disputed their authenticity. Whether or not one believes in miracles, it seems very likely that Jesus' charisma and authority made him an exceptional faith healer for those who believed in his powers. However, no one in the Synoptics seems to have heard of his nature miracles or resurrections, which require more than human faith. This suggests that Jesus' miracles consisted entirely of healings. However, the willingness of Judas Iscariot (who had learned Jesus' healing arts) to betray him suggests that Jesus' healing powers were less impressive than the Gospels depict.

Once Jesus had attracted audiences for his teachings and sermons, his key message was the gospel—the Day of the Lord, and the repentance required for the Kingdom. This message, along with Jesus' healing prowess and authority, are the three most consistent motifs in the Synoptics. The essence of his gospel was obedience to Judaism. Of course, his Judaism was the religion of his rural brethren. He observed the Mosaic Law closely, for he was never accused of any breach. If anything, he was especially strict. He also emphasized the Tanakh's ethical precepts, for he was personally familiar with the problems and injustices facing ordinary people. He paid little attention to the Pharisaic oral law, probably because it had never been part of his upbringing, and would have been a secondary issue anyway at such a portentous moment.

The major question about his religious thinking is whether he believed that Herculean perfection was required to enter the Kingdom, or whether ordinary

---

205 Vermes, *The Authentic Gospel of Jesus*, 329.

(i.e., humanly possible) Judaism sufficed. Arguments can be made on both sides, because the Gospels expound both positions without attempting to reconcile them. He may have accepted traditional observance as sufficient, for he said that he had come to rescue only the outcasts ("tax collectors and sinners"), not the healthy. Parables like The Lost Sheep strongly imply that he believed relatively few Jews needed redemption. He acclaimed the Shema and the Ten Commandments as the core religious commandments. Likewise, he "loved" or commended several Jews who were traditionally religious, and he was delighted that the tax collector Zacchaeus had been saved by rejoining Jewish society. On the other side of the ledger, his Sermon on the Mount demanded impossible virtue (although chapter 7 noted that this Sermon probably never happened as described). His warning about the great difficulty of entering the Kingdom's "narrow gates" was also harsh. So was his condemnation of Capernaum and surrounding towns, which was clearly a broad-brush indictment of most of the people he knew best, not small groups of sinners. Superficially, there occasionally seems to be a third side to the ledger as well, because he sometimes sounded as if accepting his "authority" sufficed to enter the Kingdom. We saw this when he forgave the prostitute's sins, despite the absence of evidence that she would actually reform. However, as already noted, this behavior is best understood by recognizing that he believed he understood both people's souls and God's Will, and that anyone who seemed worthy to him, or assisted his mission, must seem equally worthy to God. In short, there are several disparate strands in Jesus' theology of redemption/righteousness. Part of the problem too is the necessary of interpreting his words with a grain of salt, for he delighted in hyperbole. Too, he may have spoken rashly during his flashes of anger. Overall, understanding exactly what he believed about the Kingdom seems well nigh impossible. Perhaps Jesus, like many individuals, thought different things at different times. Or perhaps the witnesses to his actions misinterpreted his words, or their stories were corrupted or exaggerated during decades of oral transmission. In any case, it is worth noting that if he often seemed to be highly demanding, it would not be shocking. After all, most of the Jewish prophets were similarly unyielding. And Jesus had special reason to insist on perfection, for he saw the stakes in apocalyptic life-and-death terms.

Jesus seemed to have no message beyond this. For example, he never claimed to be God, either explicitly or implicitly. He upheld the Shema as the foundation of religion, personally prayed to God, and viewed himself only as an earthly messenger. Conversely, if the CSB is correct in believing that he never prophesied about his death and resurrection, it follows that he never promulgated anything resembling Paul's (i.e., Christianity's) gospel: that through his resurrection he would shoulder the sins of the world in order to redeem humanity. Even the Synoptics, all of which were written after Paul's ministry, scarcely mention his theology. Matthew's Gospel, for example, contains fifty-two references by Jesus to the Kingdom, but only two allusions to Paul's gospel. (This comparison omits Matthew's nonhistorical Nativity story.) These two "Pauline" sayings were made only privately to his Disciples, and only in his final days in Jerusalem. The pattern in Luke's Gospel's nearly identical: forty-one public and private sayings about the Kingdom, made throughout his ministry, compared to only two Pauline sayings, both made privately to his Disciples toward the end of his life. Mark's Gospel, the shortest, is similar.[206] Thus, it was the *Kingdom* that dominated Jesus' entire ministry, both in public and in private. Even the few Pauline allusions may have been too vague to be comprehensible to anyone unfamiliar with Christianity—such as the Disciples.[207]

Having summarized Jesus' message, a few other aspects of his ministry bear mention. His relations with the religious authorities were probably strained, but were inconsequential until his actions in Jerusalem. The disputes with the Pharisees over the oral law were part and parcel of first-century Jewish life. The Pharisees would not normally have cared about his attitude toward the oral law, which was ignored by most rural Galileans in any case. However, Jesus was too visible to be ignored, as was his disquieting certitude that he alone knew God's Will. His sharp ripostes to their inevitable questions generated sparks. He had no patience for disputations at such an urgent time, and demanded immediate

---

206 John's Gospel, which was written so late that confidence in the coming of the Kingdom was waning, contains only three references, none of them in the Synoptics' sense of the arrival of God's Kingdom. Instead, John believed that Jesus' presence on earth was the Kingdom.

207 Jesus' "Pauline gospel" verses in Matthew's and Luke's Gospels are:

1) "The Son of Man came ... to serve, and to give his life as a ransom for many" (Mt 20:28).

2) "This is my blood of the covenant, which is to be poured out for many for the forgiveness of sins" (Mt 26:28)./"This is my body, which is given for you ... this cup which is poured out for you is the new covenant in my blood" (Lk 22:19–20).

3) "The Son of Man ... must endure much suffering and be rejected by this generation" (Lk 17:24–25).

It is not clear whether the third verse should be included in this list, because the verse refers to a Son of Man who had not yet arrived (possibly Daniel's Son of Man).

(Jesus spoke one final "Pauline" passage that not even his Disciples heard during his lifetime, since it occurred after his resurrection: "Thus it is written, that the Messiah is to suffer and rise from the dead on the third day, and that repentance and forgiveness of sins is to be proclaimed in his name" [Lk 24:46–47]).

acquiescence to his authority. Luckily, the Pharisees were harmless and simply walked off clucking their tongues.

His real problem was with the common people. The problem was not physical, for no one ever threatened him. Luke's story of the Nazareth neighbors trying to hurl him off a cliff sounds far-fetched. But few people seemed to heed his message. They didn't believe in the imminent Day of the Lord, or his untenable demands. They would have questioned the importance of a prophet who largely restricted himself to a corner of Galilee. His authority, while enhancing his faith-healing ability, must have simultaneously raised deep suspicions. He prayed infrequently (in public) and referred to Tanakh only sporadically, yet treated most religious authorities with contempt. His fruitless association with "tax collectors and sinners" also hurt him. It might have helped immeasurably if the people had known of (and believed in) God's private message to him ("You are my Son, and in you I am greatly pleased," during his baptism), but Jesus apparently kept this a secret from everyone, except possibly John the Baptist.

Jesus' relationship with his contemporaries would have been smoother if he had been the exemplar of love and compassion portrayed by Luke's Gospel. It should be clear by now that this image is oversimplified. He was highly assertive, not meek. He never turned his own cheek to anyone, and never forgave an enemy (except, in Luke's Gospel, when he forgave his persecutors while on the cross). Instead, he often created enemies needlessly, by angrily reacting to reasonable queries and gratuitously insulting his hosts. His love of children seemed unexceptional. He interacted with them only when they were brought to him by parents, or when they could serve as metaphors for the childlike faith he demanded from others. He spoke often of his concern for the poor, but this was unremarkable in a society that was mostly poor. Not once did he actively seek out the poor, the sick, or the oppressed. The crowds that followed him appeared to be typical rural ones. Those individuals who asked for his help were as often prosperous as poor. In Luke's Gospel, for example, Jesus healed the centurion's slave immediately after proclaiming, in his Sermon on the Plain, that the poor and humble would be rewarded, and the rich and powerful punished. Yet the centurion was rich and powerful. Although Jesus was certainly right to heal the slave, he never spoke out against slavery itself, or even asked the centurion how he treated his slaves. Jesus generally felt warmly toward anyone—the wealthy, sinners, or beggars—who accepted his authority, but coolly to anyone who did not. Perhaps this explains his affinity for tax collectors and sinners. Unlike the many people who may have felt little desire to associate with Jesus, tax collectors and sinners may have welcomed his charismatic attention, especially because he seems not to have pressured them to reform. None of this is to deny that he was a good man. He was unquestionably devoted to his people and moved by their troubles and illnesses. He exerted every effort to guide them to redemption, healed everyone he could without material gain, and even sacrificed his home and possessions for his calling.

In any case, he finally traveled to Jerusalem because it was time for a pilgrimage. Or perhaps he recognized his ministry's failure and hoped that his presence in the Jewish heartland might spark a breakthrough, or even initiate the Day of the Lord. The crowds he preached to may have been enthusiastic masses, or else random knots of Jews in the packed Temple area. Either way, his challenge to the Temple authorities by both word and deed (the "cleansing") marked him as a troublemaker. He was therefore arrested by the Sadducees and/or the Romans, an unforeseen turn of events that sent his Disciples fleeing. His own shock was expressed in his heart-rending last words, "Father, why hast thou forsaken me?"

When Jesus died, many would have expected his name to disappear. His prophecies had been wrong, for the Kingdom never came. His claim of authority must also have been punctured by his ignominious death and his embarrassing failure to predict the treachery of his own Disciple. The rest of his message, that Judaism was the path to God, had been known for a millennium. So how did his memory survive? Paul was obviously pivotal. He not only transformed Jesus into a divinity of a totally new religion, but also fortuitously planted its seeds beyond Palestine prior to the First Jewish Revolt. There, the Gentile Jesus movement was able to survive while the Jews who had actually known Jesus died in Jerusalem's conflagration, or of old age. The foreign seeds sprouted even as the roots were incinerated. But Paul could never have succeeded had not the Disciples kept Jesus' memory alive. Without them, there would have been no one to vouch for Jesus' rising, or to form the Mother Synagogue. The Disciples were exceptional, being the first documented group of itinerant disciples since the ancient days of Elijah and Elisha. What was it about Jesus that so motivated these people to serve him both in life and death?

It was probably the same authority that undermined Jesus' ministry that attracted these particular twelve men to him. Jesus was absolutely confident that God had made him uniquely privy to his plans, had delegated him special powers on earth, and would grace him with an exalted role in the Kingdom. Jesus' authority is the most pervasive motif in the Synoptics, along with the Kingdom and his healing skills. Whatever Jesus had been like before joining the Baptist, he was incandescently alive thereafter. He had the galvanic energy of a Napoleon—sure of his mission and ultimate triumph, showering commands and rewards upon his followers. There had never been a prophet like Jesus. Moses had initially been so overwhelmed by his selection by God that he pleaded inadequacy to the task. Later, he was continually saddled with the frustrating task of guiding his unruly people both physically and spiritually. Similar burdens befell many subsequent prophets. Isaiah walked naked for three years as a sign of God's prophecy that the

Egyptians would be defeated by Babylon, God's agent of history, and be led naked into exile. Likewise, Jeremiah walked around with a yoke upon his neck to signify God's punishment of any kingdom that refused to submit to Babylon. Ezekiel was instructed to lie on his side for two years, to gaze upon a miniature model of Jerusalem under siege that symbolized the city's coming destruction. More typically, the prophets simply spoke words, but often frightening words, about God's intended chastisement of the people for their sins. Since these prophecies often had to be addressed directly to the rulers and the populace, sometimes during terrifying times of siege or war, the prophets often faced dangerous enmity.[208] Elijah was persecuted, Jeremiah was imprisoned, and the minor prophet Uriah was killed. No wonder many prophets saw their lives as terrible burdens:

A grievous vision is declared unto me....
Therefore are my loins filled with convulsion;
Pangs have taken hold upon me, as the pangs of a woman in travail;
I am bent so that that I cannot hear; I am affrighted so that I cannot see.
My heart is bewildered, terror hath overwhelmed me. (Isa 21:2–4)
Cursed be the day wherein I was born;
the day wherein my mother bore me, let it not be blessed.
Why is my pain perpetual, and my wound uncurable,
So that it refuseth to be healed? (Jer 20:14, 15:18)

Hence, most of the classical Jewish prophets were burdened and overwhelmed. Jesus was different. He feared no persecution until the very end, because he had no enemies in Galilee. He spoke to individual and various crowds, and then moved on. He never entered any city to challenge Herod Antipas or any powerful magistrate. Nor did he champion any social reform (of slavery, taxation, tenant farming, etc.) that might have fostered opposition. Galilee was peaceful enough for him and his Disciples to travel without undue fear of brigands. In short, although Jesus is routinely called "The Suffering Servant," he suffered very little until his last twenty-four hours. His crucifixion was certainly grisly, but hardly unique; during Jesus' youth, the same punishment had been meted out to two thousand other Jews during Judas of Galilee's anti-Roman uprising.[209]

---

208 *Encyclopedia Judaica*, s.v. "Prophets and Prophecy," 13:1149–1175.

209 Jesus' only other suffering occurred during his "temptation by the devil." Immediately after his baptism and the vision of the Holy Spirit descending like a dove, the Holy Spirit led him into the wilderness to be "tempted" by the devil (Satan). "Temptation" does not necessarily imply suffering (a "tempting offer" is enticing, not painful), and no suffering is described in Mark's original version, when Jesus was always accompa-

Finally, when the majority of people did not respond to his message, he seemed to feel little anguish. Perhaps this was due to his own excitement about the Day of the Lord. Like Napoleon before battle, he foresaw that many (perhaps most) of the people would fall, but that he and his followers would be crowned with glory. Whereas John the Baptist fasted in anticipation of the terrible apocalypse, Jesus ate and drank, and insisted his Disciples do likewise. This was a joyous time. Abba, his Father, would protect and reward them. Whatever they had sacrificed would be recompensed a thousandfold. Whether or not Jesus literally offered his Disciples judgeships in the Kingdom, no prophet in Jewish history had ever promised such boons.

The Disciples' response to Jesus was predictable. The Synoptics are too focused on Jesus to say much about them. But for these rural folk, Jesus must have been mesmerizing. He was bold, comforting, exhilarating. When the End arrived, they would ascend to untold heights. The vision was intoxicating. How they responded to their master's shocking arrest and the heart-wrenching dissolution of their dreams we cannot know. But they must have yearned to believe that things would somehow right themselves: that Jesus would reappear and reveal that everything had been part of God's plan and that they would soon be joining him in the Kingdom. Not surprisingly, this is what they saw on the third day.

---

nied by God's angels (Mk 1:13). In the Gospels of Matthew and Luke, however, no angels protected him, and Satan forced Jesus to fast for forty days and nights, so he could be tempted with the promise of food. This was presumably excruciating, inasmuch as normal humans die after thirty days without nourishment. Fortunately, the fast did not seem to have weakened him.

AFTERWORD

This book has tried to uncover both the Jesus of the Gospels and the Jesus of history. For many reasons, the attempt has necessarily been subjective. Except for the days in Jerusalem, it is impossible to reconstruct the sequence of his ministry's major events (the pericopes), or to guess what happened after he walked away. The original context of many of his key sayings remains unknown. The first 90 percent of his brief life is a void. The difficulty in assessing what is true and what is not was, of course, the motivation for Tatian's Diatessaron, and also for the Church's later discomfiture with his subjective editorial decisions. Overlaying these interpretative problems is an emotional one. Whether Christian, Jewish, or atheist, even trained scholars must constantly contend with deeply ingrained beliefs in their effort to remain dispassionately objective.

Nevertheless, this author has tried to emphasize two key touchstones that seem to provide secure mooring for this task. First, Luke and Paul provide incontrovertible evidence that Jesus must have always remained Jewish, since his Disciples remained so long after his death. The Council of Jerusalem is accepted by virtually all historians, both religious and secular, as the moment when the leaders of the Jesus sect agreed, for the first time, that Jesus followers did not have to be Jewish. This is so irrefutable that religious Christians have been forced to explain why Jesus himself did not, apparently, behave like a Christian. One major tack, pioneered by Mark, is to claim that Jesus' Disciples were too muddled to understand anything he did, and that Jesus intentionally misled the crowds he so diligently assembled, so they would not understand him. Another major tack is the doctrine of progressive revelation. This asserts that Jesus' new message was too overwhelming to be absorbed by his contemporaries, and so had to be revealed step by step after his death, starting with Peter's visit to Cornelius. However, this begs the question of why Jesus, who was simultaneously all man and all God, was incapable of explaining himself to the Disciples he lived with for over a year, whereas the all-human Paul managed to instantly comprehend everything following his brief celestial vision.

The other touchstone provided by this book follows from the first: in comparing divergent Synoptic accounts of Jesus' words and deeds, any version reporting his denial of the Mosaic Law—including its core insistence of a single, ineffable Jewish God—seems suspect. This is so logical that it bears mention that among the criteria applied by scholars to judge authenticity (e.g., the Criterion of Embarrassment) is the rather controversial Criterion of Discontinuity. This contends that Jesus' most authentic sayings are likely to be those that are most unique: i.e., that differ from anything that preceded him (e.g., in the Tanakh) or followed (e.g., the Church fathers' writings). Although this concept is certainly useful when applied judiciously, it has unfortunately encouraged some authorities to jettison anything smacking of Judaism, on the grounds that they might have been put into Jesus' mouth by a later Jewish scribe. This approach goes too far; it throws the baby out with the bathwater. Uniqueness comes in different forms, including the ability to express old ideas in vibrant new ways. Thousands of mid-nineteenth-century Americans expressed the need to preserve the United States as a unified nation based on freedom. But only Abraham Lincoln was gifted enough to express this idea in his gemlike Gettysburg Address, which remains enshrined in the memories of many millions around the globe. So too, Jesus' parables and Sermon on the Mount disclose a brilliant, charismatic orator whose loving words about his Jewish faith would easily be recalled long after his death.

This is not to imply that he never did anything controversial. In particular, his belief that he had been commissioned to spread God's Word among the people inspired an authority that was easily misunderstood as implying either autonomy from God or plain human arrogance. But careful inspection of the Synoptics makes clear that he viewed himself as a prophet: God's messenger. This would be far more obvious if these Gospels were rendered to better capture the original meanings of his words. We have seen that during Jesus' lifetime, "son/Son of God" was understood to mean any highly respected individual. Recall too that the CSB believes that "son/Son of Man" merely meant "I," and that Jesus was never called "Lord." Were the Synoptics reedited by replacing these Christological-sounding terms with "sir" and "I," Jesus' self-conception as God's messenger would be far more apparent. It would become yet more apparent if the word "save" was generally replaced with "heal," "faith" with "confidence," and so on.

Of course, this will never happen, because the existing Synoptics are too embedded in the hearts of billions of people to ever change. And this is as it should be, because modern Christianity is a religion of caring and compassion that will hopefully last forever. The days when Catholics and Protestants could slaughter one another in the Hundred Years War, which devastated Europe with the impact of the earlier Bubonic Plague, are long gone. So too are the days when burning Jews at the stake was regarded an act of spiritual grace. History turned a page when Pope John Paul II, head of the same Church that had historically vilified the Jewish people as Christ-killers, called them instead "our older brother." All religions change and revitalize themselves. Judaism too had to reinvent itself after the destruction of the Temple and the dispersion from its homeland. Moreover, like Christianity, it had to accommodate itself to the seismic societal changes that have occurred between the time of the Roman Empire and today. One of these changes, of course, has been the staggering advance in knowledge and education. Secular scholars agree that today we know more about Jesus and his times than even the Evangelists did, just as we probably know more about the Judaism of King David's era than the Pharisees did. Yet even knowledge is only a handmaiden of humankind. By itself, it leads as quickly to World War II's technologically proficient murder of fifty million people as to progress. Knowledge alone is useless without an equivalent advance in the human heart. While we all await the final coming of the Kingdom of God, our greatest goal must be the creation of a human kingdom of decency and respect. And thankfully, both Judaism and Christianity have become secure cornerstones of that kingdom. It is a hopeful sign indeed that within the Western Judeo-Christian tradition, it means less and less on which side of the hyphen each of us worships.

ABOUT THE AUTHOR

Robert Kupor graduated magna cum laude and Phi Beta Kappa from the City University of New York. After receiving a Ph.D. from Harvard University in Microbiology and Molecular Genetics, and conducting postdoctoral research in biochemistry at the University of California at San Francisco, he became an assistant professor of biology at the University of Tennessee. The efforts there of evangelicals to convert him to Christianity sparked a lifelong interest in Jesus and the New Testament. He then received an MBA in Finance from the University of Washington, and started a successful career as a biomedical analyst on Wall Street. Among other positions, he was a partner at Frazier & Co. (Seattle), the largest venture capital firm in the Pacific Northwest; senior vice president at Kidder, Peabody, & Co. (New York), one of the nation's ten largest Wall Street firms; and vice president at MDS Capital (Toronto), the largest venture capital fund in Canada. His major leisure activity aside from bicycling is reading history.

GLOSSARY

ACTS OF THE APOSTLES. The New Testament's only account of the early post-Jesus decades, written by the Evangelist Luke (author of Luke's Gospel).

ANTI-JUDAIC. In this book, this term refers to hostility against the Jewish religious authorities (Pharisees and Sadducees), as contrasted to "anti-Semitism" (hostility against Judaism or the Jewish people).

APOSTLES. Missionaries of the early post-resurrection Jesus sect. Can also refer to the Twelve Disciples.

ASCENSION. Jesus' post-resurrection ascent to heaven.

BCE. Before the Common Era (i.e., B.C.).

CANON. The accepted contents of any religion's Scriptures, such as the Tanakh or the New Testament.

CE. Common Era (i.e., "A.D.").

CHIEF PRIESTS. The highest-ranking priests of the Temple below the High Priest.

CHRISTOLOGICAL. Pertaining to Jesus' godlike (as opposed to human) nature.

CSB. The Catholic Study Bible, written by the U.S. Conference of Catholic Bishops.

DIASPORA. Jews living outside of the Jewish homeland, either voluntarily (e.g., before the First Jewish Revolt of 66–70 CE), or involuntarily (e.g., after the First or Second Revolts). Most Jews lived in the Diaspora even during the early first century CE.

DISCIPLES. When capitalized, this term refers to Jesus' twelve Disciples; when not capitalized, it refers to lesser followers.

ELDERS. The lay Jewish aristocracy.

END OF DAYS. The time when God would intervene in human affairs by establishing a perfect earthly Kingdom. In Jesus' time, the End was expected to involve a Final Judgment that would consign both the living and the resurrected death to the Kingdom or to Purgatory. Many expected a calamitous apocalypse to precede the End.

ESCHATOLOGICAL. Pertaining to the End of Days and the Kingdom of God.

EVANGELISTS. The four Gospel writers: Mark, Matthew, Luke, and John.

GALILEE. The hilly northern region of Palestine, home of Jesus and his ministry, which in his time was governed by Herod Antipas, Rome's vassal Jewish leader.

GOD-FEARERS. Gentiles who revered Judaism but would not formally convent.

GOSPEL(S). (1) The accounts of Jesus' life and resurrection, written by the four Evangelists (Mark, Matthew, Luke, and John); see also "Synoptic Gospels." (2) For Jesus and John the Baptist, the "good news" that the current world was ending imminently, and would be replaced by an earthly Kingdom of God. For Paul, however, the "good news" was his conviction that Jesus' death and resurrection had provided the means to worship and be redeemed by (the Jewish) God directly, without recourse to the Mosaic Law.

HASMONEANS. The Maccabees and their descendants, who ruled Palestine/Judea from 140 to 37 BCE.

HELLENISM. The civilization and culture of ancient Greece, which was adopted by most of the Roman Empire. It emphasized rationalism, philosophy, science, art, and physical culture.

HIGH PRIEST. The highest-ranking priest of the Temple; Caiaphas held this position during Jesus' adult life.

JN. John's Gospel.

JOHN THE BAPTIST. The Jewish holy man who baptized Jesus and is popularly believed to have hailed him as the Messiah.

JOSEPHUS. A Jew, the major historian of first-century Palestine.

JUDEA. During Jesus' time, the Jewish heartland of Palestine, consisting of modern southern Israel (including Jerusalem) and southwest Jordan. It was ruled directly by Rome, and specifically by Pontius Pilate, during Jesus' adult life. In several earlier periods (e.g., under the late Hasmonians, and Herod the Great), its boundaries had encompassed all of Palestine.

JUDEO-CHRISTIAN. In this book, this term refers both to traditional Jews who happened to believe that Jesus was the Messiah (e.g., the Disciples) and, later, to people whose religion was in the process of evolving from Judaism to the new religion of Christianity.

KINGDOM OF GOD. The perfect earthly Kingdom that God would establish after the End of Days (q.v.).

LK. Luke's Gospel.

MASORETIC TEXT. The standard Jewish translation of the Tanakh. Its wording differs from the NRSV translation of the "Old Testament," but the overall meaning of the verses is virtually identical.

MISHNAH. The written compendium of the oral law, composed c. 200 CE in Galilee.

MK. Mark's Gospel.

MOSAIC LAW. Jewish laws derived from the Torah (the first five books of the Tanakh), universally recognized in Jesus' time as the foundation of Judaism.

MOTHER SYNAGOGUE. In this book, the name of the original Jesus synagogue, established following Jesus' death by his Disciples in Jerusalem.

MT. Matthew's Gospel.

NATIVITY STORIES. Accounts of Jesus' conception and birth found in the Gospels of Matthew and Luke.

NRSV. The New Revised Standard Version translation of the Bible, which along with the previous Revised Standard Version (RSV) is the best-selling Protestant Bible in the United States.

ORAL LAW/TRADITIONS OF THE ELDERS. The Oral Law refers to additional religious laws (supplementing the Mosaic Law) that today are observed by Orthodox Jews. This Law was compiled in the Mishnah in 200 CE and was believed by contemporary sage/rabbis (and modern Orthodox Jews) to have been handed down to Moses on Mount Sinai. Scholars believe it evolved from the "traditions of the elders" upheld by the Pharisees, a small ultra-religious sect during Jesus' period.

PALESTINE. Roughly the land comprising modern Israel, the West Bank, and contiguous parts of Jordan and Syria. Although first introduced by the Romans in 135 CE, this term is useful because the Jewish nation in Jesus' time was subdivided into ministates (notably Judea and Galilee), and so lacked a unitary name.

PARABLE. A story intended to illustrate a moral or religious lesson, much favored by Jesus as a teaching device.

PAROUSIA. Jesus' "Second Coming," when Christians expect the End of Days and the arrival of the Kingdom of God.

PAUL. A Hellenistic Cilician Jew who never met Jesus. He was not a Disciple, but was an extraordinarily influential missionary (apostle) who helped transform the Jesus sect into the separate religion now known as Christianity. "Pauline" refers to Paul's writings or theology.

PERICOPE. A detailed episode of Jesus' life in the Gospels, as opposed to the connecting narrative framework.

PHARISEES. A small sect of ultra-religious laypeople who followed the "tradition of the elders" (the early Oral Law), in their quest to become as holy as the Temple priests.

PROCURATOR. The Roman commander of Judea from c. 6 to 66 CE. Pontius Pilate held this position during Jesus' ministry.

PROOFTEXTS. Tanakh passages that Christians interpret as prophecies about Jesus' coming, his ministry, and the resurrection.

Q ("Quelle") SAYINGS/SOURCE. A large collection of Jesus' sayings (often without any context) that probably existed in written form in the first century, used by Matthew and Luke as a major source for their Gospels (alongside Mark's Gospel).

SAGE/RABBIS. The religious scholars who evolved after the First Jewish Revolt from the earlier Pharisees, and created the foundations of modern Judaism. They were not rabbis in the modern sense, since they did not live among and minister to lay Jews.

SANHEDRIN. In early first century, an assembly of Sadducees, Pharisees, and laymen who provided assistance to the High Priest in matters of Jewish law, the civic administration of Jerusalem, and relations with the Roman occupiers.

SCRIBES. An ambiguous term that refers to scribe-copyists and/or scholars, who could have been Pharisees, Sadducees, or neither.

SECOND COMING. See Parousia.

SEPTUAGINT. The Greek translation of the Tanakh, written in 250–100 BCE, and used by Diaspora Jews who no longer understood Hebrew.

SYNOPTIC GOSPELS. The first three Gospels (Mark, Matthew, and Luke), which contain relatively similar accounts of Jesus, unlike the highly dissimilar Gospel of John.

TANAKH. The Jewish Bible/Scriptures ("Old Testament," to Christians).

TORAH. In this book, this term refers to the Tanakh's first five books (Genesis, Exodus, Leviticus, Numbers, Deuteronomy), which are the basis for the Mosaic Law. (Although not used here in its broader sense, Torah can also refer to the entire Tanakh, as well as the combination of the Tanakh and the Mishnah.)

WOES. Jesus' "woe to you" exclamations, particularly prominent in Matthew's Gospel, that were directed primarily against the Jewish authorities.

MAIN BIBLIOGRAPHY

Brown, Raymond. *The Death of the Messiah*. New York: Doubleday (Anchor Bible Reference Library), 1975.

———. *An Introduction to the New Testament*. New York: Doubleday (Anchor Bible Reference Library), 1997.

Cohen, Shaye J. D. *From the Maccabees to the Mishnah*. Philadelphia: Westminster Press (Anchor Bible Reference Library), 1987.

> A landmark review of Jewish society from 200 BCE to 200 CE, indispensable for understanding religious thought and practices of the Jewish sects and the common people.

Crosswalk Concordance; http://bible.crosswalk.com.

> An extremely useful free online Concordance that assists in understanding the meaning of individual words in the Bible, by listing every verse containing any word specified.

Ehrman, Bart. *Jesus, Apocalyptic Prophet of the New Millennium*. New York: Oxford University Press, 1999.

> A very good introduction to the historical Jesus with a perspective similar to Jesus Revealed, written by the (Protestant) Chairman of Religious Studies at the University of North Carolina.

———. *Misquoting Jesus*. San Francisco: HarperSanFrancisco, 2002.

———. *Peter, Paul, and Mary Magdalene*. New York: Oxford University Press, 2006.

Encyclopedia Britannica. Chicago, Encyclopedia Britannica, 2001.

Fredriksen, Paula. *Jesus of Nazareth, King of the Jews*. New York: Alfred A. Knopf, 1999.

Freeman, David, editor-in-chief. *The Anchor Bible Dictionary*. New York: Doubleday, 1992.

> This seven-thousand-page dictionary is probably the premiere English-language encyclopedia of the Tanakh and the New Testament. Books published under the Anchor Bible Reference Library imprint (e.g., see Brown, Raymond) are regarded as particularly valuable scholarly studies.

The Holy Scriptures According to the Masoretic Text. Philadelphia: Jewish Publication Society of America, 1955.

Jaffee, Martin. *Early Judaism*. Upper Saddle River, N.J.: Prentice-Hall, 1997.

Josephus. *The works of Flavius Josephus*. Trans. William Whiston. Grand Rapids, Mich.: Baker Books, 1972.

Meier, John P. *A Marginal Jew*. New York: Doubleday (Anchor Bible Reference Library), 1991–2001.

Vol. 1—The Roots of the Problem and the Person. 1991.

Vol. 2—Message, Mentor, and Miracles. 1994.

Vol. 3—Companions and Competition. 2001.

> The most ambitious (three thousand pages) and scrupulous modern effort to discover the "historical Jesus", by arguably the foremost Christian Jesus scholar of our time. Its background material contains extremely useful information about Jesus' portrait in the Synoptics. The much-anticipated Volume IV will cover Jesus' final week in Jerusalem.

Metzger, Bruce, and Bart Ehrman. *The Text of the New Testament*. New York: Oxford University Press, 2005.

O'Conner, Daniel Wm. *Peter in Rome: The Literary, Liturgical, and Archeological Evidence*. New York and London, 1969.

Reed, Jonathan. *Archeology and the Galilean Jesus*. Harrisburg, Pa.: Trinity Press International, 2000.

Roth, Cecil, general editor. *Encyclopedia Judaica*. New York: Macmillan, 1971–72.

Sanders, E. P. *The Historical Figure of Jesus*. London: Allan Lane, Penguin Press, 1993.

> A very good introduction to the "historical Jesus" that is more comprehensive than Ehrman's *Apocalyptic Prophet of the New Millennium*.

Sandmel, Samuel. *A Jewish Understanding of the New Testament*. New York: KTAV Publishing House, 1974.

Senior, Donald, general editor. *The Catholic Study Bible.* New York: Oxford University Press, 1990.

The official Catholic Study Bible of the United States, written and approved by the United States Conference of Catholic Bishops. A new edition was published in 2006.

Stark, Rodney. *The Rise of Christianity.* Princeton, New Jersey: Princeton University Press, 1996.

Throckmorton, Burton H., Jr. *Gospel Parallels.* Nashville: Thomas Nelson Publishers, 1992.

The indispensable tool for any comparative analysis of the Synoptic Gospels.

Vermes, Geza. *The Authentic Gospel of Jesus.* London: Penguin Press, 2003.

———. *The Changing Faces of Jesus.* New York: Penguin Press, 2000.

———. *Jesus the Jew.* Philadelphia: Fortress Press, 1973

Although criticized for its methodology, *Jesus the Jew* is credited with initiating the late-twentieth-century study of the "Jewish Jesus."

White, L. Michael. *From Jesus to Christianity.* San Francisco: HarperSanFranciso, 2004.

A good, modern historical overview of the contents of the New Testament, although Jesus' identity is not a major topic.

INDEX

978-0-595-42404-7
0-595-42404-X

Printed in the United States
83334LV00001B/235-273/A